What People Are Saying About
Chicken Soup for the Grandparent's Soul . . .

"If being a grandparent doesn't heal your soul and make it soar, nothing will. *Chicken Soup for the Grandparent's Soul* is another winner in this great series."

Florence Henderson

"A grandparent often plays one of the most important roles in a child's life. We have the privilege of being mentors, role models and advocates for our grandchildren and all children. This book is a touching celebration of grandparents everywhere."

Marian Wright Edelman
president, Children's Defense Fund

"Age and humor go hand in hand. That is what keeps people young at heart."

Willard Scott

CHICKEN SOUP FOR THE GRANDPARENT'S SOUL

Chicken Soup for the Grandparent's Soul
Stories to Open the Hearts and Rekindle the Spirits of Grandparents
Jack Canfield, Mark Victor Hansen, Meladee McCarty, Hanoch McCarty

Published by Backlist, LLC,
a unit of Chicken Soup for the Soul Publishing, LLC. www.chickensoup.com

Front cover design by Lisa Camp
Originally published in 2002 by Health Communications, Inc.

Back cover and spine redesign by Pneuma Books, LLC

Distributed to the booktrade by Simon & Schuster. SAN: 200-2442

Publisher's Cataloging-in-Publication Data
(Prepared by The Donohue Group)
Chicken soup for the grandparent's soul : stories to open the hearts and rekindle the spirits of grandparents / [compiled by] Jack Canfield ... [et al.].

  p. : ill. ; cm.

  Originally published: Deerfield Beach, FL : Health Communications, c2002.
ISBN: 978-1-62361-106-4

  1. Grandparenting--Anecdotes. 2. Grandparent and child--Anecdotes. 3. Grandparents--Conduct of life--Anecdotes. 4. Anecdotes. I. Canfield, Jack, 1944-

HQ759.9 .C55 2012
306.874/5   2012944877

PRINTED IN THE UNITED STATES OF AMERICA
on acid free paper

21 20 19 18 17 16 15 14 13 12   01 02 03 04 05 06 07 08 09 10

CHICKEN SOUP FOR THE GRANDPARENT'S SOUL

Stories to Open the Hearts and Rekindle the Spirits of Grandparents

Jack Canfield
Mark Victor Hansen
Meladee McCarty
Hanoch McCarty

Backlist, LLC, a unit of
Chicken Soup for the Soul Publishing, LLC
Cos Cob, CT
www.chickensoup.com

Contents

2. A GRANDPARENT'S LOVE

3. A GRANDPARENT'S WISDOM

4. PASSING ON A LEGACY

Introduction

We fashion children's values one story at a time, one experience at a time. Knowing this, it's my choice, while I'm still around, to spend the time with them that I can and not leave it to chance or television to teach them what's important.

Violet George

She'd heard it once too often—or so she thought. Your teenage daughter rolled her eyes as you launched into that story about when you were little. Now her little daughter sits on your lap and seems to actually want to hear the story! That's one of the magic moments of being a grandparent. In fact, sometimes you are allies "against" that intervening generation. Those stories you tell are the repository of your family's history, your family's values and beliefs. Without you and your stories, families would be cast adrift, not knowing anything about themselves that would make them feel special, unique, valuable. Those stories allow each family member to become part of something bigger than themselves—a tradition. So, even if your children still roll their eyes as you begin yet another story, persevere! Tell that story!

For centuries, people of all faiths often wrote two wills: one, a "real-estate" will, which detailed how someone's tangible goods and properties would be divided, and the second, an "ethical" or "spiritual" will, which discussed the beliefs, traditions, rituals, practices and family values that person wanted to impart to those left behind.

Spiritual wills from medieval times often ran forty or fifty pages, filled with the minutiae of everyday life and with exhortations to pray daily for the soul of the departed.

In today's world, we are more concerned with the well-being of our families and the continuance of the ethnic, religious and familial heritage, which we wish to pass on to them.

So many times we've heard regret, after the passing of a family member, that we "didn't ask them more about our family background, about our family tree." We need to capture those sweet stories, those family treasures, now, while we have a chance.

We've made it a practice in our families to videotape family members telling stories about family history. We discovered that they loved telling those old stories with great relish, often revealing aspects of themselves we had never known. Their storytelling reconnected us and reminded us of the value of our whole family and the many treasures hidden in their history.

Grandparents are the axle of the wheel of the family. So many people have told us of grandparents around whom their family seemed to coalesce: No holiday was complete unless the family gathered at the grandparents' home. And many told us of missing grandparents and how, in their absence, the family struggled to find its center. For many families, grandparents are the "true North" by which the family's moral compass finds its direction: We expect that our grandparents represent the values we believe are most lasting, most dear and most dependable.

Grandparents are alive and well in America. They are allies for grandchildren and have the time to really pay attention to little ones' concerns. They provide child care that enables their sons and daughters to work to support their growing families. We had the opportunity to meet or hear about some really remarkable grandparents—for example, the Rodeo Grandmas of Ellensburg, Washington. These four ladies, aged sixty-five to eighty-nine, ride and rope and yodel their way into people's hearts all over the West. During our research, we heard of Grandma Bonnie, the center of the Longaberger family, famous for their handmade baskets sold all over the world. It is her example, her values, the lessons about quality, self-reliance, building good relationships and building humor into every day that helped make it possible for her son, Dave Longaberger, to create a billion-dollar company and for her grandchildren to continue to build its success.

As we put this book together, reading the stories about countless grandparents, we found that children and grandchildren wrote about the values, the experiences, the humor and wisdom, the courage and surprising resilience of their grandparents. They did not write us about the size of their inheritance checks, or the estates of land and buildings and furniture that they had received. Instead, it was the humanness, the insights, the modeling of living by one's values that filled their letters to us. Grandparents and grandchildren wrote of sweet experiences, of treasured moments, of key events that represented a summation of all that their family meant to them.

In preparing for this book, we read each story with grandmas' and grandpas' eyes and hearts. We were touched and enlightened by stories that opened up pictures in our minds of loyalty, honor, faith and the keeping of life's commitments. We were inspired by stories of quiet courage and wisdom acquired through toil and struggle.

We were moved by stories of love expressed through being there, stepping up to the plate and doing what was right.

There are many kinds of grandmas and grandpas, from the kind we read about in stories with Norman Rockwell illustrations to incredibly active grandparents, flying all over, doing jobs they'd never consider retiring from, conquering the Internet and e-mail, and performing essential, irreplaceable services for their communities. Grandparents are living longer, doing more and refusing to accept any limitations. But they still make a difference, one at a time, for their grandchildren. In our highly mobile society, they may live far from their grandkids, but they so often serve as the anchor, the steadying point that helps give meaning and safety to those children's lives. Some grandparents are courageously parenting their grandchildren—and we celebrate them.

Join us in celebrating grandparenthood through the power of a story. Let each story touch your heart, tickle your funny bone and open new topics to talk about in your family. Let these stories be the start of your own storytelling with your children and grandchildren.

Read them, savor them, one at a time. Read them aloud to family and others you love. And then pause and tell your own stories, one at a time.

1

THE JOYS OF GRAND-PARENTING

It is remarkable how, overnight, a quiet mature lady can learn to sit cross-legged on the floor and play a tin drum, quack like a duck, sing all the verses of "The Twelve Days of Christmas," make paper flowers, draw pigs and sew on the ears of severely-injured teddy bears.

Marlene Walkington Ferber

Orange Cheeks

The reason grandparents and grandchildren get along so well is that they have a common enemy.

Sam Levinson

Willie was six years old. He lived in the country. The phone rang, and Willie picked it up. He had a habit of breathing into the phone instead of talking.

"Hello, Willie," his grandmother's voice said to the breathing.

"How'd you know it was me?"

"I just knew, Willie. Willie, I want you to spend the night."

"Oh, Grandma! I'll get Momma!"

His mother took the phone, talked a while and hung up.

"Willie," his mother said, "I never let you spend the night at your grandmother's because you get in trouble."

"I won't get in trouble," Willie burbled. He shone with excitement so his mother spoke quietly, seriously, "I don't want to get a call tonight and have to drive thirty miles to pick you up."

"No troublllllllle," he said.

"I'll tell you this: Your grandmother can be difficult late in the day," she went on. "She can be a bit of a grump."

"I'll be good. I promise."

"Well, if there's any trouble you won't go overnight again for a year. Go up and pack your bag."

Willie had won. He ran upstairs and put six T-shirts and a toothbrush in his bag.

He and his mother drove all the way into Cambridge. Willie loved Cambridge because all the houses were squeezed together. They drove around Harvard Yard, down Trowbridge Street and took a left on Leonard Avenue. The houses were all wooden triple-deckers, and his grandmother lived at number nine. They parked and Willie ran up the outside stairs, pushed the outside door open and pressed the buzzer inside.

Zzzzzzzzzzzzzzzzzzttt! The door wouldn't open until his grandmother pressed another buzzer from the inside. It made a click, then the door unlocked. It was magic. Willie pushed the door in and stood at the bottom of the stairs. The stairs were narrow and dark and filled with the wonderful smells of his grandmother's house. He could have spent the whole weekend right here, but his grandmother was standing at the head of the stairs calling him.

"Come on up, Willie."

"Here I come, Grandmaaaaaaa," he sang out.

He rushed up to the top and his grandmother leaned down for a hug. He kissed her on those wrinkled, crinkled cheeks. He loved those cheeks, but never said anything about them.

"You'll be in the guest room upstairs," his grandmother said. "There's a prize up there for you."

"Thank you, Grandmaaaaa," he said, hurrying up the stairs. His mother's voice caught up with him, "You remember what I said, Willie."

"Don't worry. No troubllllle."

When Willie ran into the guest room he saw his grand-mother had done something wonderful. She had pasted six large silver stars to the ceiling. He loved those.

The prize lay on the table. Two pieces of orange paper, a small pair of scissors, glue and a sharp pencil. Willie took the scissors and cut two circles from the paper and put glue on the back of the circles. He pasted the circles to his cheeks. Now he had orange cheeks.

Looking out the window he saw his mother driving off. "Good-bye, Mommaaaaa," he shouted with a victorious grin.

He ran downstairs and his grandmother said just the right thing: "Wonderful cheeks."

"Thank you, Grandmaaa," he smiled, jouncing his shoulders.

"We'll have tea in the dining room, but first I'll hang out wash and you'll go on an errand to Mr. Murchison's. You know him."

"The fruit man."

"Yes. He's right next door. He's expecting you. Get four pounds of bananas. Here's a dollar. Do a good job."

Willie went down the dark narrow stairs, the secret stairs, and on outside to the fruit store. He had never gone on an errand by himself before. He bravely stepped into the old-fashioned fruit store. Dark. The floor was dark and wooden and oily. Mr. Murchison stood there. He was older than the bananas. And he was curved like the bananas. "Hello, Willie," he said in a long, dark voice. "Your grandmother told me you were coming. Nice to see you again." He reached to the top of the banana rack. "I've got four pounds of bananas for you."

Willie shook his head back and forth. "I don't want those."

"What's the trouble?" Mr. Murchison asked.

"They're rotten."

"They're not rotten," moustached Murchison insisted, laughing. "They're ripe. Best way to have 'em."

"I want the yellow ones," Willie said.

Mr. Murchison replaced the bananas and took yellow ones from the rack. "Someday you'll know better," he growled.

"Think I know better now," Willie replied.

Mr. Murchison seemed to be chewing something distasteful. "I like your cheeks," he finally grunted.

Willie looked up, "I like your cheeks, too."

"Arrrrrrr."

Willie took the bananas to the backyard where his grandmother was hanging clothes on the line. "Good for you, Willie. You're a regular businessman. You go up and play till I finish, and we'll have tea."

Willie was a businessman! To him a businessman was someone who made pencil marks on the walls. Secret ones. But they were real. Willie went up and down the back stairway making small pencil marks. Then he decided to make a secret mark in the dining room.

He pushed a chair against the white wall in the dining room, stood on the chair, reached way up and started to make a tiny dot. Willie heard something. Terrified, he turned, "Grandma!" In his panic he made a scratch mark two feet long on the wall. "Oh, no. I have to go home now." He tried to erase it, but that made it worse. He spat on his hands and tried to wipe the mark off. Now it was all over the wall. It was horrible. Now he was in trouble. He jumped off the chair and ran to the window. His grandmother was hanging the last few socks. He had to do something or he'd have to go home. Willie opened the drawer in the pantry and saw a hammer and two nails. He took them into the dining room. He pulled the dining-room cloth off the table and climbed onto the chair. He nailed the cloth to the wall. Now you couldn't see the scratch mark—but you could see the dining-room cloth.

His grandmother made the tea and put everything on a tray.

"Come on, Willie. We'll have tea in the dining room."

His head seemed to be sinking into his shoulders. "Let's have the tea here," he said.

"We always have tea in the dining room," she said and went into the dining room alone.

"Willie, the dining-room cloth is not on the table," she said curiously. Then, "Willie, the dining-room cloth is nailed to the wall."

After a silence Willie said, "Which wall?"

"You come in and see which wall."

Willie came slowly in. His head sank further into his shoulders. "Oh, that wall," Willie said. "I nailed it to that wall."

Suddenly, he began to shake. His whole body trembled, and he burst out crying. "Now I have to go home." He was crying so hard the tears ran down onto his orange paper cheeks. He began to rub the cheeks, and the paper was shredding. That overwhelmed his grandmother. "Willie!" she said, rushing over, kneeling down to hold him. She was crying now, and her tears were falling onto his orange paper cheeks. She held him close, then breathed deeply, saying, "Willie, look at the two of us; this is absurd. It's all right."

"No, it isn't," Willie sobbed. "Now I have to go home. I can't come for a whole year."

"You don't have to go home," she said, standing and straightening her dress. "It's perfectly all right."

"No, it isn't," Willie persisted. "Momma says late in the day you're a grump."

His grandmother's eyes opened rather wide. "Hmmmmm, she does, does she?" His grandmother's lips pursed in thought for what seemed forever. "Well! I'll tell you this, Willie, your mother's no prize either."

They sat down at the table. "Now we'll have tea, and then we'll take care of the wall. How many sugars, Willie?"

"Five."

"One," she corrected.

The tea seemed to calm his whole body.

His grandmother took the hammer and pulled out the nails. She put the cloth on the table, saying, "I'll sew the holes up another time. For now we'll put a bowl of fruit over one hole and flowers on the other. Your mother will never know." Then his grandmother put putty in the nail holes, and she and Willie painted over the scratch mark.

In three hours, the paint was dry and the mark gone. "Now your mother won't know about this," she said with assurance. "It's our secret."

"She'll know," Willie pouted. "She always knows."

"She's my daughter. She won't know."

"She's my mother. She'll know!"

The next morning Willie was scared to death as his mother came up the dark, secret stairs. The three of them would have tea before leaving.

They sat at the dining table drinking tea. Willie was quiet as long as he could be. Finally, he looked at his mother and said, "Don't pick the bowl of fruit up."

"Why would I pick the bowl of fruit up?" she asked.

An extraordinary look of total innocence filled his face, "I don't knoooow."

Tea continued, and Willie was staring at the wall.

"What are you staring at?" his mother said.

"The wall," Willie replied. "It's a nice wall."

"Ahh!" his mother sighed. "There was trouble. What was the trouble?"

Defeated, Willie said, "Tell the trouble, Grandma."

"Well, there was trouble. The trouble was we didn't have enough time. Is that what you mean, Willie?"

"That's what I mean," he bounced.

A few minutes later his grandmother stooped over at the top of the stairs, and Willie kissed her on those wrinkled, crinkled cheeks. And then he and his mother went down the dark, narrow stairway with the wonderful smells. His mother didn't know what had happened. It was a secret.

When he got home Willie ran up to his room, unzipped his bag and took out the orange paper. He cut two circles and put them in an envelope with a note saying, "Dear Grandma. Here's orange cheeks for you. Love Willie."

Jay O'Callahan

I Love You, Grandma

"I love you, Grandma," said the child,
Grandma said, "I love you, too."
"I love you more," said the little child,
"I love you more than you."

"Well, that's an awful lot of love,"
Said Grandma then, and smiled.
"I love you, Grandma, most of all,"
More loudly said the child.

"Well, I love you back as much and more,"
Grandma smiled again.
"No, Grandma, you don't understand,
I can't love you the 'mostest' then."

Two tiny arms reach out to squeeze,
Grandma had no further words.
Such love directly akin to God's,
Unconditional and unreserved.

Virginia (Ginny) Ellis

Everybody Knows Everybody

If you look for a way to lend a hand, you will be lifting yourself as well.

Source Unknown

Today was a special day, the type of day that restores a faith of sorts.

And in that faith I found a lesson, taught to me by my six-year-old son, Brandon.

I watched him at the kitchen table carefully packing his lunch bag. I was going to take him along with me to work. As he put it, "I'm going to be a worker-man."

Carefully laid out before him was an arrangement of everything he required to get him through the day—a small coloring book, crayons, a small box of Smarties, a blueberry muffin, an egg-salad "samich" (as he called it) and three small Easter eggs.

To know Brandon is to understand that time has no meaning. I was running late and implored Brandon to "hurry up!" (I'm sure he feels the watch is a confidence trick, invented by the Swiss.)

Hurry he did. In fact, he forgot his well-packed lunch, a mistake I was painfully aware of on the forty-minute drive to town. He admonished me several times, saying, "Dad, you made me rush. Now I have no lunch." He changed the words over the duration of the scolding, but the meaning remained the same, "I need a lunch because you made me forget mine."

I purchased a sandwich and another muffin at a restaurant in town. Satisfied, he carried the bag to the van, and soon his mutinous thoughts of "no lunch, no work" vanished.

We arrived at a small bungalow in the suburbs of Kingston (Ontario, Canada). Our job: to install indoor-outdoor carpet on the porch and steps.

I rang the doorbell. I could hear the deadbolt being released, then the handle-lock and security chain. The door swung slowly open revealing an old, thin man. He looked ill. His white hair covered his head in patches. The powder-blue shirt hung from his shoulders as though on a hanger—his belt, several sizes too big.

I smiled, asking if he was Mr. Burch.

"Yes. Are you here to do the porch and steps?"

"Yes, Sir."

"Okay, I will leave this door open."

"Okay, I will get to work."

"Do you have a 'flidge'?" blurted Brandon. The old man looked down at Brandon, who extended his lunch.

"Yes, I do. Do you know where to find the fridge?"

"Yes, I do," said Brandon, walking past the man. "It's in the kitchen."

I was about to suggest to Brandon that he was being too bold by walking in, but before I could, the old man held his finger to his lips, gesturing it was okay.

"He'll be all right. He can't get into anything at all. Does he really help you?"

I nodded yes. Brandon returned, asking, in his most elf-like voice, "Do you have a coloring book?"

Again, I was about to suggest to Brandon that he was perhaps being bold. I extended my hand, beckoning him outside. The old man grasped my hand feebly. He looked at Brandon.

"Your father tells me you help him."

"Yes. I'm a worker-man," Brandon replied with pride.

I looked down, adding, "Apparently his job today is to keep the customer busy."

The old man looked at Brandon and released my hand, a faint smile appearing.

"Maybe you could do some work and show me how to color?"

With a most serious look, Brandon asked, "Dad, will you be okay?"

"Will Mr. Burch be okay?" I answered.

"We will be fine. We will be right here at the table. Come help me get out the book, worker-man."

I walked to the truck, returning with material and my notepad in time to hear Brandon comment, "You have already colored in this book. You are a good colorer."

"No, I didn't color these pictures. My grandchildren did."

"What are grandchildren?" Brandon asked curiously.

"They are my children's children. I am a grandfather."

"What's a grandfather?"

"Well, when you grow up and get married, then have children of your own, your dad will be a grandpa. Then your mother will be a grandma. They will be grand-parents. Do you understand?"

Brandon paused. "Yes, Grandpa."

"Oh, I don't think I'm your grandpa," the old man suggested.

Brandon rubbed his hair from his eyes. Studying the crayons, he selected one and continued to color.

Brandon said, "Everybody knows everybody, you know?"

"Well, I'm not sure they do. Why do you say that?" The old man looked curiously at Brandon, who was diligently coloring.

"We all comed from God. He made us all. We are fambily."

"Yes, God made everything," the old man confirmed.

"I know," said Brandon in a lighthearted voice. "He told me."

I had never heard Brandon talk of such things before, other than one time when we had gone to church to watch a Christmas play. While waiting for the play to start, Brandon had asked which door God would be coming through and if he would be sitting with us.

"He told you?" The old man was clearly curious.

"Yes, he did. He lives up there." Brandon pointed to the ceiling, looking up with reverence. "I b-member being there and talking to him."

"What did he say to you?" The old man placed his crayon on the table, focusing on Brandon.

"He said we are all fambily." Brandon paused, then added logically, "So you're my grandpa."

The old man looked to me through the screen door. He smiled. I was embarrassed that he saw me watching them. He told Brandon to keep coloring; he was going to check on the job.

The old man made his way slowly to the door. Opening it, he stepped onto the porch.

"How's it going?" he asked.

"It's going okay," I said. "I won't be long." The old man smiled slightly.

"Does the boy have a grandfather?"

I paused. "No, he doesn't. They were gone when he was born. He has a nanny, you know, a grandmother, but she is frail and not well."

"I understand what you're saying. I have cancer. I'm not long for this Earth, either."

"I'm sorry to hear that, Mr. Burch. I lost my mother to cancer."

He looked at me with tired, smiling eyes. "Every boy needs a grandfather," he said softly.

I agreed, adding, "It's just not in the cards for Brandon."

The old man looked back to Brandon, who was coloring vigorously. Turning back to me, he asked, "How often do you come to town, Son?"

"Me?" I asked.

"Yes."

"I come in almost every day."

The old man looked back to me. "Perhaps you could bring Brandon by from time to time, when you're in the area that is, for thirty minutes or so. What do you think?"

I looked in at Brandon. He had stopped coloring and was listening to us. "Could we, Dad? We are fliends. We can have lunch together."

"Well, if it's okay with Mr. Burch."

The old man opened the door, returning to the table. Brandon slid from his chair and walked to the fridge. "It's lunch time, Grandpa. I got enough for both of us." Brandon returned to the table. He removed the contents from the paper bag. "Do you have a knife?" asked Brandon.

The old man started to get up.

"I can find it. Tell me where to look," instructed Brandon.

"The butter knives are next to the corner of the counter, in the drawer."

"Found it!"

Brandon returned to the table. He unwrapped his muffin. With the care of a diamond-cutter, he cleaved two perfect portions. Brandon placed one portion on the plastic the muffin was wrapped in. He pushed it toward Mr. Burch.

"This is yours." He carefully unwrapped the sandwich

next and cut it in half. "This is yours, too. We have to eat the samich first. Mom says."

"Okay," replied Mr. Burch.

"Do you like juice, Brandon?"

"Yep, apple juice."

Mr. Burch walked slowly to the fridge. He removed a can of apple juice and poured two small glasses. He placed one in front of Brandon. "This is yours."

"Thank you, Grandpa." Brandon punctuated his eating with questions to Mr. Burch and fits of coloring.

"Do you play hockey, Brandon?"

"Yep," said Brandon, studying the end of his sandwich before biting into it. "Dad took me, Tyler and Adam in the wintertime."

"Years ago," Mr. Burch started, "I used to play for a Senior-A-team. I was almost ready to play for the NHL, but I was never called up. I did play once with a man who was called up, though. He was fine player. Bill Moore. That was his name."

My heart leapt to my throat. "Tutter Moore?" I asked through the screen.

The old man was startled. He looked at me. "Yes, that's him . . . was called up to Boston a few times. You've heard of him?"

"Yes," I said, my voice cracking. "You're eating lunch with his grandson."

The old man looked back to Brandon. He stared for a few moments. Brandon looked innocently at Mr. Burch.

"Yes . . . I see now. He looks very much like Tutter. And the nanny is Lillian?"

"Yes," I replied.

The old man clasped Brandon's hand.

"Brandon, I owe you an apology. You were right, and I was wrong. Everybody *does* know everybody."

Lea MacDonald

The Antique

My six-year-old granddaughter stares at me as if she is seeing me for the first time. "Grandma, you are an antique," she says. "You are old. Antiques are old. You are my antique."

I am not satisfied to let the matter rest there. I take out *Webster's Dictionary* and read the definition to Jenny. I explain, "An antique is not only just old; it's an object existing since or belonging to earlier times . . . a work of art . . . a piece of furniture. Antiques are treasured," I tell Jenny as I put away the dictionary. "They have to be handled carefully because they sometimes are very valuable."

According to various customs laws, in order to be quali-fied as an antique, the object has to be at least one hundred years old.

"I'm only sixty-seven," I remind Jenny.

We look around the house for other antiques besides me. There is a bureau that was handed down from one aunt to another and finally to our family. "It's very old," I tell Jenny. "I try to keep it polished, and I show it off when-ever I can. You do that with antiques." When Jenny gets older and understands such things, I might also tell her that whenever I look at the bureau or touch it, I am reminded of the aunt so dear to me who gave me the bureau as a gift. I see her face again, though she is no longer with us. I even hear her voice and recall her smile. I remember myself as a little girl leaning against this antique, listening to one of her stories. The bureau does that for me.

There is a picture on the wall purchased at a garage sale. It is dated 1867. "Now that's an antique," I boast. "Over one hundred years old." Of course it is marked up and scratched and not in very good condition. "Sometimes age does that," I tell Jenny. "But the marks are good marks. They show living, being around. That's something to display with pride. In fact, sometimes, the more an object shows age, the more valuable it can become." It is important that I believe this for my own self-esteem.

Our tour of antiques continues. There is a vase on the floor. It has been in my household for a long time. I'm not certain where it came from, but I didn't buy it new. And then there is the four-poster bed, sent to me forty years ago from an uncle who slept in it for fifty years.

The one thing about antiques, I explain to Jenny, is that they usually have a story. They've been in one home and then another, handed down from one family to another, traveling all over the place. They've lasted through years and years. They could have been tossed away, or ignored, or destroyed or lost. But instead, they survived.

For a moment Jenny looks thoughtful. "I don't have any antiques but you," she says. Then her face brightens. "Could I take you to school for show-and-tell?"

"Only if I fit into your backpack," I answer.

And then her antique lifted her up and embraced her in a hug that would last through the years.

Harriet May Savitz

Magic Snowball Time

If a child is to keep alive his inborn sense of wonder, he needs the companionship of at least one adult who can share it, rediscovering with him the joy, excitement and mystery of the world we live in.

Source Unknown

Every fall, when the frost first played freeze tag with the grass, Papa would come to our house. He would shuffle in, his soft, shiny leather shoes dancing across Momma's sunflower-yellow-tiled kitchen floor. All six of us kids knew why he was there. First frost meant magic snowball time.

Papa only came to our house once a year. He and Granny lived in an apartment upstairs from an old neighborhood corner store in the big city. Papa said they lived there to be close to the old-fashioned penny candy counter in the store.

We went to see Papa, Granny and that penny candy counter every Saturday. Unless, of course, the first frost fell on a Saturday. The first frost always meant that Papa was coming to see us.

Papa would bring an old battered coal shovel and an old-fashioned ice chest with him. He'd hustle all six of us kids out to the backyard. Then, he'd start digging and talking. He always worked as he talked.

Papa would tell us how he'd lived with the gypsies before he'd met Granny. He'd tell us about life on the road with the carnival. He'd show us magic tricks and tell us strange but true tales of gypsy powers. Then, Papa would start talking about the importance of the magic snowbank.

We'd gather around him and listen like we were supposed to, but never did, in church. He would tell us how some folks believed that if you wanted a good snowy winter, you always had to save a little snow from the winter before and put it into the magic snowbank. Then, he'd let us each have a turn digging.

The dirt would fly, as we steadily took turns digging down into the earth. We could smell the last barbequed breezes of summer, and the newly fallen leaves of autumn. Sometimes, we'd all swear that we'd smelled the peppermint, candy cane, gingerbread house and poinsettia fragrances of Christmas wafting out of that hole.

Papa would tell us how some folks believed that you have to give to the earth if you want it to give to you. He'd talk about how any good farmer knows that you can't expect to reap a harvest without planting seeds. Our snow seeds were in his old ice chest.

Soon enough, Papa would open that old ice chest. We'd crowd around it with the same amount of wonder every year. Inside, Papa would have seven perfect magic snowballs. There was always one for him, and one for each of us kids.

We'd wait politely, but impatiently as he passed them out. We could never hold them for long, as Papa said it wouldn't work if we were selfish. We didn't want to melt the snow and have nothing to offer the earth.

We would solemnly place our snowballs into the hole, quickly, if still a bit reluctantly. There's not a child I've ever known that didn't want to throw a snowball once it was placed into his or her hands. We weren't any different. We just knew that we had to give our snowballs to the earth. Our snowballs were magic. Our snowballs were the seeds for the magic snowbank.

Papa would cover our magic snowbank with the dirt that we'd shoveled out of the hole. We'd all hold hands and sing Christmas carols, as Papa buried our magic snowballs.

Then, Papa would wipe his hands on his pants and smile.

"Well, we've planted our magic snowballs on the day of the first frost, kids. It's up to the magic snowbank now," he'd say.

When the first snow came, as it did every winter, all six of us would run out into the yard and catch snowflakes on our tongues and in our mittens. We'd taste the tickly, shivery delight of falling ice stars. We'd examine the crystal beauty of bright white, frosty flakes on dark, warm mittens.

It was all Papa's magic, and we were a part of it. We would dance and hug and giggle and grin and sing, all six of us together. We never quarreled or argued on the day the first snow fell. We were too pleased with ourselves.

We knew we were magic. The first snow reminded us of Papa, the first frost and our magic snowbank deep within the earth. We knew we had a secret all our own. We had helped the snow to fall once again. We were snow farmers, and to us, first frost meant magic snowball time.

I'm all grown up now. Still, I'll tell you a secret. My family carries on Papa's magic. We have a magic snowbank in our backyard. Think of us when the first snow flies . . . as I think of my Papa and hope that someday my grandchildren will think of me.

Colleen Madonna Flood Williams

FOR BETTER OR FOR WORSE. ©*UFS. Reprinted by Permission.*

One Finger

Some things have to be believed to be seen.

Ralph Hodgson

"Mom, you should put some of your things away. Baby-proof this house," stated our oldest son Mark as he lumbered up the stairs followed by his wife, Kim, and fifteen-month-old Hannah.

Visiting for the Thanksgiving holiday, he finished unloading the luggage and took it to the guest room downstairs. After driving all day from Salt Lake to Ft. Collins, his temper showed.

"That one-finger rule may work with the twins, but it'll never work with Hannah," he insisted.

When my three granddaughters were born four months apart and the twins moved into our house at eight months, my close friend offered me her secret to entertaining grandchildren with few mishaps.

"Teach them the 'one-finger rule.'" All of her five grandchildren learned it at a young age. The success of the method surprised me.

I picked up my granddaughter and said, "Well, Mark, you just watch." I hugged her and walked all around the great room.

"Hannah, you may touch anything in this room you want. But, you can only use one finger."

I demonstrated the technique by touching my fore-finger to the African sculpture on the mantel. Hannah followed my example.

"Good girl. Now what else would you like to touch?"

She stretched her finger toward another object on the mantel. I allowed her to touch everything in sight—plants, glass objects, TV, VCR, lamps, speakers, candles and artifi-cial flowers. If she started to grab, I gently reminded her to use one finger. She always obeyed.

But, Hannah, an only child, possessed a more adventur-ous personality. Her father predicted it would prevent her from accepting the one-finger rule.

During their four-day stay, we aided Hannah in remem-bering the one-finger rule. She learned quickly. I only put away the things that might prove to be a danger to a child. Otherwise, we watched her closely, and nothing appeared to suffer any damage. Besides, "things" can be replaced.

A few fingerprints on glass doors, windows and tables remained after Hannah and her family returned home. I couldn't bring myself to clean them for days. Each one reminded me of some wonderful experience with Hannah.

Months later, my husband and I drove to Salt Lake, and I watched Mark and Kim continue to practice the one-finger rule. But I refrained from saying, "I told you so." Yet, I smiled inwardly each time they prodded Hannah to touch with "one finger."

Mark, a salesman, always gave a packet of gifts to his potential clients. The night before we returned home, Mark sat on the floor stuffing gifts into their packets.

Hannah helped.

Then she picked up one gift, held it in her hand as if it were a fragile bird, and walked toward me. At my knee, her beautiful blue eyes looked into mine. She stretched her prize to me and said, "One finger, Nana!"

Linda Osmundson

Little Marie

Learning sleeps and snores in libraries, but wisdom is everywhere, wide awake, on tiptoe.

Josh Billings

I have a great brood of grown children, many who have scattered to the far corners. We call frequently, and I send letters stuffed with coupons for diapers, baby food and things. In return, Papa and I get sent silly pictures of our growing grandchildren or crayon drawings done in school.

We love the photos and the artwork, but miss being able to go to their soccer games, dance recitals and birthday parties.

Last summer we planned a large family reunion. Finally, we'd be able to gather all our wonderful grandchildren together.

Our youngest son arrived with our youngest granddaughter. Marie was three with chubby cheeks just begging to be pinched. My daughter-in-law, well-meaning as she was, pushed Marie toward us. "Give Grandma and Grandpa kisses hello," she said.

Marie looked panicked and ducked behind her mom's legs. She held on tightly despite our daughter-in-law's urges to give us a hug and kiss. After a moment, I said that maybe Marie would like to kiss us another time, when she was more familiar with us. Our daughter-in-law, embarrassed, agreed that this might be better.

Throughout the reunion week Marie continued to hide whenever her mom asked her to give us a kiss. It pained me that my own granddaughter was afraid of me. Marie's behavior reinforced the loneliness I felt from being so far away from my children and grandchildren.

The week came to an end, and our son prepared to leave for the airport. I knew my daughter-in-law would try one final time to get Marie to kiss us. I wanted our good-byes to be happy so I decided to try something different.

Before my daughter-in-law could insist upon a kiss, I told her that I needed to say a special good-bye to Marie.

I bent over and stared right into Marie's eyes. We stared good and long until finally I had to stand up.

"What was that all about?" asked my son.

Still looking at Marie's pensive little face I said, "Our eyeballs kissed."

Slowly, Marie's face began to transform. A grin split from ear to ear and she laughed. Then she ran to me and gave me a big hug. "Silly Gramma," she whispered in my ear. "I'll miss you."

We'll miss her, too.

Angela D'Valentine

Raising My Sights

Whatever is going on is just a reflection of our-selves back to us, so that we can see ourselves more clearly.

Arnold Datent

My six-year-old granddaughter, Caitlynd, and I stopped at a Tim Horton's donut shop for a blueberry muffin. As we were going out the door, a young teenage boy was coming in.

This young man had no hair on the sides of his head and a tuft of blue spiked hair on top of it. One of his nostrils was pierced, and attached to the hoop that ran through the hole was a chain that draped across his face and attached to a ring he was wearing in his ear. He held a skateboard under one arm and a basketball under the other.

Caitlynd, who was walking ahead of me, stopped in her tracks when she saw the teen. I thought he'd scared the dickens out of her, and she'd frozen on the spot.

I was wrong.

My Grandangel backed up against the door and opened it as wide as it would go. Now I was face to face with the young man. I stepped aside and let him pass. His response was a gracious, "Thank you very much."

On our way to the car, I commended Caitlynd for her manners in holding open the door for the young man. She didn't seem to be troubled by his appearance, but I wanted to make sure. If a grandmotherly talk about freedom of self-expression and allowing people their differences was in order, I wanted to be ready.

As it turned out, the person who needed the talk was me.

The only thing Caitlynd noticed about the teen was the fact that his arms were full. "He woulda had a hard time to open the door."

I saw the partially shaved head, the tuft of spiked hair, the piercings and the chain. She saw a person carrying something under each arm and heading toward a closed door.

In the future, I hope to get down on her level and raise my sights.

Terri McPherson

Moe Birnbaum, the Fiddler

Grandchildren restore our zest for life and our faith in humanity.

Source Unknown

Moe Birnbaum hadn't made his living as a fiddle player, but no one doubted that he was good enough. Instead, for thirty-eight relentless years he had supported his family with a furniture store. He sold what in the trade they called "borax goods," furniture that was cheap and schlock. It was always peddled on credit, and the clientele was not high-class.

In his free time, Moe's fingers danced his gift. His bow cut vibrant arcs with such grace and, now retired, every day Moe made the condo caverns sing. His fiddle knew no sense of time. Moe could be heard playing at all hours, sometimes too early in the morning. Then, a shoe would be thumped on Moe's ceiling, whacked by the old couple who lived above the Birnbaums. And so Moe would wait a dutiful half hour, fingering, and with great restraint he'd keep from stroking the strings.

When he started up again, some of us applauded

behind our closed doors, then danced our way to the All-Bran boxes, poured our prune juices, and tapped our feet waiting for the kettle to whistle. We remembered all the fiddle-playing weddings we had known, and all the catering halls where we had done the hora and downed all that chopped liver smeared on Ritz Crackers.

Moe Birnbaum was definitely the music maker in his family. Esther, his wife, had her charms, but sadly, music was not among them. Stuffed cabbages she could do, but Esther's strings involved beans. Yet she had encouraged their two kids get into violins. While Moe was at the furniture store, it was Esther who monitored the practicing. She knew it was their inheritance.

The kids are grown now. They come to Florida to visit the old folks two times a year: Hanukkah and Passover. Moe and Esther help with the airfares.

The fiddling music during those twice-a-year visits rocks the humid Florida nights. It goes long, and it runs late. Everyone was always invited to come hear the generations play. Even the old couple upstairs would sit on their balcony and listen, the glazed look of lost memories on their faces.

The Birnbaums couldn't roll up the rugs, not the wall-to-wall built-in condo carpeting, beige and pilled, but they danced anyhow. People brought potluck canapes. It got competitive, and there were always plates full of lox and smoked whitefish scattered among the chopped herring and the Rye Krisps.

Moe and Esther were blessed with four grandchildren, and as could be predicted, they didn't play trombones. Instead, every year, as the children grew, another grandchild would have learned on the passed-down miniature Suzuki fiddle, built for tiny fingers, and they'd join the more experienced Birnbaum violins, fitting right in. Moe would cry openly, making no effort to pretend he didn't feel this inordinate pride in his blooming reality; his brood could fiddle.

The unkind years brought arthritis, and it nibbled at Moe's fingers. Esther, too, found it harder to stuff cabbages. But Moe kept playing, moving from quick-fingered dance tunes, to slower, romantic dinner music. We noticed the difference, but we were dancing slower ourselves and welcomed Moe's changes.

One grim day, Moe had a stroke, two weeks before Hanukkah. His bowing arm lay curled and hopeless at his waist, supported by a sling. People who called on them looked above it, pretending not to see it. Moe couldn't speak, but his eyes showed where the pain really was. The music was over for Moe. His fiddle sat in the corner of the living room. Esther dusted it every time she thought of it.

In the days after the stroke, their kids were on the phone constantly, wanting to rush right down, but Esther said, "Come when you were going to come. I won't let him die before you get here. It will be better and cheaper. You already have your tickets. Keep it that way. Just bring your fiddles."

Sitting up in their bed, Moe overheard her. He turned his head into the pillow and cried, tears dropping on his sling. The late afternoon sunlight painted mauve shadows on the ceiling.

The two weeks dragged, but then they finally arrived— his two kids, their tender spouses, complete with the four grandchildren and six violins. Months ago, Esther had arranged for them to stay in the empty condos of two friends who had gone up North to see their own children. It was one of the folk rituals of condo life.

Esther fed everyone at the groaning table. With all of its extensions, it filled the living room. Moe sat in the wheelchair at the head, silent, but his eyes were bright.

There was chicken from two Crock-Pots, buckwheat groats, steaming plates of vegetables, baskets of breads and enough salad to feed the rest of the condominium. She finished them off with her famous apple compote.

Esther had a job for everyone. When the dishes were cleared and the leftovers put away, only then did she give the okay, declaring that the kitchen was cleaned to her high standards. It was then that they opened the violin cases and all six of them began playing a song, one written just for Moe. It was filled with musical jokes and lots of family history. Soundlessly, Moe laughed. His eyes flooded with tears, and so they played it all over again.

For the second song, they had planned an amazing thing. The oldest granddaughter, in her first year in high school, ceremoniously opened Moe's own violin case and tucked Moe's fiddle under her chin. Very tenderly she raised his good arm and cradled his fingers on to the strings. Then standing behind him, she whispered in his ear, and with a sense of triumph she started bowing for her grandfather.

Moe's fingers found the Russian lullaby he had played for her when she was a baby and later fiddled for each of the new grandchildren as they came along during those years when Esther and Moe had baby-sat while the baby's parents were out on one of those too-rare married dates.

Moe didn't miss a note. The granddaughter bowed with Moe's flair. Everyone sang the Russian words. And once again Moe Birnbaum's fiddle echoed up out of the court-yard canyons at Spoon Lakes Condominium.

Sidney B. Simon

The Last Man on the Moon

Love doesn't make the world go 'round. Love is what makes the ride worthwhile.

Franklin P. Jones

Too many years have passed for me to still be the last man to have walked on the moon.

One evening, as the moon climbed full and achingly bright above the hills, I scooped my five-year-old grand-daughter Ashley into my arms, just as I had once held her mother, Tracy, beneath a similar night sky. I thought that now perhaps she was old enough to understand, to remember, and I prepared to tell her the story.

Before I could speak, she pointed straight up and declared in an excited voice, "Poppie, there's your moon." She had always called it that, never knowing why.

"Do you know how far away it is, Punk?" I asked.

She seemed puzzled, for a child of that age could not possibly grasp such a distance, so I rambled on, using words familiar to her.

"It's way, way far away in the sky, out where God lives," I said. "Poppie flew his rocket up there and lived on that moon for three whole days. I even wrote your mommy's initials in the sand."

Ashley gazed at it a little longer, then lowered her eyes to meet mine, and she saw not some mighty suited-up space hero from an age before she was born, but only her silver-haired grandfather.

"Poppie," she said, "I didn't know you went to heaven."

Eugene Cernan and Don Davis

The Priceless Gift

May you have enough happiness to make you sweet, enough trials to make you strong, enough sorrow to keep you human, enough hope to make you happy and enough money to buy me gifts.

Shawna Whitmore

I love to give and receive presents; they are always so much fun to open. One day my grandson, Justin, sent me six dollars and thirty cents. I could not think of one good reason why he would send me that amount of money. I thought about it for a couple of days and then called my grandson.

I asked him, "Why did you send Grandma six dollars and thirty cents?"

Justin told me that I always did such nice things for him, that he wanted to give me everything he had.

After hanging up the phone, this old grandma sat down and had a good cry. I knew in my heart that I would never again receive a gift given with such pure and innocent love.

Irene (Seida) Carlson

Same Agenda

Grandchildren are loving reminders of what we're really here for.

Janet Lanese

We were sitting in the crowded auditorium waiting for the program to view the performance of our seven-year-old grandson, Tanner, in his school's annual Christmas pageant.

It was difficult to say who was more excited—the children or the audience. I looked around and spotted my son and his wife, with their four-month-old baby boy, and Tanner's maternal grandparents seated several rows behind us. We acknowledged each other with a smile and a wave.

Then I saw them—Tanner's "biological" paternal grand - parents. My son and Tanner's mother had dated briefly as sixteen-year-olds, split up, then became reacquainted shortly after their high-school graduation when Tanner was just six months old. Even though my daughter-in-law never married Tanner's father, his parents had fought for grandparents' rights and won. Tanner may call my son

"Daddy," but Tanner is bound by court order to go every other weekend for visitation with the parents of his "biological" father.

We had taken Tanner into our hearts as our own, and we weren't very willing to share him.

This had always been a particular sore spot for me. We did not know them well, and I feared the worst when he went with them on their weekend. In retrospect, we should have viewed it as commendable that they were interested enough in Tanner to pay a lawyer and go through the complicated legal system.

So there we were, separated by a few rows of folding chairs. There were only a few instances where we had been thrown together, and each of these meetings had been uncomfortable. I saw the woman look at us, nudge her husband and whisper in his ear. He immediately looked back at us as well.

My ears were burning as if on fire. I attempted to remember why we were here—our common bond, a child that meant so much to us.

Shortly thereafter the program started, and for the next hour we were enthralled. Before we knew it, the lights were on, and we were gathering our things to leave. We followed the crowd into the hall and searched for our grandson.

We soon found him, and suddenly three sets of grandparents were thrown together, each waiting to take our turn in congratulating Tanner on a fine performance. We eyed each other and spoke a brief "hello."

Finally, it was our turn to hug Tanner and discuss his job well done. His eyes were shining brightly, and he was obviously proud to be the object of so much adoration.

I leaned down to hear what he was saying. "Grandma, I'm so lucky!" Tanner exclaimed, clapping his hands together.

"Because you did such a fine job?" I innocently asked.

"No, because all my favorite people are here! My Mom, Dad, little brother, and *all* my grandmas and grandpas are here together, just to see *me!*"

I looked up, stunned at his remark.

My eyes met those of the "other" grandma, and I could see she was feeling the same shame as I was. I was horrified at my thoughts and feelings over all these years.

What had given only me the right to love this little boy? They obviously loved him as much as we did, and he obviously loved each of us. They also no doubt had their own fears about us. How could we have been so blind?

As I looked around, I could see we were all ashamed of our previous feelings on this subject. We visited briefly, said our good-byes and went our separate ways.

I've thought a lot about our encounter since that night, and I admit I feel that a weight has been lifted off my shoulders. I don't fear Tanner's weekend visits like I used to.

I discovered that we all have the same agenda—to love a little boy who truly belongs to all of us.

Patricia Pinney

Buying Something for Herself

The soul is healed by being with children.

Fyodor Dostoevsky

Our granddaughter Tanisha jumped down from the giant yellow school bus and ran up the sidewalk, back-pack swinging, waving something in her hand. I opened the door and in she flew.

"Papa! Grandma!" she yelled excitedly. "I didn't know you were coming to visit."

Papa picked her up and swung her around. "What's this in your hand?" he asked.

"It's my report card," she replied, handing it to him.

Papa turned to me and said, "Look at this, Grandma, it's all As!"

"Wow! That's wonderful," I replied, giving her a hug.

"All As deserve something special. What would you like me to buy you?" Papa asked.

"I don't know, Papa."

Digging into his pocket, he produced a five-dollar bill.

"Here you go. You can buy something for yourself. How about that?"

"Thanks, Papa!" she squealed.

"That's from your Grandma, too," he said as he gave me a look that asked if it was okay.

Tanisha turned to me and echoed, "Thanks, Grandma."

"You're welcome, Sweetheart. We are very proud of you. Spend it wisely," I added.

As I watched her bound from the room with her treasure, I thought of how we miss this bright-eyed, curly headed little granddaughter of ours. Tanisha had lived the first few years of her life with us in sunny California, while her parents spent their mandatory time at sea with the navy. Now, she is with her mommy and daddy as well as her little brother and sister. They live in military housing in Washington, D.C. At seven, she is already in the second grade and getting so tall we hardly recognize her.

As with most grandparents who visit grandchildren only a few times a year, we try our best to spoil them when we actually see these precious little cherubs! The five dollars for the report card was just part of the spoiling. We did not think about this being more money than she had ever had. We did not realize what an awesome responsibility this was going to be for this seven-year-old little girl.

While on outings during our week's visit, we asked if there was anything she saw that she wanted to buy with her money. She searched the shelves for the perfect item. She sighed and scrunched up her nose and thought hard as she looked carefully, but she could not find one thing she wanted to buy with her newfound wealth. She said she wanted to save it for something very special.

"When you see it, you'll know it," I said. "Don't worry about it."

After a week of books and movies, ice cream and Playland at McDonald's, it was time for Papa and I to return home. We did so with long faces and sad eyes. We were going to miss the fun Tanisha and our other two little grandchildren brought into our lives during our stay. But work beckoned, our vacation at an end.

Once home and back to the daily routine, Papa and I forgot about the report card reward we had left with our eldest granddaughter. It was not until months later that I remembered our gift and asked her, "By the way, what did you buy with that five dollars Papa and I gave you for getting all As on your report card? I hope it was something special."

"Oh, it was," she said. "But I didn't buy anything."

Confused, I asked, "What do you mean?"

"I spent it. I just didn't buy anything. I put it in the collection plate at church."

"Oh," I said with a proud lump in my throat. "That was very nice of you."

"There was a special collection at church for poor people. I figured their kids needed it more than me. So when they passed around the plate, I dropped it in," she said, as if it was no big deal.

"How thoughtful of you." Tears rolled down my cheeks as I thought of her unselfishness. "I'm proud of you all over again," I continued. "I love you very much."

"I love you, too, Grandma. Can I talk to Papa?" she asked.

Papa looked at me with worry. He whispered, "Why are you crying?"

I pushed the phone into his hands and said, "Here, she wants to talk to you."

We had wanted our granddaughter to buy something special for herself. In the end, that's exactly what she did. She bought something for herself that we could never have given her. She bought the gift of giving to others, of doing something for someone in need.

Without knowing it, she bought us gifts as well. She bought us the knowledge that we had not failed her during her formative years when she lived with us—and a special pride in calling her granddaughter!

Karen Brandt

The Gift of Giving

*Kindness is more important than wisdom, and
the recognition of this is the beginning of wisdom.*
Theodore Isaac Rubin, M.D.

Gram and Gramps lived on the other side of the country, and although we called and wrote often, it had been twenty years since I'd seen them in person. Their health was failing, and age kept them close to home. My responsibilities at home with a husband, two young children and a part-time job, kept me from visiting.

I did make a point of going in March one year. I'd spoken to Gram and realized that, in their eighties now, they weren't going to be around forever—as much as I would like them to be. I made the arrangements and flew there for a week.

The moment I walked in the door, I was home again. The memories from a childhood long past, immediately returned. The cookies baking in the warm oven, watching Gram ice the fairy-tale cake and letting me dig in the bowl of icing when she was done. The beautiful clothes she'd sewed, smocked dresses and shorts with pop-tops to match.

As she often did in her letters, she told stories of what I was like as a little girl and how she'd given me Muriel as my middle name. I never told her how much I was teased as a child because of that name—suddenly, it was prettier somehow and its very uniqueness was so like Gram.

Gramps talked of the two wars he lived through, and I told him how proud I was to know he'd served his country so well. He made me laugh, and I believe I made him feel young again, if only for awhile. In turn, he made me cry. He told me that he and Gram had given up on celebrating Christmas about ten years back. They were just too old.

How can one let Christmas pass by unnoticed? I remembered best the Christmas as a child, when they lived with us. They loved the season and always went to midnight Mass. Gramps took my brothers, sisters and me to cut down the tree, while Gram baked every Christmas cookie imaginable, then decorated the tree just so. Our house had been filled with the love and togetherness I had always associated with Christmas. I couldn't believe they had stopped celebrating it.

Gramps explained that they were too old to bother with a tree and their friends too old to travel to see it. Even shopping, now, was too difficult, and they had all of the necessities delivered. I wanted to cry for the joy they'd once had—and lost.

That week remains one of the most joyous of my life. Knowing that it might be the last time I saw either of them saddened me, but I was determined to make it a happy visit. I took the two of them out to dinner—something they hadn't done in well over two years, since Gram had her hip surgery. I know they had a good time.

Saying good-bye was difficult. Gramps, the brave, strong hero of mine, cried and Gram did her best not to. She never succeeded. I cried on the plane all the way home.

As Christmas approached, I thought of them more than ever. I wanted to do something so they would know I was thinking of them. The idea came to give them back Christmas, and I set about to do just that.

First, I found a small artificial tree and decorated it with miniature bulbs and fine gold ribbon. With this, I added colorfully wrapped presents for each of them; slippers, chocolates, a hand-knit scarf for Gramps and a pretty bed jacket for Gram. I made up a box of cookies and bars; many of the recipes were from Gram's cookbooks. Then I filled stockings for each of them with toiletries wrapped and tied with ribbons.

In the card, I wrote that they had given me so many wonderful memories throughout the years that I wanted to give them some new ones. I asked both of them to promise to set the tree up in the living room and stack the gifts around it. My last instruction was, "Do not open 'til Christmas!"

I mailed the parcel, barely able to contain my excitement. Gram called as soon as it arrived. She was crying and, this time, not even attempting to hide it. We spoke for a long time, reminiscing about Christmas past, and when I knew for certain they had the tree up, I promised to call Christmas morning.

When my boys had opened every gift and were digging through their stockings, I made the long-awaited call. Gramps answered on the first ring. I thought he sounded strange, and we only spoke briefly, then Gram took the phone.

"We were like two kids," she told me. "Neither of us got any sleep last night. I even caught Harry in the living room, shaking one of the packages and had to make him go back to bed. Honey, this is the first time in years we've been so excited. Don't tell your grandfather, but after he went to bed, I just had to rattle a few of the gifts myself."

I laughed, imagining the two of them sneaking out to guess at the presents I'd sent. I wished there was more money to send more expensive gifts, and told Gram that maybe next year they would be better.

"Your grandfather can't talk right now because he's too busy crying. He keeps saying, 'That's one heck of a granddaughter we have there, Muriel.'"

Hope Saxton

Computer Granny

Other things may change us, but we start and end with family.

Anthony Brandt

My eyes filled with tears as I kissed my family good-bye at the Sydney, Australia, airport. Because the trip from America is so expensive, I knew I wouldn't be returning to be with my son, my Australian daughter-in-law or my precious grandchildren for at least two more years.

Tracy, nine years old, and Phillip, eleven, were born there. I'd seen them only five times in their short lives—one month every two years. I so wanted to be a good grandma to them, like my grandma was to me. I wanted to bake them homemade cookies, visit their schools, watch Tracy's dance recitals and Phillip's bowling tournaments. I wanted them to be able to come to me when they were hurting and let me wipe their tears and give them hugs. I wanted to be able to talk with them every day—to listen to their laughter, to know their dreams, to say "I love you."

Each time we parted, my heart ached a little more. But on this visit Tracy and Phillip had given me exciting hope for the future. They had talked incessantly about their new computer and how, if I bought one, we would be able to communicate daily!

"Remember, Granny," Tracy squealed as I waved goodbye, "get a computer! And write to us!"

"Every day!" Phillip shouted. "We'll write to you, too."

And so it was that I abandoned my outdated typewriter and made a frightening leap into this fast-paced, high-tech era of e-mail. Everything about my new computer scared me. I was afraid to touch the keyboard for fear I'd delete something important or do some sort of damage. I even had trouble getting started with the one-page, loose insert of quick tips:

Click on the Windows Icon.

(Wait! I wanted to scream. *How do I turn on the computer?)*

Click on the Start button, located on the Taskbar.

(What's a taskbar?)

Point to Programs with the mouse cursor.

(What part of this silly-looking mouse thing is a cursor?)

Gramps started questioning my sanity when he heard me talking to my machine, aloud, on a regular basis:

WARNING! Invalid MAPI.DLL present. Cannot provide MAPI.DLL service.

(Did I ask to be serviced?)

WARNING! This program has performed an illegal operation and will be shut down.

(So shut down already. I don't want to work with something illegal anyway.)

WARNING! A printer time-out has occurred.

(What?! My printer is taking a break? Who's in charge here?)

My first few weeks of learning were not fun. I spent full days and nights reading tutorials. I bought *Windows for Dummies*. I waited on hold for hours, the phone glued to my ear, trying to connect to a live helper on the "helpline." I harassed my friends with annoying calls—at 7:00 A.M., at meal time, at bedtime—pleading for a simple escape from some program jam that had me trapped in limbo.

The machine became my nemesis, and at the same time, the hero that could link me to my family. It was definitely a love/hate relationship. But no obstacle, technological or otherwise, could deter me from the possibility of hearing from my grandchildren every day!

I've missed out on so much of their lives. But with electronic mail, everything has changed. Now, one month and dozens of messages later, I'm up-to-the-minute with news from Tracy and Phillip!

By e-mail, Phillip tells Gramps and me about his role in the school play. He regales us with his account of getting caught in the rain on his bike. And he makes us proud as he announces his test scores in math.

On my last visit I taught him a goofy language called "Op." He recently sent a complete e-mail message using our "secret code"—no easy task. The best part was *Opl lopove yopou sopoopoopoopo mopuch!* Translation: I love you soooo much!

Tracy turned ten last week. We were in on the birthday plans from day one—the porcelain doll she was hoping for, the anticipation of a slumber party with three of her friends and a Lion King cake.

On the night of her sleepover we smiled at the computer message from her dad complaining about the unbearable noise level. We quickly responded to Tracy by saying, "We had to close our windows because we could hear you and your friends all the way across the ocean!"

Her mom immediately replied, "I just went in and read your message to the girls. They started to apologize, then realized it was a joke. The look on their faces was priceless!"

Before long we received a short note from Tracy. It was

almost as though we were right there enjoying her party in person.

The kids write to me when they're happy. And they write when they are hurting. They share some secrets they don't even tell Mom and Dad, and they ask me questions that only a grandma could answer.

I can't wipe their tears or put my arms around them and hold them close. But I can "listen" and show how much I care with my empathy and advice. I can send them funny jokes and precious poems. I can tell them how much I love them—every day.

I still make lots of mistakes on my computer, and my heart still jumps when I get one of those obnoxious, threatening, WARNING! alerts. The most recent one said I had committed a "fatal error." *Fatal!* I nearly threw in the mouse pad! But on the same day we received a message from Tracy saying, "I love you guise bigger than the entire world!"

For *that* I'll take any abuse this whiz-bang wonder of chips and a motherboard dishes out.

Just call me Computer Granny!

Kay Conner Pliszka

Here with Me

*God gave us loving grandchildren as a reward
for all our acts of kindness.*

Roger Cochran

Last weekend marked one of the nicest days so far this spring.

It was warm with a tiny breeze; the sun penetrated through lightweight sweaters to warm the skin; the male choir was warming up, and the graduates were milling around the lawn behind the throng of six-thousand-plus observers.

With all of the parents, sisters, brothers, grandparents, aunts and uncles, the state university was a hub of activity. My nephew was going to receive his bachelor's degree. Who would have guessed that four years would go by so quickly?

As the crowd of freshly polished and scrubbed candidates wandered, joked, hugged and chattered behind the bleachers, I heard several cell phones ring. There were several nonsensical conversations going on with the accompanying giggles of the not-quite-mature students, but then one conversation in particular caught my attention:

"Yes, Grandma, I'm really graduating. I can't believe it, either! I never thought I'd be here today, you know? Really! Like, I know it! Yup, it's a very special day. . . . Oh, what did the doctor say? He did? I know, Gran . . . I know you wanted to come. . . . It's okay. . . . No, really, please don't cry. . . . It's a very happy day, you know?

"Hold on, we're lining up . . . okay, all set . . . yup, the center aisle . . . the grass is awesome! Smells really good, too . . . Oh wow, they've got like a zillion balloons they're going to release! Yes, Kelly's here. . . . Okay, I'll give her your love . . . here we go! Gran, I'm graduating!

"Love you, too, Gran. I'm so glad you could be here with me!"

And somehow, my initial surprise and disdain at the use of cell phones during such a serious occasion left me. For these little representatives of modern technology had joined a young woman and her doting Gran to share a very special moment in time.

Gail C. Bracy

2

A GRAND-PARENT'S LOVE

*Grandma and Grandpa, tell me a story and
  snuggle me with your love. When I'm in
  your arms, the world seems small and
  we're blessed by the heavens above.*

Laura Spiess

The Red Mahogany Piano

People only see what they are prepared to see.

Ralph Waldo Emerson

Many years ago, when I was a young man in my twenties, I worked as a salesman for a St. Louis piano company. We sold our pianos all over the state by advertising in small-town newspapers and then when we had received sufficient replies, we would load our little trucks, drive into the area and sell the pianos to those who had replied.

Every time we would advertise in the cotton country of Southeast Missouri, we would receive a reply on a postcard that said, in effect, "Please bring me a new piano for my little granddaughter. It must be red mahogany. I can pay ten dollars a month with my egg money." The old lady scrawled on and on and on that postcard until she filled it up, then turned it over and even wrote on the front—around and around the edges until there was barely room for the address.

Of course, we could not sell a new piano for ten dollars a month. No finance company would carry a contract with payments that small, so we ignored her postcards.

One day, however, I happened to be in that area calling on other replies, and out of curiosity I decided to look the old lady up. I found pretty much what I expected; the old lady lived in a one-room sharecropper's cabin in the middle of a cotton field. The cabin had a dirt floor, and there were chickens in the house. Obviously, she could not have qualified to purchase anything on credit—no car, no phone, no real job, nothing but a roof over her head and not a very good one at that. I could see daylight through it in several places. Her little granddaughter was about ten, barefoot and wearing a feed-sack dress.

I explained to the old lady that we could not sell a new piano for ten dollars a month, and that she should stop writing to us every time she saw our ad. I drove away heartsick, but my advice had no effect—she still sent us the same postcard every six weeks. Always wanting a new piano, red mahogany, please, and swearing she would never miss a ten-dollar payment. It was sad.

A couple of years later, I owned my own piano company, and when I advertised in that area, the postcards started coming to me. For months, I ignored them—what else could I do?

But then, one day when I was in the area something came over me. I had a red mahogany piano on my little truck. Despite knowing that I was about to make a terrible business decision, I delivered the piano to her and told her I would carry the contract myself at ten dollars a month with no interest, and that would mean fifty-two payments. I took the new piano in the house and placed it where I thought the roof would be least likely to leak on it. I admonished her and the little girl to try to keep the chickens off of it, and I left—sure I had just thrown away a new piano.

But the payments came in, all fifty-two of them as agreed—sometimes with coins taped to a three- by five-inch card in the envelope. It was incredible!

So, I put the incident out of my mind for twenty years.

Then one day I was in Memphis on other business, and after dinner at the Holiday Inn on the Levee, I went into the lounge. As I was sitting at the bar having an after-dinner drink, I heard the most beautiful piano music behind me. I looked around, and there was a lovely young woman playing a very nice grand piano.

Being a pianist of some ability myself, I was stunned by her virtuosity, and I picked up my drink and moved to a table beside her where I could listen and watch. She smiled at me, asked for requests, and when she took a break she sat down at my table.

"Aren't you the man who sold my grandma a piano a long time ago?"

It didn't ring a bell, so I asked her to explain.

She started to tell me, and I suddenly remembered. My Lord, it was her! It was the little barefoot girl in the feed-sack dress!

She told me her name was Elise and that since her grandmother couldn't afford to pay for lessons, she had learned to play by listening to the radio. She said she had started to play in church where she and her grandmother had to walk over two miles, and that she had then played in school, had won many awards and a music scholarship. She had married an attorney in Memphis, and he had bought her that beautiful grand piano she was playing.

Something else entered my mind. "Elise," I asked, "it's a little dark in here. What color is that piano?"

"It's red mahogany," she said. "Why?"

I couldn't speak.

Did she understand the significance of the red mahogany? The unbelievable audacity of her grand-mother insisting on a red mahogany piano when no one in his right mind would have sold her a piano of any kind? I don't know.

And then the marvelous accomplishment of that beautiful, terribly underprivileged child in the feed-sack dress? No, perhaps she didn't understand that, either.

But I did, and my throat tightened.

Finally, I found my voice. "I just wondered," I said. "I'm proud of you, but I have to go to my room."

And I did have to go to my room, because men don't like to be seen crying in public.

Joe Edwards

[EDITORS' NOTE: *In loving memory of our friend Joe Edwards—your stories live on in thousands of hearts you've touched.*]

A Grandpa's Love

The person who has lived the most is not the one with the most years, but the one with the richest experiences.

Jean-Jacques Rousseau

I stared from the deck of my hotel room, intrigued. An older gentleman was assisting a young girl as she struggled to walk down the beach. *He must be her grandfather,* I thought. Somehow, I was drawn to the drama of the twosome, and winced as she fell. The graying man helped her to her feet, and she continued painstakingly plodding through the sand.

That evening, I ate in the hotel restaurant, and watched as the same young girl proceeded to get up from the table and reach for her walker. She grasped it firmly with both hands, and, leaning heavily, she made her way out of the restaurant, smiling as she went.

As I sipped my coffee in the lobby the next morning, I noticed a sign tacked to the announcement board. "Special Olympics Relays." *Ah,* I thought, *that must be what the walking lessons are about.*

Over the next three days, I watched as the grandfather patiently worked with his student. "You can do it, Sweetheart. Let's get up and try again." And at this encouragement, she would struggle again to her feet.

On the morning of the Olympics, as I visited with friends in the lobby, a beautiful bouquet of roses was delivered to the front desk. The girl soon appeared for her delivery, her face brightening at the sight. She smiled as she read the card.

As she walked away, the card slipped from her fingers and she continued down the hallway. I stepped quickly to retrieve it, glancing at the handwritten words as I hurried after her, "To my sweet Elizabeth—you have been the greatest encouragement to my heart these last few days. I love you and am proud of you. Win or lose, you will always be my little miracle from God. Love, Grandpa." She had disappeared around the corner, so I put the card in my pocket to give to her later.

Now attached to the little girl and her grandpa, I felt compelled to watch her Olympic event—a quarter-mile. She definitely was a fighter. I cheered as she crossed the finish line—second place. She smiled as she stood on the awards platform, and a tear slipped down her cheek as the medal was placed around her neck. She told the crowd, "I especially want to thank my grandpa for believing in me when I had no one else."

I found her later, and returned her card. I said, "Congratulations!" As we talked, she revealed that she and her parents were hit by a drunk driver three years prior. She was the only survivor. Her grandfather shook my hand and said, "By the grace of God alone, this little girl is alive and able to accomplish what she did today."

Elizabeth smiled and hugged her grandpa. "Everyone gave up hope that I would ever walk again. My grandpa was the only one who didn't."

Scot Thurman

Gift from Another Grandmother

The measure of love is not how much that child loves me but rather how much I dare to love that child.

Lois Wyse

Our son, Bob, placed a little stranger down in the middle of our living room. "Mom, Dad, this is my Bridget." Bridget, two and a half, stood there and just smiled, her hazel-brown eyes dancing from one of us to the other. She had been born in the northernmost part of Canada where the aurora borealis can be seen from her yard. This was her first trip to Washington State, and she took my breath away.

We hugged and laughed and greeted one another, then I asked if Bridget would like to help me in the yard. We gathered all the tools, and as I kneeled in the pansy beds beneath our birch trees, Bridget wiggled her plump body close. "Grandma, are you allowed to get dirty?"

"You bet. And so are you."

The next morning we threw our sleeping bags and groceries into the trucks and headed for the ocean. Bridget sat straight and tall between her grandfather and me. As we started off down the driveway, she smiled up at me and carefully took my arm, cradling it between both of her chubby hands, and just hung on for two hundred miles.

Bridget had learned the word, "Grandma," from our daughter-in-law's mother, who lived near their homestead. So we didn't need time to get acquainted. "Run, Grandma, run," Bridget called as we held hands, lifted our faces to the wind and ran toward the ocean waves. She giggled and splashed as the sun and surf painted rainbows across our toes at the water's edge.

That night Bridget never left my side as we toasted marshmallows, our cheeks and fingers melding together with traces of white, sticky sweetness. At bedtime, she rolled out her bag and put it on the canvas floor beside my old army surplus cot in our nine- by nine-foot tent. Grandpa was already snoring and the other grandchildren chose to sleep under the stars with Uncle Brian. As Bridget and I talked about taking our pails to the beach in the morning, she lifted my hand to her lips, "Grandma 'Rean says you're nice." And we drifted off to dreams as the auspicious drone of waves and shifting sand washed across our world.

In the middle of the night a noise awakened me. And in the faint, first light of morning through the tent screen flap, I saw Bridget sit up in her bag and lean onto my cot. She reached across my stomach and hugged me, then brushed her lips across my cheek. Very carefully she patted my arm. Then scooted back inside the Mickey Mouse bag, closing her dark lashes, snuggling her ponytail into the pillow.

I caught my breath, and lay very still, allowing warm tears to wash the memory of Bridget's visit deep into my bones. I held a treasure, my grandchild's ready, open heart, the gift of Grandma Mearean, up north nearly two thousand miles away.

Doris Hays Northstrom

We'll Never Divorce You

What the heart knows today the head will understand tomorrow.

James Stephens

Dear Grandchild,

Grandma and Grandpa know that you're hurting right now because Mommy and Daddy are breaking up. It's called "divorce," and you probably know some other children who have gone through this, too. It happens a lot, more than anyone would like, but we want you to know that you're not alone. When you're at school, ask around, and you're sure to find lots of other kids who have been through what you're going through. And they are surviving. You'll survive, too, although Grandma and Grandpa know that you probably don't feel that way right now.

It's no fun at all, is it? Just a little while ago, things looked fine, everything seemed to be just right, and now everything seems to have fallen apart. We really wish we could somehow "kiss all the boo-boos" and make everything right, but, sadly, Honey, we can't.

We want you to know that this time is difficult for us, too. It makes us very sad to see the hurt and uncertainty in your eyes. When we sense that you are hurting, we hurt, too.

Mommy and Daddy have found that, for whatever reasons, they can't go on living together. You must know that Mommy and Daddy still love *you* very much even if they are having problems with each other.

We want you to know several important things, things that we hope will help you to go through this scary and difficult time.

The first thing that we want to tell you is this: *It is not your fault!* You know, whenever a divorce happens, almost all children think that they did something that made it happen. And we want to promise you this—that is almost *never* true! Mommies and daddies who break up are doing so because they are having some big problems in their relationship. And you are not to blame. If you are blaming yourself, even a little bit, please let us know. Talk to us or write us, and we'll be your special friends and listen to your feelings.

The second thing we want you to know is that *you probably can't fix it.* Lots of kids imagine that they might be able to find just the perfect thing to say or do and, magically, Mommy and Daddy will start loving each other again. We're sorry to tell you, that almost never works. Sometimes mommies and daddies *do* get back together again after a time apart and some time for healing, but that happens because *they* found their own reasons to do so.

The third and maybe the most important thing we want to tell you is this: *We will never divorce you!* We will *always* be there for you when you need us. Sometimes we may be far away, but you can call or write us. We'll answer as soon as we can. And you can always talk to us because we promise to be the very best listeners we can for you.

You need to know that we won't ever take sides between your mommy and your daddy. The only "side" we're going to be on is *yours*. Instead, we'll be good listeners, and we'll also help you find good things to do and great ways to spend your time. We'll search for fun, and we'll make some of our own, too.

You might think that you'll never be happy again or that things will never feel right again. We can understand those feelings. But we want you to know something that we've learned because we've lived so long and seen and experienced so many things—you *will* laugh again; it *will* get better. You'll laugh and grow and experience joy again. Good things will happen. You will have many good times with Daddy and many good times with Mommy again, we assure you. It won't be the same as it was, but your life will be a good one. And the love that surrounds you—from your parents, your grandparents and the rest of the family, and all your friends—will heal and help.

Now here's a list of the things you can count on:

Nothing you can ever do or say will make us stop loving you. We'll love you forever. When we're in heaven, we'll still love you. There *are* things you can count on now, when the world seems so shaky, and one of them is our love for you.

We'll be good listeners for you. Share your feelings, both good and bad. It is a healthy way to help yourself get past these rough times.

We'll give great hugs and warm, long back rubs.

And we'll still make your favorite foods whenever you ask us.

You can contact us easily. We're enclosing a card with our address, home phone number, cell phone number and e-mail address. So no matter where you are, you'll always be able to reach us. If you have to, you can call us "collect." We've also included a pack of stamped postcards addressed to us, so you can always send us a card. And there's a stack of stamped, addressed envelopes for when you have bigger, longer things to write or a nice picture to send us.

Honey, you're not alone. Your mommy and daddy still love you, even if they are breaking up. And we'll always love you, no matter what. And remember: *We will never divorce you. Never.*

Love,
Grandma and Grandpa

Hanoch and Meladee McCarty

The Grandma Video

*To love what you do and feel that it matters,
how could anything be more fun?*

Source Unknown

From the day of my first grandchild's birth, my daughter thoughtfully has sent frequent pictures and videos of him. Even though we live over three hundred miles apart we have always felt we are an active part of his life. As Matthew's second birthday approached, we knew we could not be with him to celebrate it, so we made a short video wishing him a happy birthday. We ended it by setting the camera on a tripod so my husband and I could sing (a bit off-key) a happy birthday duet to him. Even at two, Matthew seemed to understand the video and watched it over and over again.

It doesn't take much to encourage me, so when my daughter reported back the success of the video, I began to do videos periodically whenever we saw or did something that we would have shared with Matthew had he lived closer. It was an interesting turn of events from them sending us videos of Matthew!

Our videos are short, often with just a single subject. We have one of a pasture, not far from our house, filled with cows. We are showing the cows to Matthew and talking about them. We ask him questions, which his mother reports he eagerly answers from his seat on the couch as he watches the video. "Look at that one chewing his food. Isn't he silly?" I ask. Matthew nods and laughs as Grandpa zooms in for a close-up of the cow's face. Just then the cow unexpectedly moos, and it is perfect.

Then I tell Matthew when he visits we can go to see the cows together. It's a good way to keep from being strangers and is also a learning experience as we show him things that might not be readily available in his area.

When the almond trees in our yard bloom, we take a short video of the trees with a close-up of the flowers, explaining that they will turn into almonds and assure him we will send him some to taste when that happens in the months ahead.

For Christmas, we toured our house as Grandpa pointed out the items his mother had made as a child and I showed him my special nativity collection. We saw the lights outside our house after dark and the crackling fire in the fireplace. Our younger daughter was home from college that weekend, and she even got into the act by showing us the cookies she was baking. Matthew especially liked that part.

We watched snowflakes drifting down around our swimming pool in a rare desert snowfall and a shepherd tending his flock of sheep a few miles from our home. Matthew has watched his grandpa hammering and sawing in the garage and Grandma washing dishes. As the camera roams around our home, Matthew sees the bed he will sleep in when he visits and the stack of special books we saved for him from his mother's childhood. "We'll read these books together again when you visit our house, okay?" I ask. I'm told that Matthew smiles and says, "Yes," every single time he sees that part.

The videos are obviously unprofessional, the camera bounces around a bit and sometimes I can't find the object I want to zoom in on. "Oops," you can hear me say. "Where did those flowers go?" My husband and I laugh, but Matthew certainly doesn't mind.

The "Grandma Videos" have continued for over seven years now, and four more grandchildren are viewing them. We enjoy taking the videos and sometimes wonder if we enjoy them more than the grandchildren do! It's fun for us to look at things from a child's perspective again, and I find we have a renewed interest in the simple little objects we often took for granted. We delight in sights we would normally drive past and barely notice. We literally stop and smell the California poppies when they bloom because we want to share them with our grandchildren on a video. The flowers take on a more intense beauty as we walk among them for the very best shot. While on vacation, instead of driving along the beach, we stop and examine the seashells and write the children's names in the sand.

These videos only take half an hour or so from start to finish and cost a minimal amount to mail. My own children saw their grandparents only once a year, but ours can literally have their grandparents at their fingertips anytime they wish.

Oops! I gotta go. It's time to star in another chapter of the Grandma Video!

June Cerza Kolf

Pumpkin Magic

The closest friends I have made all through life have been people who also grew up close to a loved and loving grandmother or grandfather.

Margaret Mead

The heat is just beginning to rise, steaming the earth lightly under my feet. It smells of fresh-turned dirt and young corn, heavy ripe blackberries and climbing beans, sunflowers and peonies and pine trees.

The scent clears the sleep from my head, and I breathe in deeply, drinking it down to the bottom of my lungs. I scuff my toes in the soft grass on the edge of the garden.

Grandpa is strolling through the rows of young growing plants, pulling a weed here, plucking a bean there, testing and touching and studying. I love it here, out in the huge growing field that seems to stretch for miles beyond the acre lot. I watch as Grandpa paces his domain.

"Come here, Sweetheart. I have a surprise for you." I hurry after him, stumbling a little in my attempt to keep up with his long-legged stride. He's headed to the far left edge of the garden, past the rows of corn and tomatoes and cabbage, past the beans and peas and cucumber. He stops at the last row, pausing in front of several low, flat-leaved viney plants. I stand back as he lifts the broad leaves aside, searching for his surprise. Then he nods and beckons me forward.

It is a small, still-growing pumpkin, slightly green, not fully ripe. Its stem is still attached to the vine, and it lies on the ground at an angle. I can see a scar on the far side, and I'm slightly disappointed, sad for Grandpa that his surprise is damaged.

Then he turns the pumpkin over, brushing the dirt away, and I can see that it's not a scar at all; it's my name, growing there along with the pumpkin! MY NAME, borne on this fresh and growing plant, living there in the dirt and sun and wind. I stare at it, run tiny fingers along the edge of the letters. They are rough and solid. When Halloween comes, this pumpkin will be mine and no one else's. I turn wide eyes to Grandpa, standing in the field with the sun behind him. "How did you do that?" I asked.

"Well, it's a long process," he begins. "First, you take a pumpkin seed and a very small knife. . . ."

His eyes sparkle as he discusses magnifying glasses and special planting techniques. I turn and look at the house. Grandma is standing in the doorway waving. "How about breakfast?" Grandpa asks. "I'll make oatmeal with raisins cooked in."

We begin the long walk back to the house. I think about the fresh peas with dinner and the just-picked black-berries over vanilla ice cream, the ripe plums in the bowl on the counter and the corn that won't be ready until the next visit. And I think about my very own pumpkin and my grandpa who can work magic in his special garden. I place my hand in his and walk up the hill to breakfast.

Kati Dougherty-Carthum

Lemon Love

Love is a little word; people make it big.

Source Unknown

My grandfather gave me the world when he gave me his love.

I never had to guess if the wonderfully weathered old man, whose eyes smiled brighter than his mouth, loved me. Unlike many of his generation, he believed in saying so. It was high praise since I was the twenty-fourth of twenty-seven to be delivered into his happy embrace.

Grandpa would have done anything for me, but since love is all about the little things, he was always willing to busy himself with some project meant for my happiness. There was the double-benched swing, crafted in his farm workshop, upon which I spent endless afternoons inhaling the scent of spring wildflowers, while prairie clouds morphed from tempestuous oceans, to families of waddling ducks, to snow-crested mountain peaks only as far away as my imagination made them.

In the house, where my grandmother tended an oven that never went cold, I carried baskets full of romping kittens each spring, played tuneless melodies on an antique pump organ and felt safer than I ever have since.

Summer months meant that I could spend more time away from the confinements of city life. Only a twenty-minute drive from our home, my mother often made the trip with me, past fields of golden wheat, and into the company of my grandfather.

On one visit that was meant to be short, I soon forgot myself in the midst of childish bliss. On a tireless red wagon, I pulled all the ingredients of a lemonade stand to the edge of my grandparents' property, where a county road intersected a sprinkling of homes, and where other children walked the dusty path to visit friends and family.

Excitedly, I peddled my refreshments to the few people who passed by, counting the meager change that was far from the point of my endeavor.

My enthusiasm withered, however, when the approaching form of my mother reminded me of an appointment I knew I would not be permitted to miss. "But who will sit at my lemonade stand?" I wanted to know, imparting it all the importance unlost innocence always does.

"I guess you will have to pack it away until another day," she replied with regret. Mournfully, I began to obey, slowly replacing my handmade sign, cups and pitchers into the wagon before loading on the table and chair.

From the house, where I had been visible through the window, Grandpa came stepping across the expanse of grass with a stiffness reminding me my best friend was not my own age.

Without a word, he gently touched my cheek with a rough finger and bent to undo the work I had reluctantly done. He seated himself in the chair and unfolded a newspaper. "It is a nice day for lemonade," he said. "Hurry back, and we'll share some."

When we returned later, Grandpa was still at my post, the newspaper abandoned in favor of a needle and thread and some clothes in need of mending. In the small box where I had begun to deposit my earnings was more change than could be accounted for had the entire village showed up for a drink.

Together we sat by the road for a little while longer. As the sun began to go down and Grandma called us in for supper, we dismantled our stand and walked back to the house.

Darcie Hossack

The Play

The hands of a grandparent are like the comfort of a favorite blanket. They surround us and warm us emotionally while protecting us from life's little bumps and bruises.

Hanoch McCarty

She smiled a lot when she spoke to us, but it was not a smile that showed any human warmth. Her smile was for punctuation and for eliciting our choral response.

"Isn't that nice boys and girls?" Smile.

"Yeeeeeeessssssss, Miss Stellwagon."

"Aren't you glad about that?" Smile.

"Yeeeeeeessssssss, Miss Stellwagon."

She saw her work with us as her personal burden: training her fourth-grade Brooklyn street urchins to use the King's English.

"Jack in the booox," I practiced, watching my unruly tongue flick out, off-cue, in the little hand mirror. "Awl shuttt uppp tyytte." When it was my turn to come up to her desk and perform my language feat, her cold, hard smile formed around her thin lips, and I knew I was the source of great displeasure.

When we were well into the spring of that school year, she told us we were to give a play so that she might show off to the rest of the school her success in teaching us to speak properly. We sat very still, sweaty hands folded politely, as she explained behind the joyless smile that every one of us was to have a part.

"And who would like to play the king?" Eager hands danced in the air and collapsed, deflated, after she named her choice. "Bobby will make an excellent king, don't you think, boys and girls?" Smile.

"Yeeeeeeesssssss, Miss Stellwagon." But none of us had truth in our hearts.

"And now, who would like to play the part of the fairy godmother?" Smile.

I thought I would explode with longing, as my hand shot up, waved and then fell with my hopes, as Arlene Herbst was named. I felt my overweight body, dressed in Irma Klebanoff's cast-off clothes, like a penance and knew that I'd never be chosen. Never.

She continued to call out the parts, selecting the few more attractive children from a flurry of hand-waving hopefuls. Her choices had already been made, but she kept up the deception, teasing us with the possibility that we still might be named. We, unsuspecting, continued to play her cruel game.

The characters with speaking parts had now all been identified, and I sat there nervously, biting my thumbnail, my ugly brown shoes tripping on Irma's too-long dress, hoping for a miracle. To be unchosen is the great pain of grade four. The unchosen were the detritus of classroom life.

"Now, who wants to play the role of the announcer?" Smile.

Melvin Taub and I were the only ones who dared to brave one more rejection. We shot our hands up. Her bird-like eyes took all of me in, like a candid camera, from Irma Klebanoff's dress, down to the world's ugliest brown shoes, and without smiling, she turned to Melvin. It was my last hope to be chosen, and I'd have cheerfully knocked Melvin off to increase my chances to move out of the rejects.

Her eye fixed on me again.

"Do you think you can do this? It's an important part you know." Smile.

I almost cried out loud with my reassurances. I could. I could. Oh, please. I could.

"You need a white blouse and pleated skirt for this part. Do you have one?"

"Oh, yes," I lied. "Yes. I have one."

"All right then."

I never gave another thought to Melvin, who ended up as one of a small chorus of elves, that nondescript group of back-stage castoffs. As it turned out, a far luckier fate than mine.

That afternoon I told my mother the hard news. I had a part in the class play. The *announcer*. I had to have a white blouse and a pleated skirt. The teacher said so.

My mother fell into her quiet fury, the most terrible expression of her anger. We were in the midst of the Great Depression, and my father hadn't worked in months. There was no money. There could be no new blouse and skirt. I would have to give up the part, and the teacher would have to choose someone else.

She didn't understand that that was impossible. To give up after having been chosen was simply, totally impossible. I cried. I wailed. I sulked. Never did I think that the cost of a new white blouse and pleated skirt was a week's food budget; that we ate lung stew because lung cost five cents a pound because that was what we could afford. So we went to war, my mother and I, using every verbal weapon we owned. I told her that she was a bad mother. She said that I was too fat to wear a pleated skirt and would look like a baby elephant. We knew exactly where to aim—the most vulnerable and tender parts of the psyche. When my father came home, we were both casualties.

My parents spoke quietly for a long time, and after supper my mother took me to the shop around the corner on Blake Avenue and outfitted me in a week's food budget worth of white blouse and pleated navy skirt. She was right about one thing. I did look like a baby elephant.

The next day at school the class was herded in a long, single line to the auditorium for the first rehearsal. Miss Stellwagon pinched an edge of cloth from the shoulder of the leader's dress and held her at arm's length as she led the file down to the front of the hall. We were instructed to sit, and we settled, in an unnatural quiet, into the two first rows in the center, just under the sign etched DO UNTO OTHERS AS YOU WOULD HAVE OTHERS DO UNTO YOU.

Miss Stellwagon began by organizing a tableau of look-alike, gunny-sacked elves rear stage, admonishing them in advance about any bad behavior. Walking authoritatively to center stage, she pointed her index finger at me and beckoned me to come up and begin the announcement.

With equal amounts of nervousness and eagerness to please, I rushed from my seat toward her, the toe of my brown shoe catching the lip of the platform step. In a thud that echoed in my heart for the next twenty years, I fell face down at the feet of my fourth-grade teacher, pleats billowing, rump exposed.

She looked down at me, her eyes cold and unforgiving. The words, precisely formed in perfect King's English, fell from that cold, hard mouth, like stones. "Get up and return to your seat. You could never be the announcer for our play. Suppose you fell during the actual performance? You would make the entire class a laughingstock."

I watched from my seat as Melvin Taub replaced me, and I sat there numb with shame, as the hands of the clock made their painful way to 3:00. I could feel every classmate's eye on me, sucking the breath from my body.

When the bell sounded, I ran out the door and down the block, past my own apartment, and over to Wyona Street, to my grandmother's house. She was waiting at the window, and all she needed was to see was my face, to know the burden I carried. She opened her arms, and I fell into them, weeping. Her apron smelled of apples and cinnamon, and I buried my face into her largeness, her touch, like magic fingers, erasing the pain.

"Come, *mameleh,* and help me finish making the strudel," she said in Yiddish. We rolled the dough together, stretching it over the large dining-room table, careful that it would not tear. She gave me the bowl of cut-up apples, sprinkled with cinnamon, sugar and lemon peel, and told me to spread the apples evenly over the dough. Together, we placed bits of sweet butter over the apples. Then, for the first time ever, she allowed me to roll the dough up without her help. The unbroken strudel stretched from one end of the table to the other, the apples nearly bursting through the fragile pastry. My grandmother looked at my handiwork, and I could see the pleasure in her face. She put her arms around me and said in Yiddish, "You did that all by yourself! The first time! I'm going to tell your grandpa! I'm so proud of you."

Safe in my grandmother's house on Wyona Street, I knew that I could face the world again.

Selma Wassermann

A Doll of a Christmas

God does notice us, and he watches over us.
But it is through another person that he meets
our needs.

Spencer W. Kimball

Often, as adults, we tend to remember the Christmas toys we wanted as children, but never received, and to forget the ones we were given. Later in life we sometimes indulge ourselves with collections of these never-acquired toys. Some women collect teddy bears or delicate music boxes to compensate for the ones they didn't get as little girls, and some men like to collect model cars and train sets to replace the ones they wished for but never found under the Christmas tree.

I suspect that's why, for as long as I can remember, I've collected dolls: big ones, small ones, dolls of all sizes, styles and shapes. And I suppose that's why I display my collection proudly every Christmas season.

Perhaps the events of one Christmas morning, many, many years ago, inspired my devotion and interest in dolls. It all began the year my family moved in with my immigrant grandparents, in their two-story home on the west side of town.

As a little girl growing up in an immigrant household, I experienced a time when money and jobs were scarce for our family, and the only gifts we could afford on holidays and birthdays were an abundance of family love and my grandma's wonderful homemade pasta dinners.

Traditionally, my family celebrated Christmas Eve by attending a solemn midnight mass at the nearby church. It was also traditional to hang one of Grandma's long, black cotton stockings on the mantel every Christmas Eve. Come Christmas morning I would awake to find the stockings filled with fruit and nuts, a generous gift from the "Christmas Angel," or so Grandma told us. Santa Claus had never paid our house a visit; only the Christmas Angel came bearing fruit and nuts.

Coming from a poor, small town in Italy, where it was a struggle to make ends meet, Grandma and Grandpa frowned on the New World's tradition of spending hard-earned money on frivolous gifts. For that reason I stayed indoors on Christmas day, with a faked bellyache, rather than face my new neighborhood friends, who all received bright and shiny new toys on Christmas morning.

However, as time went by, Grandma and Grandpa began to mellow to the modern ideas and rituals of their new country and eventually welcomed the new traditions of Christmas gift-giving.

I can vividly recall that Christmas Eve when Grandma and Grandpa set up their very first Christmas tree. It happened in December of 1945. The family had just welcomed the birth of a new baby. It was a time of great joy and family happiness, prompting Grandpa to gallantly announce that, come that Christmas Eve, for the first time in his home, there would be a decorated Christmas tree and beneath that tree a generous gift for each family member.

That year, my grandpa was working as a store clerk in a busy downtown department store. It was there he'd seen me admiring a lovely hand-woven wicker doll carriage in the store window. The doll carriage was a popular seller that season; every little girl in my neighborhood owned one, except me. I longed to own one of these buggies so that I would fit in with my new modern little girlfriends.

Come Christmas Eve, I was the first to open my gift from Grandpa. I tore eagerly away at the plain brown paper wrapping. A moment later, I was gloriously surprised to discover the beautiful doll carriage I'd seen in the store window. Grandpa, knowing how much I wanted to emulate my new friends, had spent all of his Christmas bonus to buy it for me.

I found it impossible to sleep that night; I was filled with anticipation for Christmas morning. This year, I would have a brand-new gift to share with my friends.

At the first sign of daylight, I ran outside into the front yard, clutching my fine new toy in my hands. I strutted and strolled my carriage like a fine peacock as Grandma and Grandpa watched proudly from the kitchen window. I paraded my doll carriage up and down the sidewalk until, at last, a group of my little friends began to gather inquisitively around my new toy. I stood there, anticipating words of praise and envy, but instead my smiles soon turned to tears.

As Grandpa and Grandma looked on from the window, they heard my little girlfriends cruelly poking fun and laughing at my empty doll carriage. It seems my well-meaning Grandpa had "put the cart before the horse" so to speak, or in this case "the carriage before the doll." He had given me a doll buggy but forgot that I didn't own a doll!

I stood there, humbled before my peers. Humiliated, I dashed back into the house with my empty carriage. Grandpa, who wanted peace at any price, tried to console me by offering to buy me a new doll for my birthday. I appreciated the kind gesture, but my birthday was a month away, and I needed a solution right away. It was Grandma, in her infinite wisdom, who came up with the idea that solved my problem and made that Christmas a day I'd always remember. As far back as I can remember, my extended family has always been there for me, and that day was no exception.

After a few minutes, I reemerged from the house, but this time I was the envy of all the little girls in my neighborhood. Although I didn't have a dolly to call my own, I did have a brand-new baby cousin, who fit snugly into my new doll carriage. Grandma had dressed the new baby in her finest clothes and placed her in my doll buggy, allowing me to take the new infant for an unforgettable stroll around the block.

Fifty years later, I remember that Christmas morning as though it were yesterday. I also remember that one of those little girls offered to trade me her doll for my little baby cousin, and Grandma never knew how close I came to making the trade. It was quite a temptation, but I finally said, "Naw, I'll keep this one. It's got all movable parts!"

Cookie Curci

3

A GRAND-PARENT'S WISDOM

*Chains do not hold a family together.
It is threads, hundreds of tiny threads,
which sew people together.*

Simone Signoret

TRUDY By JERRY MARCUS

"Thanks to Grandpa, we won't have any trouble finding our car at the mall anymore."

Good Medicine

When you are ready, come to me. I will take you into nature. In nature you will learn everything that you need to know.

Rolling Thunder, Cherokee Medicine Man

As a young boy, I fondly remember my grandfather.

He was tall in physical size, but he was also larger than life itself, in my eyes. As a Cherokee Indian, he loved to tell the old stories that had been passed down from generation to generation in the tribe, located in the Great Smoky Mountains of North Carolina. His zest for life and his love of nature was passed on to me through the experience there in the mountains of western North Carolina.

On a warm spring day when I was a young boy, my grandfather and I were sitting on a large rock on the edge of the Oconaluftee River in Cherokee. I was looking into a small puddle of water that was caught in an etched indentation of a rock. The large rocks were worn away by water action, and we would sometimes fish on the rocks and watch the fish travel downstream between the rocks. This particular day, I was more interested in the small minnows moving around the puddle of water that seemed to be caught in the rocks. I must have stared endlessly at the minnows wondering how they would get back to the larger body of water and their parents for safety. After all, I had my grandfather there to protect me. Who would protect them from the warm sun and from being eaten by animals, or other fish? *Wow,* I thought, *I was glad I was not a fish!*

My grandfather would glance around every few minutes to see what I was doing. He saw me looking at the small fish and asked, "What do you see when you look into the water?"

Always wanting to please my grandfather to show him how smart I really was, I looked quickly downstream and said, "I see the little fish swimming around, but they have no place to go."

"Are you afraid for them, or yourself?" My grandfather would often ask two questions at once.

"The sun is hot, and I am afraid they will get too hot in the shallow water. Besides, what if they don't get back to their parents in the river?" He softly spoke, "Well, maybe they are all right in this special little pool of water. They might get out into the large river and a larger fish might come by and eat them for dinner."

"Grandfather, what will they eat to stay alive? What if they stay there and grow too big for a little pool of water?" I guess I must have learned to ask two questions, as well, from my grandfather.

"Grandson," he said, "you do not need to worry because Nature will take care of them. Whatever happens is all part of a greater plan of life. It is the Great One's plan."

I am sure I must have looked perplexed by this statement, but I didn't really know what to ask. Even at that young age, I knew he would be quiet to allow me to respond, then he would share more with me.

"What do you see when you look into the water?" asked

my grandfather. I would look closely to see the water rushing quickly downstream. My eyes would catch the glimpse of the fish, flies touching the water, the water beetles moving quickly down the river, a piece of wood floating with the movement of the water, and the beautiful green plants. I must have explained all these things to him.

There was a long pause, then he said, "What else do you see? Look deeply into the water."

I looked as hard as I could, then he said, "Now look at the surface of the water." My eyes began to water as I stared, wanting to make my grandfather proud of my ability to see everything he saw.

"Ah, I see my reflection," I proudly responded. He quietly said, "That's good." A smile came across my face.

"What you see is your whole life ahead of you. Know that the Great One has a plan for you, as well as the little fish in the puddle of water. Sometimes we don't understand why things happen the way they do, but there is a plan."

By this time I had forgotten about the little fish and asked, "What is the Great One's plan for you and me?"

"Well," he replied, "my way is working itself out as I am growing older. I am an elder now, and I am to be the 'keeper of secrets' just for you. You will be the keeper of stories and much that you will experience in life to be a helper to others. You are a keeper of all living things."

As I listened to my grandfather, I got excited. "Even the keeper of the rocks and the little fish?" I exclaimed. "Yes," he said with a grin, "because they are all your brothers and sisters, even the rocks, because they had the same elements of you and me."

That special day seems so far behind me now. Shortly after that day my grandfather was taken to do better work, as he would say, in the "great skyvault above, where all things are perfect."

What I remember most about that day was that he taught me to give thanks every day for all things, even the little fish and the rocks that we sat upon together.

As he said, "Always remember to walk the path of Good Medicine and to see the good reflection in everything that occurs in life. Life is a lesson, and you must learn the lesson well to see your true reflection in the water, as well as in life itself."

J. T. Garrett, Ed.D., M.P.H.

Learning to Listen

Grandmothers have the time they never had as a mother—time to tell stories, time to hear secrets, time for cuddles.

Dr. M. De Vries

"When I grow up I'm gonna be a boy!" my four-year-old granddaughter announced. Ignoring the concerned look on her father's face, she calmly bit into a slice of pizza.

My son shot me a worried glance across the table. "Now Hilary," he said to his daughter, "we've talked about this before. You know you can't turn into a boy."

"But I want to," she smiled.

"That won't make it happen. Besides, it's good to be a girl. Girls are just as smart as boys. Girls can do anything boys do."

"No, they can't."

As I sat listening to my son reel off a long list of careers girls could have and sports they could play, I wished I knew how to help. The truth was, I was still pretty new to the grandmother business. My son had married early, quickly produced three children—and then suddenly found himself a single parent, struggling to be a good dad and a good provider at the same time. Everything had happened so fast, I hadn't had a chance to perfect my grandma technique.

And another thing: Hilary was a girl, and I had no first-hand experience with raising little girls. I had two sons and two stepsons. I knew all about Cub Scouts, football, Power Rangers and burping contests, but I didn't have a clue about the mysterious world of girl-children. Being female myself should have helped, but somehow it didn't. Things had changed a lot since I was little.

After dinner, Hilary and her two younger brothers played in the family room where their grandpa was watching TV, while my son visited with me in the kitchen.

"I don't know how to handle this, Mom," he said over a cup of coffee. "It just started this week. Hilary came in from playing and told me she wanted to be a boy. I didn't pay much attention to her then, but after she talked about it three or four times, I started to get worried. She's the only girl in a house full of males. Do you think I treat her brothers better than her?"

"Of course not. Don't spend too much time worrying about this; it's probably just a passing idea. She'll forget about it after a while." I was just as puzzled as my son, but I tried to sound reassuring. Hilary was spending the night at our house. It was a special treat to stay with Grandma, where she could play undisturbed by annoying little brothers, stay up past her bedtime and receive plenty of one-to-one attention.

That evening as I watched her at the kitchen table drawing pictures with bright new crayons, I thought about my own grandparents. I had loved Grandma and delighted in hearing her stories about how she grew up on an island in Canada, the youngest of seven daughters in a fisherman's family. But it was Grandpa I truly adored. During the first few years of my life, my father had been overseas with the Marines in Korea, so Grandpa was my substitute Dad. I remembered following him around the yard, jabbering happily to him as he pruned his roses. A quiet man with a gentle sense of humor, he let me wear his gray fedora and clomp around in his shoes. Had I thought I would grow up to be a boy back then, simply because I admired Grandpa? I couldn't remember.

As I put away the supper dishes, I continued to think about my grandfather. I hadn't been the only person to enjoy his company. Everyone sought him out—family, friends, business associates. What was it that made people want to tell him about their troubles and triumphs? I thought I knew the answer: Grandpa was a great listener. From the time I toddled around in his footsteps to the day he passed away when I was thirty-five, I knew I could tell Grandpa anything—and he would listen quietly, without judgment. Even though there were times when he must have disagreed with my decisions or opinions, he respected my right to say what I thought. Was I as good a listener as Grandpa?

The next day I was driving Hilary home through rush-hour traffic. My little granddaughter sat in the seat beside me, chattering nonstop about her neighborhood friends, her brothers, and her cat Francis. We stopped at a red light, and Hilary said matter-of-factly, "Grandma, I'm gonna be a boy when I grow up."

This time I wasn't going to offer her a dozen reasons why she should enjoy being a girl. I decided to simply listen. "So you want to be a boy. Why's that?"

The answer came immediately. "Because I want to chew tobacco!"

I struggled to keep a straight face. "I see. Who do you know who chews tobacco?"

"My friend Lucy's Uncle Jack. I saw him do it when he came to visit them. It looks really cool!"

"Oh?"

"Yeah. You get to carry the tobacco around in this pouch thing, and then you get to spit it out on the ground! I asked her Uncle Jack if I could have some of his tobacco, but he said only boys get to chew it. That's why I want to be a boy!"

Hilary's two brothers greeted her with noisy enthusiasm. They'd missed their big sister, even though she'd only been gone for one day. Soon the three children were out on the sidewalk blowing bubbles that I'd brought them, so I had a chance to speak with my son.

"You'll never guess why Hilary wants to be a boy," I began and told him about our conversation on the way over. My son howled with laughter.

"Well," he said at last, "I guess this isn't as serious as I thought. But what did you say to her after she explained about Lucy's Uncle Jack and the cool tobacco pouch?"

"Oh, I think we worked it out pretty well," I replied, suppressing a grin. "I just told her she didn't have to be a boy to chew tobacco. I said it's a free country, and when she grows up she can chew all the tobacco she wants."

Ann Russell

The Smooth Stone

When I was a boy I didn't know I loved my grand-mother. Being around her was more fun than being around most people, and I thought of her as the center of all good things. She could make taffy that just disappeared in your mouth and sent bright sparks of vanilla playing on your tongue. She could find any herb you might need for a stomachache or cough or sore muscles somewhere in the woods near her farm. She could tell a better story than you might ever hear anywhere else, and she could understand me when I tried to sort out the confusing parts of life.

What lasts in recall of her is how she helped people—including me—put confusion to rest. She didn't lecture or explain how things ought to be; she just walked along beside me, and we looked at the world together.

One summer when I was fourteen and having a rough time with growing up, I spent the month of June with her. My parents, I think, were eager to be rid of me after the school year. I have no idea now why I fought with them in the way that I did, but I know that fighting back seemed important to do. I wasn't going to let anyone run rough-shod over me even if I knew I was in the wrong about staying out late, or taking the car on my own, or going into the city to see a movie.

My grandmother lived in a very small town in the mountains of Kentucky. Everyone knew her, and everyone knew me. She did not drive and had no car so there was no problem about my driving anywhere, and there was nowhere in the county to stay out late because most people were farmers and "went to bed with the chickens" as people used to say.

I spent my days working on the land, helping mend fences or hauling rocks, and often in the afternoon my grandmother and I would go walking. I called it "hiking." She said it was "walking" because "hiking" meant you were going someplace.

"Honey," she said to me that day, "we don't know where we're going. We're just out in creation and takin' things in."

We walked for a time along the edge of the woods that bordered her property and led eventually down to a fast-flowing creek that had clear, sweet water even in summer. She walked in an easy deliberate way that gave her time to spot four-leaf clovers or mushrooms. We stopped many, many times to look at something: a snake's dusky burrow or a red-winged blackbird's nest.

There was something on my mind, but I didn't know exactly what it was. After a time, we climbed down the stony bank of the creek and waded in the cool, fast water. I liked to watch it roll over the rocks in the creek bed and the feel of it between my toes.

A fallen trunk of an old maple tree almost spanned the creek at one point, and my grandmother took off her shoes and left them on the bank. Then she waded into the water to the old tree and sat on it so that her feet were in the water up to her ankles.

For some reason or other I began to collect stones. Small

egg-shaped stones, gray and white. Stones shaped like little hard cookies and—the prime object of my quest—
stones that were almost round. I was very picky about
what I chose to keep and often would toss back something
I found after I'd examined it closely and found that it came
up short of my expectation.

Then I heard myself say, "My dad would never do this."

"Do what, Honey?"

"Sit on a log and watch me hunt stones."

"Oh," she said. And nothing else.

I worked my way down toward the edges of the stream
where the best stones often were and continued my hunt
in the dappled, leaf-filtered light. The air was warm and
smelled faintly of mint. My father was much in my
thoughts lately because I had so much trouble with him.

He was a doctor, and it seemed to me he thought he
knew everything there was to know. He pushed me pretty
hard, I thought. Just then, as I was thinking about him, I
reached my hand into the water and out it came holding a
perfectly round piece of white quartz. It was round as a
marble almost. I splashed through the water to show it to
my grandmother.

She took it from me and held it between her thumb and
forefinger. She looked at a long time, turning it this way
and that in the light.

"Right pretty," she said. "You'll keep this one?"

"Oh, yeah, I sure will. It's perfect. Isn't it?"

"I'd say so," she said. She gave it back to me. Then she
said, "Why don't you just pick up rocks from the bank
instead of going to all the trouble of searching the water?"

"There aren't any good stones on the bank."

"What do you mean? A stone is a stone."

I looked closely at her to see if she was teasing me and
saw that she was very serious.

"No, Grandmother," I said patiently. "The stones on the bank are all rough."

"You like smooth stones?"

"Yes, I do." I held up my newfound treasure and thought again how lucky I'd been to find it.

"You know how they get that way? How they get smooth like you like?"

"The water does it," I said, glad that I knew that.

"Yes. And it does it by rubbing the stones together. Over and over. Years and years. Until all the rough edges are gone. And then the stones are beautiful. Sort of like people."

I looked directly into her eyes—they were almost the color of cornflowers—astonished that I suddenly, somehow knew what she meant.

She rubbed her hand through my hair, messing it up. "Think of your daddy like the water, Honey, and one day when you are a splendid man, you'll understand how you got that way." And that was all she said that day to me about important things. And it was enough.

Walker Meade

Nana's Mysterious Panache

In youth we learn; in age we understand.

Source Unknown

She was grand! But Nana adamantly disclaimed the title, explaining, "No one is grander than your own mother."

Picture Rosalind Russell's portrayal of Auntie Mame and you get a glimpse of my grandmother. Strong and independent, she drove the first car in town, wore pants when that was still scandalous, and she never minded a bawdy joke. Nana vivaciously dashed through life, lighting up the lives of everyone she met. I wondered why the slings and arrows of life never seemed to overwhelm her.

Domestic chores, even the making of lard soap, were performed effortlessly and cheerfully. I'd watch as she scurried about, emptying ashtrays into the silent butler. How unique that was! Yet, upon seeing a bored child, she'd immediately drop her towel and sit down to teach a game of solitaire.

Basking in the warmth of her sunny presence, I'd watch as the last hairpin was pinned in her brightly hennaed hair.

"Want to walk to the grocer's with me, Honeypot?"

"Oh, yes." I was always proud to walk with her. Tall and slender, and dressed so impeccably (she was the only grandmother who wore spike-heeled shoes—an important distinction to me), Nana energetically marched along, calling out, "Hello there, Little Miss Pumpkin. Bunny Boy, how's your lovely mama today?" as neighborhood kids waved and shouted, "Hi, Mrs. K." They sensed here was a woman who knew—and believed—in kids.

Deliverymen and visitors always lingered at Nana's gracious home. Laughing and chattering, she discussed politics or recipes with equal enthusiasm; her gold cigarette holder waving through the air, punctuating the discourse with grace. Framed by a strong, square jaw and prominent cheekbones, her wonderful smile—wrinkles danced as she spoke, and sparkling green eyes watched for signs of trouble. The surly became cheerful; crudeness was treated with gentility. Nana gave strength to the sorrowful, calm to the hysterical, and everyone left feeling touched by her love. Why, I pondered, did she never seem cranky?

Widowed at age fifty-two, she invited me for sleepovers more often. Mornings, waking to her raspy voice singing in the kitchen, brought new adventures in food.

"Your breakfast is served, my queen." Pretending to be my lady-in-waiting, Nana pulled out the chair with a flourish. Elegantly set, my place held a juicy, ripe mango and a boiled egg standing in a delicate little cup. Fine crystal and bone china were used daily, never stored away.

Some evenings, after the dinner table was cleared, Nana would throw a sweater over her shoulders and go out into the night. Finally, I asked, "Nana, where are you going . . . can I come?"

"No, darling," she'd chuckle. "This is my alone time." I sensed an air of mystery in this.

One evening, after Nana had slipped out, I climbed out the bedroom window and followed her—at a distance;

Nancy Drew stories had taught me well. Nana walked swiftly down two lamplit blocks and went inside the neighborhood church (churches never closed back then). I hid behind a massive pillar as Nana knelt down in the pew; no prayer book in her hand. After a few moments, she bent her head. When she finally looked up, I saw, in the glimmer of dozens of candles, her face shining with tears. Nana was crying! She stared at the altar. Slowly, ever so slowly, the corners of her mouth began to curve upward. The gentle curve grew and grew. At last, that unique and wonderful smile returned. A moment longer she sat, then, as though consummating a business deal, she briskly arose, genuflected once, and bustled away.

Once back snug in bed, I contemplated what I'd just learned. Bring my sorrows to church. Leave them there. In the face of adversity, put on a smile; before long, it will be genuine. Nana had struggles just like the rest of us; she just refused to succumb to them.

Lynne Zielinski

Through the Windowpane

Grandchildren and grandparents are joined at the heart.

Source Unknown

Riding the crest of a desert arroyo, our property becomes a passageway for wildlife. We keep our eyes open for the animals and birds that come to visit. One season, a mother quail nested on the ground of our open atrium, where we could eavesdrop on her developing brood through the windowpanes.

When our Midwestern grandchildren came to visit, it was seven-year-old Hannah who pressed her nose against the glass and became resident companion to the mother quail. Hannah sat on the tile floor, guarding the nest from inside the house for long stretches of time. Whenever we wanted to find Hannah, we knew just where to look. I sat there a fair amount, finding the tranquil time often not available when grandkids' visits are brief and energy rides high. Sitting together and watching the quail family cast a special aura around us. We were inches away from the birds, yet we didn't frighten them because of the glass that separated us. If we were still, if we were quiet, we could see the chicks bob and scratch around their mother as they learned the ways of nature.

Hannah and I were watching together on the day the mother quail began to lead the chicks over the four-inch ledge out into the desert. Hop. Skip. Up and over. Hop. Skip. Up and over. Each little bird did the calisthenics required to leave the protected nest and proceeded to conquering the unknown. The mother called to each one softly, offering encouragement. All went according to the designated plan until the turn of the tiniest chick. The little bird hopped again and again but couldn't make it over the concrete ledge to reach the rest of the family. The height was too great. The mother coaxed and cajoled, then finally abandoned the last bird in the window well to care for the rest of the youngsters who foraged for seeds nearby. Hannah and I listened to the heartbreaking cheeping sounds of the forlorn, feathered babe. We were upset, too. I'd been told that once quail leave the nest, they do not come back, but I didn't want to share this information with Hannah. I knew she expected me to solve the problem. Her eyes held mine, searching for my answer.

Then I did have an idea. I grabbed a sturdy piece of heavy cardboard and explained the plan to Hannah. We hurried outside with the makeshift material. I let Hannah slip the ramp into place for the last chick, angling it to present an easy slope to the top of the ledge. We quickly retreated back to the inner window.

When the little bird scrabbled up the cardboard and scooted out to join the others, we sighed in relief. It was a matter of cardboard and common knowledge, sympathy and simple wisdom.

The words of a poem by Emily Dickinson came to mind, and we went to the bookshelf and found her words. Now the lines could be understood in a new light, for Hannah and for me.

> *Or help one fainting robin*
> *Unto his nest again,*
> *I shall not live in vain.*

On that sunny desert morning, my granddaughter Hannah and I had not lived in vain.

Connie Spittler

Home Run

Sometimes you don't know how courageous you are until disaster strikes and you find yourself, much to your own surprise, doing what needs to be done.

Wilfred Rand

I was ten. Life that summer was softball, climbing trees, pollywog hunting and bike riding, in that order.

Our city street was made for softball. A well-hit grounder could skip for a mile down that paved "field." There was, thankfully, very little traffic to disrupt our practice and games. Whenever a car would approach, we simply ambled off to the curbsides, waving to the driver as he or she passed.

Amazingly, I remember not a single accident, mishap or problem with this arrangement . . . except one. Just one.

The instant that softball shot off from my bat, I knew I had messed up. Big time. In a neighborhood graced with houses lining both sides of the street, room for error was limited. Hours upon hours of practice greatly improved our odds of keeping the ball between curbs and thereby avoiding houses, lawns and cars parked in driveways. Any ball hit beyond either curb was, by necessity, a foul.

Immediately following the earsplitting shatter of that enormous square of glass, my teammates split to parts unknown. This was indeed a grave situation and not the time to contemplate the obvious fact that I had a flock of chickens for friends.

Now, the Hansons were not trolls. Well, at least as long as no one was trip-trap-trip-trapping over their lawn. Up to this point, they had never, as far as I knew, killed any neighbor child. But, this was a serious offense.

Being one of eight kids and the daughter of a milkman, I was aware that, mostly, money was for essential things—not to be taken lightly. I also knew, instinctively, that my dad would replace that window. I was a minor child. My dad was my dad and responsible for me—for better or worse. He would pay for the window because I broke it. Simple as that. The Hansons had a giant jagged gaping hole in the front of their house, and I had put it there.

I finally set my bat down, not wanting to carry a smoking gun with me on this particular journey. Suddenly, each leg weighed about a hundred pounds, as I trudged up the walkway to the porch of the House of Horrors.

No need to knock. Mrs. Hanson wasted no time greeting me, with the door wide open, and escorted me inside to this new vantage point of the crime scene. Like a stoic wooden judge, her grandson's highchair stood starkly in that very room. Mrs. Hanson was saying, "What if he had been sitting there?" Even though the baby was not in the house, the highchair was several yards from the window, and the window screen was still intact, I absolutely felt as if I had killed the baby.

About a year later, I was released and walked down the sidewalk, toward home. I wondered if it were possible to feel any worse. Now, I had to face my dad with what I had done.

I was surprised to see Mr. Terryberry leaving my house. He was an across-the-street neighbor and had never come over before. His son and daughter were on my street softball team—part of the chicken clutch.

I wondered briefly if perhaps his kids had told him what I did. Or, maybe he was an eyewitness, and he had come over to squeal to my dad.

I knew I was not going to get hit. I knew I wouldn't even get yelled at. But, my dad would no doubt say, "Man!" in an agitated manner, and he might grumble for a few seconds, before walking next door to apologize and measure the hole where the window belonged. Then he would drive off to buy the replacement.

He would be disappointed. And, it was my fault.

When I walked in the door and stepped into our living room, my dad was right there to meet me. I avoided looking right at him, but plainly heard what he said: "I am proud of you."

Oh great. There was some kind of enormous misunderstanding. Anxious to enlighten him and get the truth out, I blurted, "I was the one who hit the ball!"

"I know," my dad said. He had kind eyes. "Mr. Terryberry saw the whole thing."

I was still confused. I was missing something here. My dad, Mr. Character, was proud of me?

He told me Mr. Terryberry had seen his son pitch the ball to me, saw me belt it, saw the window shatter, and could hardly believe his eyes when his kids and the others hightailed it and left me standing to face the music alone. He thought that I would surely drop that bat and follow the others. He said that he was pleasantly surprised to see me walk up, instead, to face Mrs. Hanson.

Mr. Terryberry told my dad, "I am as proud of your kid as I am ashamed of my own."

And, it was Mr. Terryberry who bought the replacement window—and would not accept any argument.

My dad was proud of me and I was on Cloud Nine . . . until he said no more batting in the street—only ball and gloves.

But, Cloud Eight didn't feel too shabby.

Alison Peters

PICKLES. ©2001, The Washington Post Writers Group. Reprinted with permission.

Grandpa and Me Fishing

A little boy was asked, "Where is your home?"
"Where grandpa lives," was his reply.

Source Unknown

My grandfather was my father figure in every way that my real father should have been. He taught me respect, a work ethic, humor, the importance of stories, social and people skills, the meaning of a handshake, fulfilling a promise, commitment, appreciating my education, the intricacies of relationship, and probably most importantly . . . how to fish. Much of his wisdom came to me while holding a fishing rod down on the dock at his place on the lake. I was shaped in his image by his words as they floated over the water, down that pole and into my soul. I wrote this poem to sum up some of these lessons taught to me in life:

My Grandpa

The small bills go in front and the bigger ones behind.
You have to use your head boy! You got to use your mind!

And when you change that filter, run some oil 'round the lip.
Or else you'll fry your motor in the middle of your trip.

When I went to school, I walked a mile through the snow.
I'd shoot some dinner on my way home. A pheasant or a doe.

If you wanna catch the big one, you tie your line just like this.
Tease it just a little. Don't yank too hard or you'll miss.

*Keep your eyes on the road boy! Don't drive too fast! Slow
     down!*
*And don't you tell your grandma 'bout those milkshakes back
     in town!*

Treat her like a lady, son. Do it every day of your life.
Respect her and take care of her. Mother . . . daughter . . . wife.

I miss my grandpa.

                                                        Michael W. Curry

Grandpa's Little Buddy

Hope is putting faith to work when doubting would be easier.

Jean Wasserman McCarty

As Steven stood awkwardly on the bank of Lake Malone in Western Kentucky, his grandfather watched his "Little Buddy" desperately attempt to get just one of the many flat rocks he'd gathered to skip over the lake's sun reflective surface. "Keep at it, Son!" his grandfather shouted with much enthusiasm. "Grandpa," Steven asked in his pre-adolescent and breaking voice, "why am I no good at anything I try? I want to be a great pitcher like you used to be!"

His grandfather gently touched his shoulder while observing his grandson's eyes beginning to brim with tears. "Little Buddy, let me tell you why you are already a great pitcher and will be a better pitcher than your old grandpa ever was. Can I give you a little advice, Son?"

Steven looked intensely into his hero's eyes and replied, "Yes, Grandpa! I'll do anything to be great like you!"

His grandfather sat him down on a hollowed-out log and pulled him in close. "Little Buddy, I want you to remember what I am about to tell you and all I ask is that you never forget what I had to learn the hard way. Do you promise you will remember?" Without pause, Steven assured his grandfather he'd remember anything and everything he told him.

His grandfather continued, "If you think someone is better than you, always remember that you are the only one who is thinking the other guy is." His grandson looked at him inquisitively and caught his grandfather off-guard with his response.

"So, you're saying that I need to use my brain. Is that what you said, Grandpa?"

"You got it, Little Buddy! Many folks focus on what they are doing wrong, but the winners figure out what they are doing right." His grandson replied with yet another super insight based on what he'd heard his grandfather say. "So I need to tell myself that I am good?" he asked. His grandfather smiled and went further.

"Not only do you need to tell yourself that you're good, but you must always believe that you are great! You see, Little Buddy, you've got determination and grit. I've been watching you throw those stones for over two hours, and anyone who stays at it that long has what it takes to be a winner even though he may get a bit down on occasion!"

As they walked back up the hill to the home Steven's grandfather built for himself and his wife twenty years earlier, his grandfather took hold of his Little Buddy's hand and stated the last piece of wisdom Steven would ever hear him provide. "You'll be at the pitcher's mound next season, and I'll be there, too, Lord willing. When you're on that mound, I want you to repeat to yourself what I'm about to tell you when you start to throw each ball. Are you listening, Son?"

Steven glanced at his grandfather and boldly stated, "Yes, Sir!"

"Okay, then, I want you to repeat this right after me. 'When I feel down, I know God will lift me up!'" His grandson repeated it three times before they finally reached the front porch.

The next season came, and Steven looked into the stands searching for his grandfather's always eager and proud face. "Mom, I don't see Grandpa anywhere! Where is he?" he anxiously asked his mother of very strong faith. "Steven, Grandpa won't be here today because God called him to be with him last night." Steven began to cry as his mother consoled him with a firm and comforting hug. "Steven, Grandpa told me last night before he passed away to be sure to tell you that he loves you and to repeat what he told you to say to yourself when you get up to that mound." Steven's dark brown eyes steadied as he wiped his tears away with his baseball shirt's sleeve. His tears wiped away, he immediately looked up and stated, "When I feel down, I know God will lift me up." His mother's eyes began to water as she patted him on the back and directed his eyes towards the pitcher's mound. As he walked to the mound, his mother continued to hear him repeat what his grandpa instructed him to repeat.

With two strikes and three balls thrown awry in the bottom of the ninth inning, the crowd watched as Steven paused, knelt to one knee, muttered something and stood upright and proudly. He gazed into the eyes of the batter and shouted loud enough for the entire crowd to hear. "When I feel down, I know God will lift me up." Oddly, he held the ball like the stones his grandfather had watched him throw that sunny day only one year ago. Steven poised himself with his gaze remaining in the batter's eyes. Before the pitch was released, he remembered his grandpa's other words of wisdom—"If you think someone is better than you, always remember that you are the only one who is thinking the other guy is." He released the ball with a furious and awkward sidearm pitch that the "more-than-a-little-bit" intimidated batter never seemingly saw curve over the middle of the plate. "You're out!" the umpire shouted and to Steven's surprise, the crowd mostly comprised of the parents of both teams stood up and gave Steven a roaring applause. His team and the opposing team both rushed the field and carried him off the field.

Things had settled down after all the pomp and circumstance, and Steven noticed an old man walking his way. "That was a heck of a pitch you threw, Son," the old man stated with the same look of pride his grandpa often had shown on his face.

"Sir, thanks a lot." Steven appeared confused and asked, "Sir, do I know you from somewhere?" The old man grinned, and touched Steven gently on his shoulder before uttering, "No, Son, you don't, but your grandfather did." Steven excitingly exclaimed, "You knew my grandpa?"

The old man's eyes began to fill with tears as he told Steven, "Your grandfather struck me out just like you did that boy when we were 'bout your age. He told me something I'll never forget just before I got signed on with the National Baseball League." Steven's eyes lit up as he waited for what the old man would say next. "Your grandfather told me that my greatest asset in the Big League wouldn't be my throwing or batting. He told me that if I ever thought someone was better than me, to always remember that I was the only one who thought the other guy was. What he never told me was what you shouted while standing out there on the mound. Your mother called me long distance late last night and asked that I come on down. I was feeling down on the trip to get here, but thanks to you, Son, God has lifted me up!"

Brian G. Jett

4

PASSING ON
A LEGACY

*Each of us leaves a thumbprint on the world,
a record that we were here and who we
were and what we did. Your only choice
is what kind of thumbprint to leave.*

Sidney B. Simon

Grandmother Nature

You don't need to be a super grandma for your grandkids to cherish you. One treasured memory can last a lifetime.

Janet Lanese

When I was a small child, I was one of nine first cousins who spent summer vacations together at my grandparents' cottage on Deep Creek Lake in Maryland. My older cousins would be sailing and water-skiing, and the younger boys would play trucks in the sand near the water.

That's when my grandmother would find me sitting alone on the screened-in porch feeling left out and out of place. She would take my little hand and talk me into a nature walk. It was a pretty easy sell.

Nature walks with my grandmother were always an adventure. We would visit patches of bubble-gum pink mini-mushrooms floating atop mounds of lime-green moss edged by matchstick moss that looked like toy soldiers with reed hats.

One time we found a fairy ring—a natural circle of mushrooms about four feet across. Other times we would find lady slippers or black-eyed Susans, Queen Anne's lace, Dutchman's-breeches or wild blueberries.

Deeper into the woods there were rotting tree stumps, home to spiders, salamanders and Indian peace pipes. Everywhere we went we found interesting bugs, stones and plants.

In the spring, I would visit her in Ohio, and we would head out for the woods to find wildflowers—trout lilies, trillium, rattlesnake plant. We would trudge through forest floor softened by spring rains. Onward through the fiddlebacks, past the skunk cabbage and over the partridge berry until we found her mark. I would hold the newspaper open as she shoveled in twenty or more jack-in-the-pulpits. They were destined for small paper cups to be delivered to an inner-city Head Start program.

No matter what time of year it was, we always found adventure, and we always found some wonderful prize to bring home—a used hornets' nets, monarch larvae to raise, large pinecones or different-shaped acorns. Each new discovery was a reminder to me that God was with me in this wonder-filled world, and I was not alone on this planet.

Twenty years later I found myself as a single mother with two young girls. Remembering the peaceful joy of my walks with my grandmother, I would take their little hands and start off for the woods. It was on those walks with my own children that I finally understood the joy of sharing the secrets of nature with small children. The honor of introducing a child to her first tree toad or garden snake, or watching her face as a monarch butterfly pumped its wings for the first time on the end of one of my children's fingers. It helped put things in perspective.

I found solitude in those long, quiet walks where the simple pleasures of finding a praying mantis or listening to the rustling of the trees would stir my heart and renew my peace. And again, as in the days of my own childhood, it was as if I knew that at the end of my long walk there would be at least one small miracle of God to remind me that I was not alone on this planet.

As I write this, it has been forty years since those walks with my grandmother. My daughters have graduated college and live in their own homes. It was on a recent visit to see my grandmother, who is now ninety-eight, that I was reminded of those rich and wonderful walks in the woods.

As I sat across from her, holding her frail hand, I was eager to talk about our walks. I wanted to tell her at long last what children often forget to say. I wanted to say "thank you" for giving me a wonderful tradition and a legacy that I will pass down to my own grandchildren. I wanted to say thank you for noticing me sitting on the screened-in porch all alone when I was so small. And I wanted to share the delight of discovering God's world together one more time.

Sorrow and frustration grew in my heart as I realized that she could not really understand me. Her blue eyes had become cloudy with blindness, and her hearing was all but gone. I knew she was feeling all alone, trapped in a body that had given up way before her spirit was ready. As alone as I had felt as a child at the summer cottage.

How could I tell her what it had meant to me when she reached out when I was all alone? How could I reach her in her time of loneliness? How could I bring back the joy of our adventures and discoveries? I was overwhelmed by the obvious odds. I could not make her see or hear or walk. I was powerless.

When she took her afternoon nap, I slipped out for a walk. It was a clear, crisp October day, and I started to pray. First I asked God to forgive me for never letting her know the gift she was to me. Then I begged that he would show me how to reach her. As I was walking I had absentmindedly started picking up acorns and autumn leaves. I looked down and there in my hands I saw God's answer.

I spent the next hour gathering together a basket full of nature's treasures as full of texture as I could. There were nubbly wart-covered gourds and spiny pinecones, smooth acorns and crunchy fall leaves. I even found a farmer's stand that sold me a very bumpy small pumpkin with folds so deep it looked like an orange accordion. It was topped with a coarse stem all twisted and turned like driftwood.

I returned to the house. When my grandmother got up for dinner, I put the basket in her lap. She reached in and took out each treasure one at a time. She identified each one correctly, describing from memory the color—maple leaves of scarlet, green and yellow gourds, tan acorns, an orange pumpkin, silvery milkweed pods, brown oak leaves. She held each one up to catch the pungent smells and laughed until her eyes filled with tears.

After forty years, I was showing my grandma the wonders of nature a whole new way. By concentrating on what she could do instead of focusing on what she couldn't do, she went on a nature walk using her fingers and nose.

It must be true what they say, that when you lose one sense the remaining ones become stronger. Because touching and smelling those goodies in the basket was so powerful that it brought back Grandma's memory of all the other senses. For a moment she was my strong and sturdy "partner in crime" discovering the mysteries of the deep woods.

God had given us a nature walk in a basket. And as always, the peace of God filled my heart as I was experiencing another little miracle to let me know that I was not alone on this planet after all.

Sally Franz

A Valentine for Grandma

Families will live on through the stories we tell our children and grandchildren.

Carolyn J. Booth and Mindy B. Henderson

It was just a harmless prank, that's all that it was. And it wasn't as though Old Lady Hayes didn't deserve it. The way she used to scream at us for borrowing a few of her precious raspberries, like we were stealing gold out of Fort Knox . . . well, she had it coming.

At least, that's the way it seemed to us as George finished tying the string to the red, heart-shaped box. We giggled as Ron added the final touch: two plastic red roses, glued to the lid of the empty valentine box.

"I wonder what will surprise her most," I asked as George and Albert practiced jerking the box out of reach by yanking on the used kite string we had attached to it, "seeing a box of candy on her step, or watching it fly away when she tries to pick it up?"

We laughed as we watched George make Albert chase the empty box around the dusty garage. For a chubby ten-year-old Navajo, Albert did a pretty good imitation of Mrs.

Hayes's hunched-over hobble and her seemingly perma-
nent scowl. And we howled when he picked up a broom
and pretended to ride it through the midwinter air while
shouting, "I'm Old Lady Hayes, the driedest-up old prune
in the West!"

Ron was the first to notice my dad in the doorway.
Within seconds, Ron's anxiety was shared by all but Albert,
who, unaware of Dad's presence, continued to swoop
around the garage, cackling and screeching all the way,
until he came face-to-belt-buckle with our silent observer.

For a few moments, the only movement in the suddenly
quiet room came from mouths. Albert pulled a face, grop-
ing in his mind for some way to conceal the evidence now
stacked so neatly against him—and us.

Dad broke the stillness by walking slowly to the empty
candy box lying on the floor at Albert's feet. He picked it
up and dangled it by the string, watching it swing incrimi-
natingly back and forth. Then he looked into the eyes of
the six frightened boys who anxiously watched his every
move. And, as was his custom, he looked into their hearts
as well.

"It doesn't seem so long ago that I was pulling
Valentine's Day pranks myself," he said as he laid the
heart-shaped box on the workbench. At first it was difficult to picture my dignified father pulling the kind of
prank we were planning. But then I remembered a picture
I had seen of him as a child, with fiery red hair, a freckled
face, green eyes and wearing a tight, impish grin. It was
possible, I thought.

"One Valentine's Day my cousins and I decided to pull
a good one on my Grandma Walker," he continued. "Not
because we didn't like her. She was the sweetest grandma
a boy could ever have, and we loved her. We were just
feeling a little devilish and decided to have some fun at
her expense.

"Early in the evening we snuck up to her doorstep with a can of red paint. Grandma was hard of hearing, so we didn't have to worry about being very quiet. Which was a good thing, because every time we thought about how funny it was going to be to see Grandma try to pick up a valentine that was just painted on her doorstep, we couldn't keep from laughing.

"It didn't take long to finish. It wasn't very artistic, but for a bunch of farm kids and an old woman with poor eyesight, it would do. As soon as we were satisfied with the painting, we kicked the door and ran to hide behind bushes and trees to watch the fun.

"There was a lot of giggling going on as we waited in the snow for Grandma to open the door. When she finally appeared she stood in the doorway for a minute, peering into the darkness, her gray hair pulled back tightly into her usual bun, wiping her hand on her usual white apron.

"She must have heard the commotion in the bushes because she looked in our direction as she spoke loudly enough for us to hear: 'Who could be knocking at my door this hour of the night?' My stomach and cheeks ached from trying to hold back the laughter. Then she looked down at her doorstep. Even from fifteen yards away we could see the joy that sparkled in her eyes when she spotted the splash of red at her feet.

"'Oh, how wonderful!' she exclaimed. 'A valentine for Grandma! And I thought I was going to be forgotten again this year!'

"She bent down to retrieve her prize. This was the moment we had been waiting for, but somehow it wasn't as much fun as we had planned. Confused, Grandma groped at the fresh paint for a moment. She quickly became aware of our prank. Her delight at having been remembered by a sweetheart on Sweetheart's Day was short-lived.

"She tried to smile. Then, with as much dignity as she could muster, she turned and walked back into her house, absently wiping red paint on her clean, white apron."

Dad paused for a moment, allowing stillness to once again settle over the cluster of attentive boys. For the first time I noticed that my father's eyes were moist. He took a deep breath. "Grandma died later that year," he said. "I never had another chance to give her a real valentine."

He took the candy box from the workbench and handed it to me. Not another word was spoken as he turned and left the garage.

Later that night a red, heart-shaped box with two plastic roses on it was placed on Mrs. Hayes's front doorstep by six giggling boys. We hid behind snow-covered bushes and trees to see how she would react to receiving a full pound of candy and nuts.

With no strings attached.

Joseph Walker

Harvest Moon

The secret of happiness is not in doing what one likes to do, but liking what one has to do. Stand by your word; it speaks to who you are.

J. M. Barrie

My grandfather had a small farm where he raised beef and some grain for feed. He also worked diligently as a factory laborer and country pastor. He was a good neighbor and well-respected for honoring his word.

When harvesttime came, he'd piece together his old one-row corn picker and oil it up for the season. He pulled it behind a little Ford 9-N tractor with a wagon hooked on the back. It was a noisy contraption unlike the modern machines you see these days devouring the golden armies of grain in wide gulps.

His whole operation was like that. Basic. In fact, his life was like that, too. He worked hard, helped others, and you could count on him to keep his promises. That's what made it so hard one autumn when difficult circumstances closed in on him.

He had promised to harvest a few ribbons of corn that

wound around the hills on a friend's farm, but after harvesting his own corn, Grandpa's little corn picker
coughed, sputtered and quit. It would be out of commis-
sion until a particular part could be ordered, but that
would take far too long to help this year. Then the odds of
being able to help out his neighbor got even worse; the
factory where grandpa worked began to require overtime.
In order to keep his job there he had to leave the farm
before dawn and didn't get home until well after sunset.

One autumn night, while harvesttime was running out,
he and his wife sat at the kitchen table sipping bitter black
coffee and trying to figure a way out of their dilemma.

"There's nothing you can do," said my grandma. "You'll
just have to tell him that you can't help with the corn this
year."

"Well that just doesn't sit well with me," said my
grandpa. "My friend is depending on me. I can't exactly let
my neighbor's harvest rot in the field, can I?"

"If you don't have the equipment, you just can't do it,"
she said.

"Well, I could do it the way we used to do it. I could harvest it by hand," he said.

"When do you think you'd have time to do it?" she
asked. "With the overtime you've been working you'd be
up all night . . . besides it'd be too dark."

"I know of one night that I could do it!" he said, running
to the bookshelf. He grabbed the *Farmer's Almanac* and
started flipping through the pages until he found what he
was looking for. "Aha! There's still one more full moon in
October." As it happened, the harvest moon had yet to
pass. They say it's called the harvest moon because it gives
farmers more light and more time to collect their crops. "If
the Lord gives us clear weather, I think I can do it," he said.

And so a few days later, after a long shift at the factory,
my grandpa made his way to the field where my grandma

met him in the truck with dinner and a steaming thermos of strong, black coffee. The weather was cold but clear, and the moon was brilliant. He worked through the night to keep his word.

I know this story well, because I've spent hours on that old tractor's fender talking with my grandpa. We've even suffered through some of that same bitter coffee together. I'm proud to say that my parents named me after him.

Sometimes, when I'm tempted to cut corners or to put off responsibilities, I think of my grandfather with his scythe cutting wide arcs of corn in the light of the harvest moon. I hear the ears of corn hit the floor of the wagon and the music of geese crossing the cold October sky. The chilly autumn morning darkness envelops my mind and I see my grandpa, his work finally done, crawling into the seat of the old tractor and making his way home. Behind him in the pale moonlight, row after row of corn shocks stand at attention in respect for a man who keeps his word.

Kenneth L. Pierpont

Passing the Torch

Pretty much all the honest truth-telling there is in the world is done by children

Oliver Wendell Holmes

Summer 1964, a northwoods lake.

"Get up! Get up!" my mother whispers.

My eyes flash open. Confusion clouds my brain. Where am I? Is something wrong? I quickly look around.

I'm sandwiched between frayed woolen blankets and the sagging mattress of an old metal bed on the porch of our family log cabin. Looking almost exactly as it did when my grandparents built it in 1929, it sits high on a hill surrounded by the pine and musty fragrance of the woods.

Through sleepy eyelids I take in the dark-green porch swing, the birch leg table, and the smoky glass of the corner kerosene lantern reflecting the stillness of the lake below.

Having escaped the steamy cornland of my home for a few summer weeks, I believe I'm in heaven on Earth. My face feels the coolness of the early morning air. I relax and curl deeper beneath the blankets' warmth.

"Get up!" my mother's voice whispers again. "You must

come now. The sunrise is simply glorious!"

The sunrise? Get up to see the sunrise? Who's she kidding? The last thing this fourteen-year-old wants to do is leave a warm bed to go see a sunrise, glorious or otherwise. It's 5:00 A.M. and freezing out there.

"Hurry!" my mother urges.

Being careful not to let the screen door slam, she sets off down the forty-nine long steps at a determined rate of speed to the lake below.

In the twin bed opposite me, my seventeen-year-old sister Nancy stirs. She pushes back the covers and plops to the floor. Not to be outdone, I make a supreme effort and struggle out of bed as well. In our thin cotton nighties, we grab my father's WWII pea-green army blankets from the foot of our beds and wrap them tightly around our shoulders.

As our bare feet touch the cold porch floor, we are thunderbolted awake. Our pace quickens. One of us misses catching the screen door. It slams. Like a couple of water bugs hopscotching across the lake in avoidance of fish jaws, we gingerly pick our way over slippery rocks and prickly pine needles down the forty-nine dew-covered log steps to the lake shore.

When we feel we've saved our feet from any horny toads or big black spiders that might be crazy enough to be up this early, we catch our breath and look up. Our mother's silhouette is outlined against a rosy dawn, the first light catching the soft red of her hair. She is right. It is a glorious sunrise.

Across the lake a sliver of the most brilliant red crests the top of the shadowed forest. Hues of lavender, rose and amber begin to pulsate into the sky like a heavenly kaleidoscope. High above in the soft blueness, a lone star still sparkles. Silver mist rises gently from the smoothness of the lake. All is still. In the sacred silence, my mother, sister and I stand reverently together against a backdrop of tall pine and watch the magic of God's dawning unfold.

Suddenly, the curve of a brilliant sun bursts through the dark forest. The world begins to awake. We watch a blue heron rise up from a distant shore and gently fan its way over still waters. Two ducks make a rippled landing near our dock while the black and white beauty of a loon skims along the edge of a nearby island hunting for its morning food.

Breathing in the chill air, the three of us draw our blankets closer. The soft hues of the sunrise turn into the brightness of a new day and the last of the stars fades. My sister and I take one more look, race up the steps, and jump into our beds to grab a few more hours of sleep.

My mother is more reluctant to leave the sunrise's amphitheater. From the renewed warmth of my bed, it is a while longer before I hear her reach the top step and gently close the porch door.

Summer 1994, a northwoods lake.

"Get up! Get up!" I whisper to my adolescent sons sleeping dreamily in the same old metal beds of our family's cabin porch.

"Come see the sunrise! It's awesome!"

Amazingly, I watch as this fourth generation of cabin snoozers rouse themselves from cozy comfort. They snatch the WWII pea-green army blankets from the foot of their beds and stumble out the porch door. It slams. Gingerly they maneuver slippery rocks and prickly pine needles down forty-nine dew-covered log steps to the lakeshore.

Their seventy-four-year-old grandmother is already there. Her red hair, now streaked with white, reflects the first light.

She greets her grandsons with the quiet of a bright smile, gathers her blanket closer, and turns toward the east to observe once again God's dawning.

My sons' faces watch intently as the rich colors of the sunrise soar up into the sky like the brilliant plumage of a great bird. It isn't long before the flap of a blue heron's wing or the melodic call of a loon awaken the lake with activity.

"Isn't it beautiful?" I whisper.

The boys nod in silent agreement. Their grandmother smiles at them. Before long, they grab the tails of their frayed blankets and race back up the steps to the welcomed warmth of their beds.

My mother and I stay a little longer. Standing close, we watch the swirls of pearl mist rise and the sky bloom into the shades of a morning rose. We are rewarded this morning by the graceful glide of an eagle high overhead. The gentle rays of the early sun warm our faces.

Eventually, we turn to begin our slow climb up the old log stairs. Halfway up, I catch my breath and look back to see how my mother is doing. But she is not there. She has changed her mind, and through the treetops I can see her, still on the lakeshore, lingering in the light.

Marnie O. Mamminga

He Was a Hero, Like All Grandfathers

My grandfather didn't only provide a guide to living; he lived life fully and modeled for me how to do it—mostly with love and kindness.

McAllister Dodds

A while ago, a legend entered my life in the most common of ways, disguised as a grandfather. His name was familiar, and I knew what he did long before I met him in a sticky, half-empty middle-school gym. We were watching a basketball game. I was there to see my son, and he was there to see his grandson. They play on the same team—a pretty good team, like a lot of other pretty good teams that play in gyms across the city every Saturday afternoon. Their fans are vocal and intimately tied to the players. Mother. Fathers. Siblings with nothing better to do. Sometimes grandparents. I saw him every week.

His past made him extraordinary, and periodically I would watch as people stopped to shake his hand. I assumed that he had gotten used to that, as well as to the deference and muffled whispers that followed him wherever he went, a long time ago. I wondered if that made life harder or easier, but as I watched him I decided that he had gotten used to that, too, and it was clear that although he enjoyed it, he had given it a place. A nice place, to be sure, but certainly somewhere below watching his grandson.

Over the years, his grandson and my son became friends. They did things that any other middle-school friends do. Movies. Football. Basketball. But interspersed with the routine, there was always the reminder of the legend.

"Mom, can I go to the Hall of Fame luncheon with Jeb and his grandpa?"

And visits to Jeb's house were followed by, "We went to Jeb's grandpa's house. He has a really cool trophy room."

"I imagine he does," I would reply.

"No, this is *really* cool. He has a copy of his Hall of Fame bust."

I don't know why, but each time the reminder came, it took me by surprise.

Last week after school, for no other reason except that he likes to draw, my son came home and drew a copy of an autographed publicity shot Jeb's grandpa had given him. He worked on it for hours. He finally brought it over.

"It's very good," I said and for the first time I really looked at the photo. It had been taken about forty years ago. I compared the photo and the drawing. "You've done the body perfectly," I said.

And he had. He had copied in detail the body of the athlete kicking a football. But the face in the photo and the face in the drawing didn't match. The face John drew was not the face of forty years ago. The face in the drawing was the mature face that he knew. John had drawn the face of the grandpa.

"But it's not the best I've done," he said.

"Well it's not a perfect copy, but it's very good," I replied. "You should give it to him."

The next morning my alarm went off at five, and, as is my routine, I lay in bed and listened to the radio's news broadcast. The broadcaster was talking about The Toe.

I knew before they said it why The Toe was the lead story. Legends become lead stories when they are gone.

I listened for a while and went downstairs. The drawing was sitting on the kitchen table. "Lou Groza," it said, "Hall of Fame, '74."

When John came home from the funeral, he mentioned a passage that had been read. It was titled, "Little Eyes Upon You."

"And what did it say?" I asked.

"It said that older people should watch the steps they take because little kids are watching. Because to little kids, older people are heroes."

Older people. Not legendary sport stars. Ordinary grandpas and grandmas and aunts and uncles and fathers and mothers.

This time the grandpa and legend just happened to be the same man.

I was wrong about the drawing. It was perfect.

Sue Vitou

The Boys of Iwo Jima

*The service we render others is the rent we pay
for our room on Earth.*

Wilfred Grenfill

Each year I travel to Washington, D.C., with the eighth-grade class, from Clinton, Wisconsin, where I grew up, to videotape their trip.

I greatly enjoy visiting our nation's capital, and each year I take some special memories back with me. This fall's trip was especially memorable.

On the last night of our trip, we stopped at the Iwo Jima Memorial. This memorial is the largest bronze statue in the world and depicts one of the most famous photographs in history—that of the six brave soldiers raising the American flag at the top of a rocky hill on the Island of Iwo Jima, Japan, during WWII.

We piled off the buses and headed towards the memorial, where I noticed a solitary figure at the base of the statue. As I approached him, he asked, "Where are you guys from?" I told him that we were from Wisconsin. "Hey, I'm a Cheesehead, too! Come gather around,

Cheeseheads, and I will tell you a story."

His name was James Bradley and he just happened to be in Washington, D.C., to speak at the memorial the following day. He was there that evening to say goodnight to his dad, who had passed away. I videotaped him as he spoke to us and received his permission to share what he said from my videotape.

Touring the incredible monuments in Washington, D.C., is spectacular, but it can't compare to the insight we received that night. When we had gathered around him, he reverently began to speak. . . .

"My name is James Bradley, and I'm from Antigo, Wisconsin. My dad is on that statue, and I just wrote a book called *Flags of Our Fathers* which is number five on the *New York Times* bestseller list right now. It is the story of the six boys you see behind me. The six boys who raised the flag.

"The first guy putting the pole in the ground is Harlon Block. Harlon was an all-state football player. He enlisted in the marine corps with all the senior members of his football team. They were off to play another type of game. A game called 'war.' But it didn't turn out to be a game. Harlon, at the age of twenty-one, died horribly. I say that because there are generals who stand in front of this statue and talk about the glory of war. You guys need to know that most of the boys in Iwo Jima were seventeen, eighteen and nineteen years old.

"You see this next guy? That's René Gagnon from New Hampshire. If you took René's helmet off at the moment this photo was taken, and looked in the webbing of that helmet, you would find a photograph. A photograph of his girlfriend. René put that in there for protection, because he was scared. He was eighteen years old. Boys won the battle of Iwo Jima. Boys. Not old men. The next guy here, the third guy in this tableau, was Sergeant Mike Strank. Mike is my hero. He was the hero of all these guys. They called him the 'old man' because he was so old. He was already twenty-four. When Mike would motivate his boys in training camp, he didn't say, 'Let's die for our country.' He knew he was talking to little boys. Instead, he would say, 'You do what I say, and I'll get you home to your mothers.'

"The last guy on this side of the statue is Ira Hayes, a Pima Indian from Arizona. Ira Hayes walked off Iwo Jima. He went into the White House with my dad. President Truman told him, 'You're a hero.' He told reporters, 'How can I feel like a hero when 250 of my buddies hit the island with me and only twenty-seven of us walked off alive?'

"The next guy, going around the statue is Franklin Sousley from Hilltop, Kentucky. A fun-lovin' hillbilly boy. Franklin died on Iwo Jima at the age of nineteen. When the telegram came to tell his mother that he was dead, it went to the Hilltop General Store. A barefoot boy ran that telegram up to his mother's farm. The neighbors could hear her scream all night and into the morning. The neighbors lived a quarter of a mile away.

"The next guy, as we continue to go around the statue is my dad, John Bradley from Antigo, Wisconsin, where I was raised. My dad lived until 1994, but he would never give interviews. You see, my dad didn't see himself as a hero. Everyone thinks these guys are heroes, 'cause they are in a photo and a monument. My dad knew better. He was a medic. John Bradley from Wisconsin was a caregiver. In Iwo Jima, he probably held over two hundred boys as they died. And when boys died in Iwo Jima, they writhed and screamed in pain.

"When I was a little boy, my third-grade teacher told me that my dad was a hero. When I went home and told my dad that, he looked at me and said, 'I want you always to remember that the heroes of Iwo Jima are the guys who did not come back—did *not* come back.'

"So that's the story about six nice young boys. Three died on Iwo Jima, and three came back as national heroes. Overall, seven thousand boys died on Iwo Jima in the worst battle in the history of the marine corps. My voice is giving out, so I will end here. Thank you for your time."

Suddenly the monument wasn't just a big old piece of metal with a flag sticking out of the top. It came to life before our eyes with the heartfelt words of a son who did indeed have a father who was a hero.

Maybe not a hero for the reasons most people would believe, but a hero nonetheless.

Michael T. Powers

FOR BETTER OR FOR WORSE. ©*UFS. Reprinted by Permission.*

The Stories Grandma Told

Courage is a sort of endurance of the soul.

Laches

I can recall being five years old and knowing the stories of how my grandmother and grandfather came to the United States. Both came at different times, Grandpa from Spain and my Portuguese grandmother from Trinidad. Along with those stories came how they met and various tales of family members long gone. I was always fascinated to be entertained by these stories even into adulthood when I had heard them so many times before, however, one night the story of my grandmother's passage to the United States became a teaching method that I will never forget.

My sister and her family were moving to Utah, which might as well have been Mars in its relationship to the sunny shores of Florida, where we all had migrated from the sidewalks of New York where my grandparents laid down their American roots. The time had come to say good-bye. My sister tried to be strong along with her husband so not to upset the other family members. My grandmother watched intently as I said my farewells. First to my sister and brother-in-law then to my two-year-old nephew, Jesse, and finally the most difficult and heart-breaking good-bye to my beautiful twelve year old niece, Carmen. She and I had always shared a special bond, and I could hear her sob along with me as I stroked her mahogany tresses all the while thinking of all the mile-stones in her life that I would no longer be a part of. As I looked up for a brief moment I saw the tear-stained faces of my family but noticed that my grandmother was the only one who was composed. Before I could contemplate what I had seen, Carmen had broken away and locked herself in the bathroom to cry alone. All of us made attempts to get her to open the door to no avail. Then we heard her say, "I'll let Aunt Susan in." Once I was inside with the door closed we sat on the floor together crying. There was nothing I said to her that would console her. I felt so helpless. Here I was, the only female in the history of my family to graduate from college and hold a master's degree, and a teacher whose job it was to help children to understand, but I had no words of wisdom for the child who means more to me than my own life.

Soon the faint knock of my ninety-year-old grand-mother came to the door. Her voice barely audible through the door said, "I would like to tell Carmen a story." Carmen slowly opened the door and the five-foot frame of my grandmother gently entered. As Carmen and I stood together, I listened as my grandmother began to tell the story of her journey to the United States. Suddenly, I was an observer of a great teacher at work. The story that I always perceived as entertainment was being used to teach faith, hope and courage. Her eyes burrowed into my niece's with the pride and dignity of my family that had been passed to me so long ago. In very few, but healing words the story of how my grandmother at fifteen years of age left her grandmother and aunts behind began to unfold. Boarding the ship headed for Ellis Island, filled with fears of never seeing them again was not any different than Carmen's fear two generations later. The story came to a close with my grandmother's family arriving in the United States one year later. I saw my niece's face transform from expressions of despair to expressions of hope in a matter of minutes. I realized at that moment what a wise woman my grandmother was. She knew all along that we had to express our pain of the separation and when the time was right she would simply tell the old story that we had all heard many times over the years.

That night changed the way I listen to the old stories now. To this day, I look beyond the entertainment and listen for the deeper meanings of my grandmother's stories. They are stories of courage, pride, love, happiness and sadness each with their own hidden messages to soothe, comfort and guide the generations that have come after her. Truly with age comes wisdom.

Susan Garcia-Nikolova, M.S.

Worms and All

Laughter is the lightening rod of play and the public and private sharing of joy.

Source Unknown

I stood in my grandparents' kitchen, watching the steam curl through the air above the big pot on the stove. It was an annual ritual as far back as memory would take me. Grandpa was making jelly.

Unable to stand for long periods of time because of arthritic knees, Grandpa would get his juices cooking, then drag over one of the kitchen chairs and sit next to the stove. With an elbow propped on the countertop, he stirred the big pot with a wooden spoon. I would tiptoe to see what it looked like, but I was too small to peek over the top. From what I could tell, though, Grandpa couldn't stretch high enough to see in, either.

"How can you tell when it's ready, 'Pa?"

"I can tell."

He could smile at my impatient fidgeting. Most children like jelly, but to me, Grandpa's was special. It was made from the plums we picked in the yard. While he picked the ones still swinging high in the branches of the little plum tree, I picked up the ones that had been knocked down. Green, overripe or bruised, my contributions were tossed right along with his into the bucket.

Washing the plums in the sink, Grandpa would sort out and discreetly dispose of the unsuitable fruit. Then we steamed the plums, strained the juices and prepared the jars. Quite possibly I was more of a hindrance than a help, but Grandpa never complained or lost patience.

I can remember the first time he told me his recipe.

"There's an art to making good jelly," he lowered his voice and told me. "Worms an' all, Pammy, that's the secret. Worms an' all."

Aghast, I'm sure I made faces while telling him I'd never eat worms. No way! Grandpa threw back his head and laughed. Amusement danced in his eyes.

Then at long last the jelly was ready to eat. Jelly jars sat in rows on the tabletop, with the sunlight shining through the window behind. The deep maroon color would lighten to a brilliant red, and the gold tops and rims would glow. We spooned jelly onto bread and folded it over into sandwiches.

I watched Grandpa take that first bite. Surely if there were worms involved, he wouldn't be eating it, would he? Feeling assured that it was another of Grandpa's jokes, I began to eat, too.

Grandma eyed us both suspiciously.

"Merle, have you been telling her there were worms in those plums? Mercy! Don't you be listening to him, Girl. He just says that so they'll be more jelly left for him."

Grandpa laughed deeply as he spooned more jelly onto the bread.

Each year was the same. While stirring the juice over the stove, Grandpa would share his recipe with me. He would lower his voice and bend over so he could look me in the eye, telling me, "Worms an' all, Pammy. That's the secret." Then the laughter would come. I imagined that this was a secret he was passing down only to me. Quite possibly, though, he spoke softly just so Grandma wouldn't hear from the next room.

The year after Grandpa passed away, my new husband and I moved into a little home in the country. There was a lovely little wild plum tree in the backyard. I waited eagerly for those tiny hard, green plums to ripen so I could try my hand at jelly-making. It took almost a week of gathering daily to get enough to make even one batch of jelly. I carefully sorted, washed and double-checked the fruit.

Following what I could remember from watching Grandpa all those years ago, I succeeded in making a passable plum jelly at my first attempt. Proud of my accomplishment, I showed the shelf full of jelly jars to my dad.

He held one up and admired the sunlight shining red through the glass. I imagined his taste buds watering for his first bite. Then I mentioned that I had used Grandpa's recipe.

The look of delight faded from Dad's face as he turned slowly to look at me. Then he asked, "Worms and all?"

I nodded.

At the end of his visit, Dad only took one jar home with him. His lack of interest in my culinary skills didn't bother me, though.

As I spread a sweet spoonful onto a bit of toast, I thought with a smile, it just leaves more jelly for me!

Pamela Jenkins

THE FAMILY CIRCUS®   By Bil Keane

"Can I talk to Grandma?
Can I talk to Grandma?
Can I talk to Grandma?"

Perennial

Thoughtfulness is a habit—a way of life well worth cultivating and practicing.

Brough Botalico

The garden in front of my grandparents' red brick house is where the jonquils, tulips, crocuses and irises bloomed. Other bulbs remained beneath, still hidden in the darkness of the moist soil. As the days grew longer and stretched into summer, the deep pink star-gazers and trumpet-shaped lilies of pure white would also spring forth from the loamy earth and leaf debris.

In the springtime, a dear old friend who had known my grandparents for decades longer than I had even been alive, came over to help with removing the storm windows. The air was warm, and any threats of wintry weather seemed to have passed.

After the task had been completed, he and my grandmother walked around to the front of the house where my mother and three aunts had spent their childhoods.

There, in the plot beside the front porch, a colorful congregation of flowers waved merrily in the breeze, a statue of St. Francis presiding over the petals.

My grandmother stopped to admire the flowerbed.

"I've been noticing these past few weeks," she said, pausing in contemplation, "and it just seems to me that the flowers are even more beautiful than usual, there just seems to be more colors."

The friend chuckled quietly. "Well," he said in response, "that probably has something to do with the extra bulbs Joe planted in secret last fall."

Joe was my grandfather, and although it was my grandmother who took most of the pride in the beautiful blossoms in front of their house each year, it was he who was the primary tender of the garden.

The friend shook his head, "Leave it to Joe to not tell you something like that." He continued, "I suppose the flowers speak louder than any words could anyway. And he was never one to make a big fuss over things, nor did he like it when other people would—especially when the fuss was being made over him."

"Well for heaven's sakes," said my grandmother. "But when could he have done it? We were together so much of the time."

"I reckon all those times he went to working on projects in the garage, he wasn't necessarily in the garage the whole time. And you did go to your ladies' meetings at church."

They both stood looking at the flowers.

"And he wanted it to be a surprise for you this spring." The man blinked several times in quick succession and cleared his throat, looking around the yard. "Is there anything else I can do for you today, Mary?"

She shook her head gently. "No, you've been such a big help already. Thank you so much."

"Well," he said brusquely, clearing his throat, "then I must be going now."

He rolled down his window in his car before pulling out

of the driveway. "Mary, you be sure and let me know if there's anything you need."

She smiled and waved.

The car disappeared down the street, and my grandmother went to the porch swing. She sat down in a sunbeam, a small solitary figure with gray curls, swaying slowly back and forth. She gazed at the flowers, bathed in the warmth of the sunshine and thoughts of her romantic husband.

As long as she had known him, he was forever giving her thoughtful gifts. They were a duo who had weathered a childhood in the Depression, and later had channeled much of their energy and financial resources into raising four children. Frivolous objects were a foreign concept to them, and the gifts he had given were never flamboyant or expensive. The few pieces of jewelry he had presented to her had been hard-earned after months and months of scrupulous saving.

She treasured the jewelry, but it was perhaps the other gifts that meant even more to her. The purchase prices had been smaller, but she recognized the thought that went into them, which made them so precious.

Throughout their courtship he had given her books that they would read sitting together on park benches. While he was overseas during the war, my grandfather wrote her letters almost daily, and sent photographs and small trinkets when he could. In 1944, he returned safely, and they began their lives together. Although he returned from Europe and they could see one another every day, he still sometimes wrote her love letters.

Even during the busy parenting years of crying babies, potty-training, skinned knees, school plays and proms, he still made time to be romantic, giving small gifts. The gifts and notes continued to appear, through the course of fifty-six years of marriage.

She turned her blue eyes again to the garden, breathing the sweet fragrances. A tear ran down her cheek, and the flowers became a blurred watercolor as her eyes welled with more tears.

He always found a special way to remind her and let her know how much he loved her.

Even now, three months after the cancer had so abruptly taken him, an angel gardener blew her kisses, carried on the scents and colors of the flower petals.

Tinker E. Jacobs

The Silver Sugar Bowl

The love of my family is my estate.

Horatio Nelson

I was traveling home to New Hampshire after visiting with my grandma and grandpa.

While waiting to go through security at the airport, I noticed an older lady in front of me struggling to open her carry-on bag. Apparently, there was something in her bag that looked "strange" on the X ray.

After emptying everything on to the table, she pulled out a silver sugar bowl. The security inspector checked it over and then waived her through. As she struggled to re-pack her things, I offered to assist her. We got everything back into her bag, but the unpacking and packing had made her rather upset. I tried to calm her down, and we headed towards the gate.

We looked at our boarding passes and realized that we were sitting next to each other on the plane.

We talked about many things during our three-hour flight, including our families. She told me that she was going to visit her great-grandson. His wife had just given birth to her first great-great-granddaughter, and she just had to get to Vermont to see her before it was "too late."

"You see, I have cancer," she explained, "and I'm not going to be around for much longer. I just want to be able to see my new grandchild and give her parents the silver sugar bowl. It's been in our family for many, many years. My great-great-grandmother gave it to my father more than eighty years ago."

She looked up toward the overhead bin where I had put her bag and the bowl.

"Yes," she continued, "that bowl may be well-worn from all of the loving hands that have polished it over the years, but it's part of our family and it has to be given in person."

As we were talking, I discovered that I actually knew her great-grandson. He was a vendor at the small store I was working in at the time.

Walking off the plane, I thanked her for the most enjoyable conversation.

With a twinkle in her eye, she agreed, "Yes, dear, the time seemed to fly right by."

I carried her bag for her and she held on to my arm as we approached the arrival area. She was met by her great-grandson and her new great-great-granddaughter who was honored with the same name as her great-great-grandmother, Marion.

The luster and shine of the silver sugar bowl seemed to return as the family embraced. Tears streamed down the old woman's cheeks when she saw little Marion's smiling face reflected in the small vessel.

I wished them a wonderful visit, and I didn't see her great-grandson until two or three weeks later. He told me how much his great-grandmother had enjoyed our "little talk." When I asked how she was doing, he told me that sadly she had passed away just one week after she arrived.

Apparently, only days before, she had written down the

history of the silver sugar bowl for little Marion in the hope that one day she, too, would pass her family's precious heirloom on to the next generation like her great-great-grandmother Marion had done with her—in person.

Karen Carr

My Grandmother's Shell

My grandmother was a great teacher, and her influence on me only grows over time.

Source Unknown

Above my mantel is a painting of a little girl with a conch shell. As she holds it up to the light, the sun streams through, turning the smooth, inner surface into glowing pink satin. No matter what the season, the painting's sunlight fills my study with summer brightness.

Looking at the painting, I remember the story of its creation. The little girl is posing for her father, a painter. Her arms grow heavy, her neck aches, she longs to rest a bit. "El, El, look into the shell," her father murmurs, and she remembers what a privilege it is to pose for him, how sought-after his paintings are. "Just a bit longer," he promises, "and then we'll stop for tea."

Eleanor was my grandmother, and the painting—one that her father could not bear to part with—has been handed down through the generations. For as long as I can remember, the shell in the painting sat on my grandmother's desk. In the winter, when cold fog rolled in off the sea, she would hold it up to the lamp and its rosy sheen would fill her with summer's warmth once again.

Grandmother found it washed up on the rocky shore of the little island in Maine that was her family's summer home. She used to tell me how, when the morning's silvery mists had lifted, she and her sisters and brother would run across the open meadows with their kites or pick bouquets of wildflowers or gather the wool left behind on the bushes by the wild island sheep. The children would hunt for blackberries and watch birds with their father, who taught them the birds' names and all their many songs. After tea, they often explored the wide beaches looking for pirate treasures. It was on one of these adventures that Grandmother found the shell, scoured smooth by the waves, bleached clean by the summer sun. As generations before her had done, she placed the shell to her ear and heard the sound of the sea.

By the time my mother was born, Grandmother had left that island home and created a new summer place for her own children. They spent hours sailing in little dinghies, galloping their ponies across the marshes, and gathering shells on the broad white beach that bordered Cape Cod Bay. In this new home, Grandmother recreated many of her childhood loves: She seeded meadows with wildflowers, designed perennial borders and planted blackberries. And from the porch she could look out across the tidal river and see ospreys nesting in a tall pine tree.

When we grandchildren began arriving, she set aside a part of her garden so we could know the joy of planting vegetables and flowers. How proud we were to place a plate of our radish harvest—ruby globes scrubbed shiny and clean—on a dinner table made brighter still by vases filled with our flowers. She taught us the birds' calls, and told us how they returned each summer to her woods and meadows, just as we did. And she let us listen to the ocean in her shell.

Each autumn, as my family and I returned to our Midwestern home, I ached for the sounds of the shore; the cry of the gulls wheeling overhead, the low mournful song of the foghorn, so deep I seemed to feel more than hear it. The tangy smell of the salt air was replaced by the smoke of burning leaves. But I missed the tides and the wildness. Grandmother knew my yearning.

One year, shortly after Thanksgiving, the postman brought a large box mailed from Massachusetts. Mother hid it in that secret place she kept all boxes that arrived in December. On Christmas morning I opened my grandmother's present and saw, nestled in tissue paper, the delicate pink and white of her shell. I picked it up and held it to my ear, and there was the ocean, murmuring. Outside, snow was falling softly past the window, but in the shell, cupped in my hand, waves lapped on a summer shore.

This year I have a granddaughter of my own. Her birth heralds the beginning of a new generation. When she comes to visit, I shall hold the shell up to her ear and she will hear the sound that has always drawn the women of our family to the ocean. It is the sound of her own heart.

Faith Andrews Bedford

Grammy's Gifts

Children have more need of models than of critics.

Joseph Joubert

"What are you looking for?" my husband, Peter, asks, watching me dig through a box in one of our closets.

"Stuffed cabbage," I reply. It was always a family Hanukkah tradition, served with crisp latkes. I haven't seen my grandmother Miriam's recipe in years, but I know exactly where to find it: in the large cardboard box of mementos I had labeled "From Grammy" when I was thirteen years old.

The box contains photos of a chubby toddler splashing around in a pool in water wings. When I was terrified I would drown in the deep end, Miriam taught me how to float on my back, supporting my shoulders and assuring me she'd never let go.

The box also contains a graduation card with the words "You always make me so proud. Love, Grammy" scrawled in a thin, shaky hand. And it has her gold wedding band, the one I wore when I took my marriage vows last January.

Miriam knew the most amazing things. She could spell Mississippi backwards. She could keep an omelet from sticking to the pan. She could comb the knots out of my long, matted hair without it hurting one bit.

When I was six and she was in her sixties, she showed me how to Charleston. "I was an extra in a Gloria Swanson movie, you know," she'd say, swinging one leg high out in front of her to demonstrate. "It was a party scene with lots of people dancing, and the director put me up front because he thought I had great legs."

On the nights when my parents went out to dinner and she was babysitting, we'd dress up in bangles and boas, and belt out "Boogie Woogie Bugle Boy" to an imaginary audience. My grandmother and I were kindred spirits. We laughed and cried at the same things, and we understood each other. I told her we'd travel around the world together, and she showed me how to touch the stars by closing one eye and balancing them on my fingertips.

She taught me how to paint my toenails a perfect shade of Redcoat Red and never gave away my secret when I stalked around the living room in sweat socks. When my mother would scold me for hanging upside-down on the monkey bars or riding my bike with no hands, Grammy would nod and wink. "Go on," she'd whisper in my ear. "Do something spectacular with your life."

She was the first person who ever encouraged me to dream and to put those dreams down on paper. When she became almost completely bedridden and shook with Parkinson's disease, I would sneak into her room—a makeshift space we had walled off from the dining room— in the middle of the night and crawl under her covers. We'd stare up at the ceiling, watching the darkness fade into dawn, and tell each other stories. We called the cracks in the plaster our cloud pictures and squinted to see an assortment of characters take shape in the shadows.

"Right there's a one-legged ballerina," she told me once, pointing her chin in the direction of a paint splatter. "Do you see it?"

I nodded, straining to make out a woman in a *tutu en pointe*. "She lost her leg because she danced too much in tight shoes," she whispered so my parents down the hall wouldn't hear us and chase me back to bed. "She should never have bought them on sale at Macy's."

Miriam's lessons are the ones that stuck with me—not all the algebra formulas or Spanish verb conjugations I studied for years. She taught me important basics: how much constitutes a pinch of salt; how to use seltzer to get a stain out of a silk blouse; how to sew a button on so it stays put. She helped me appreciate the simple things, like cream cheese and tomato sandwiches, towels warm from the dryer, and the quiet moments at dusk when the whole world is draped in a curtain of blue light. She liked the springtime most of all, when the air was warm and the breezes gentle. "This is soft weather," she explained to me. "Not too hot, not too cool, just soft."

But I don't need to rummage through my box to recall Miriam's lessons. My senses often bring them and her back to me: the gardenia fragrance of her hand lotion at a department store counter; an Andrews Sisters tune playing on Muzak in the dentist's office; the taste of her favorite sticky-sweet cherry cordial. Sometimes I see the back of a head on a bus and recognize the snowy-white hair falling in soft waves. Or I catch myself laughing her laugh, a hearty, joyous cry that makes my shoulders shake and my cheeks ache.

I'm reminded of all those little words of wisdom she instilled in me, about life, love and loss: "Every time a door closes, a window opens," "There's a lid for every pot," "Don't cry over spilled milk."

My husband calls these little phrases old wives' tales

and teases me when I tug on my left ear each time I sneeze as she advised me (to ward off bad luck). But I cherish her sayings. Miriam's lessons have gotten me through many terrible times—when I lost my job, when I broke up with a boyfriend, when I failed a test or when I simply burned dinner.

As I stir a big, boiling pot of stuffed cabbage on my stove, I can picture the past as if it were yesterday: My sister, Debbie, and I are spinning a dreidel and snacking on Hanukkah gelt, as my mother and grandmother work diligently in the kitchen. Miriam sprinkles a dash of sugar into the pot of cabbage for sweetness and squeezes in just enough lemon juice to "give it a kick."

And I can't help thinking that "life is like that"—sometimes sweet, sometimes sour, and always a challenge to blend both parts perfectly.

Sheryl Berk

The Secret of Grandma's Sugar Crock

The best portion of a good woman's life is her little, nameless, unremembered acts of kindness and love.

William Wordsworth

World War II had recently been declared. On the surface, there appeared to be little change in Grandma's ranch. Grandpa worked the fields and orchards every day, just as he had done before, and Grandma tended to the chores and harvesting as usual. But in fact, there had been a big change in the old homestead. The ranch was without the manpower of their five youngest sons, who were now on active military duty somewhere in the Pacific. Both Grandpa and Grandma would have to work twice as hard now to compensate for the absence of their five strong sons.

During World War II, a government-issued flag, imprinted with five blue stars, hung in the front window of my grandparents' old farmhouse. It meant that five of their sons were off fighting in the war. Without the boys to work the land, the ranch was shorthanded. Grandma worked doubly hard now to harvest a bountiful fruit crop.

During that time, every member of the family pitched in to help, including grandkids like myself. Even so, it was a difficult time for Grandma: Rationing was in effect, there was little money for luxuries, and worst of all was the constant worry over whether her five sons would come home safely to her.

The old ranch was a lovely place, especially in the spring when the orchards were white with plum blossoms, and the song of the meadowlarks filled the fields and rolling hills of the surrounding valley. It was this beautiful ranch and returning to Grandma and Grandpa that their five sons focused on all during the war years.

In the summertime, while the rest of the family harvested the plum crop, Grandma was in the kitchen cooking up delicious fine Italian dinners. We would all sit on blankets spread out on the orchard ground, enjoying not just the wonderful food, but also the satisfaction of being part of such an important family effort.

To encourage the ripe fruit to fall, Grandpa used a long wooden pole with an iron hook at the top to catch a branch and shake the plums loose from the trees. Then the rest of us would crawl along, wearing knee pads that Grandma had sewn into our overalls, and gather the plums into metal buckets. We dumped the buckets of plums into long wooden trays, where the little purple plums were soon sun-dried into rich, brown prunes.

After a long, hard day I would walk hand-in-hand with Grandpa through the orchards while he surveyed what had been accomplished that day. I'd enjoy eating fresh plums off the trees, licking the sweet stickiness from my fingertips.

On each of these walks, Grandpa would stoop down and pick up a handful of soil, letting it sift slowly and lovingly through his strong, work-calloused hands. Then with pride and conviction he would invariably say: "If you take good care of the land, the land will take good care of you." It was this respect and belief in the soil that helped bolster his generation.

As darkness fell on the ranch, we'd all gather together on the cool, quiet veranda of the front porch. Grandpa would settle comfortably into his rocker, under the dim glow of a flickering moth-covered lightbulb, and there he'd read the latest war news in his newspaper, trying to track the whereabouts of his five young sons.

Grandma always sat nearby on the porch swing, swaying back and forth and saying her perpetual rosary. The quiet squeak of Grandma's swing and the low mumbling of her prayers could be heard long into the night. The stillness of the quiet ranch house painfully reflected the absence of the five robust young men. This was the hardest part of the day for Grandma; the silence of the empty house was a painful reminder that her sons were far, far away, fighting for their country.

On Sunday morning, Grandma was back out on the porch again, repeating her rosary before going into the kitchen to start cooking. Then she and Grandpa sat at the kitchen table, counting out ration slips for the week ahead and what little cash there was to pay the bills. Once they were finished, Grandma always took a portion of her money and put it in the sugar crock, placing it high on the kitchen shelf. I often asked her what the money in the jar was for. She would simply say, "A very special favor."

Well, the war finally ended, and all five of Grandma's sons came home, remarkably safe and sound. After a while, Grandma and Grandpa retired, and the family farm became part of a modern expressway.

I never did find out what the money in the sugar crock was for until a week or so before last Christmas. Completely on impulse, perhaps feeling the wonder of the Christmas season and the need to connect with its spiritual significance, I stopped at a little church I just happened to be driving past. I'd never been inside before, and as I entered the church through the side door, I was stunned to come face-to-face with the most glorious stained-glass window I'd ever seen.

I stopped to examine the intricate beauty of the window more closely. The magnificent stained glass depicted the Holy Mother and child. Like an exquisite jewel, it reflected the glory of the very first Christmas. As I studied every detail of its fine workmanship, I found, to my utter amazement, a small plaque at the base of the window that read, "For a favor received—donated in 1945 by Maria Carmela Curci-Dinapoli." I couldn't believe my eyes. I was reading Grandma's very words! Every day that Grandma had said her prayers for her soldier-sons, she'd also put whatever money she could scrape together into her sacred sugar crock to pay for the window.

Her quiet donation of this window had been her way of saying thank you to God for sparing the lives of her beloved five sons.

The original church in which the window was placed had long ago been torn down. Through the generations, the family had lost track of its existence. Finding this window at Christmastime, more than half a century later, not only brought back a flood of precious memories, but also made me a believer in small but beautiful miracles.

Cookie Curci

Grandma Hattie

You don't develop courage by being happy in your relationship every day. You develop it by surviving difficult times and challenging adversity.

Barbara De Angelis

Going through the Christmas cards in our mailbox today, I came across one from my dear old grandma in Illinois. She never fails. Never missed a birthday, Christmas, or anniversary as long as I've lived. Quite a gal, old Grandma Hattie. There's always a nice little letter inside wrapped around a crisp five-dollar bill she can't afford to send.

I read the letter—newsy stuff about her holiday baking and the weather (no snow there yet, either). Then as always, there was the postscript at the end: "Just a little Christmas treat. Love, Grandma." So I tucked the five-dollar bill into my shirt and promised that my wife and I would do something extra-special with it. At least as special as five bucks will buy you these days.

Then, as I was reading through the rest of the mail, I came across another card from Grandma. I'll be darned. Must be our anniversary card, being as we were married the day after Christmas, same as her birthday. She never forgets. I was wrong. It was another Christmas card with another newsy little letter and another brand-new five-dollar bill she couldn't afford to send. Well, what do you think of that?

She must have gotten confused somehow and forgotten to cross us off her list. Or maybe she doesn't have a list. She may do it from memory, and eighty-seven-year-old memories can play tricks like that at times. She may have thought she already sent us one but wasn't altogether sure, so she sent another one just in case. That would be just like her. Rather than take the chance of missing one of us by mistake, she'd send two just to be sure. There aren't many of us who *can* afford the five dollars that would do that. The heck of it is that I don't dare send it back. She'd be so embarrassed by the mistake, it would do her no good, and I'm sure we can get it back to her in other ways.

There are probably not a whole lot of Christmases left in Grandma Hat, and the world will be the worse for it when she goes. She's endeared herself to friends, family and strangers alike for many, many decades. My mom tells a story of her from the Depression years.

At the time, Grandma and Grandpa owned a dairy. It was right next door to the house, where the garden is now, and they ran it themselves. They lived near the train tracks, and being that it was during the Depression, they used to get their share of hoboes coming around looking for handouts.

They were hard-working folks, my mom's family, and believed that everybody else should be, too. They'd give the "bums," as she called them, food and milk, all right, but they'd have to wash milk cans, scrub floors, shovel snow or some such thing to get it. Those were the rules, and nobody complained.

Mom says they got pretty popular on the hobo circuit and got that inevitable mark on their front gatepost. Just a little X on the post in white chalk to let the other hoboes know this was a place where a guy could get a handout. It was common practice at that time and was supposed to be on the sly. But Grandma knew it was there. She never did bother any with that chalk on the gatepost, except just once.

It was Christmastime, and my mom was just a little girl. They didn't have any snow yet, but right before Christmas they had a big wind and rainstorm. Coming back from church that Sunday, Grandma noticed that the chalk mark had been washed clear off the post by the storm.

It got cold right away like it will on the Midwestern plains and snowed to beat the band. She sat that day in the front room saying the rosary with Grandpa like they always did on Sunday. They saw the hoboes walking down from the train yard going wherever it is hoboes go in a snowstorm. They looked so cold and defeated, but none of them was stopping at the gate or knocking on the dairy window like they always did. Then it struck her why. Of course—the little white X wasn't on the post anymore. Now, where another person might have been relieved to be left alone the Sunday before Christmas, Old Grandma Hat, and she wasn't that old then, put on her overcoat, went right out to the gatepost, and put a great big white X there where nobody could miss it.

I don't know if they got to feed any hoboes that day or not because Mom usually stops telling the story about there, but it doesn't matter. It told me something about Grandma, and I've carried this story with me a long time. She put that X on the gatepost way back then for the same reason she sent us two Christmas cards this year. She didn't want to miss anybody, even if it did cost an extra five bucks. I always think of that story when I'm starting to feel a little broke and put out at Christmastime; then I'm ashamed of myself.

Tom Bodett

Finger Play

Four-year-old Kayla nestled on Opa's lap while he read their favorite Dr. Seuss book—again. As she fought sleep, her dimpled fingers plucked idly at the roadmap of veins ribbing the backs of her grandpa's hands. First one, then another, she pulled each dark blue vein into a ridge and watched it melt back down.

Suddenly, she leaned forward for a closer look. Opa paused to watch as she inspected his weathered skin and compared it to her own baby-plump pink hand, touching first one, then the other. Satisfied at last, Kayla looked up.

"I think God must've practiced on you first, Opa," she said. "'Cause he did much better making me!"

Carol McAdoo Rehme

5

WHEN THE KIDS TEACH US

I worked as a chief business executive for over forty years. I made major decisions. I worked side by side with powerful men and women. But one grandchild has changed me more than any of those people I worked with, and I have learned more from watching my children be parents than I learned in all those forty years in the workplace.

A Grandfather

Behind the Mirror

If it were not for hopes, the heart would break.

Thomas Fuller

When I was a little girl we lived in New York City just down the block from my grandparents. Every evening my grandfather would go for his "constitutional." During those summers of the mid-1960s I would join him for the walk, and he'd tell me how life was when he was a little boy.

As we walked past storefront windows reflecting the setting sun, he described a world of horses instead of cars, outhouses instead of flush toilets, letters instead of telephones, and candles instead of electric lights. As he pointed out all the hardships, my little mind wandered and I asked him, "Grandpa, what was the hardest thing you ever had to do in your life?"

I expected a tale of physical labor that those tough times demanded of him, but when Grandpa stopped walking and stared silently at the horizon I knew he was reliving an experience much harder than working long hours. He knelt down and took my hand. With tears in his eyes he began to speak.

"Grandma got very sick after your Aunt Mary was born. This was when your mom and your uncles were still little children. Well, Grandma had to go to a place called a sanitarium for a long time to get better. Since there was no one to take care of your mom and uncles, I had to send them to an orphanage where nuns could take care of them for me so I could work two and three jobs until your grandma got well. The hardest thing I ever had to do was put my babies in there. I went every week to see them, but the nuns wouldn't let me talk to them or hold them. I could only watch my children play from behind a one-way mirror. Sure, I brought them candy every week, but I could only hope they knew it was from me. I would keep both hands on the glass for the thirty minutes I was allowed to see them, hoping they would see me and come to touch my hand—but they never did. I endured a whole year without touching my children, but I know it was even harder for them. I'll never forgive myself for not making the nuns let me hold them. But they said I would do them more harm than good, and they would have even more trouble living there. So I listened."

I had never seen my grandfather cry before. He held me close, and I told him that I had the best grandfather ever and that I loved him. It was a strange and powerful reversal of roles, me reassuring him as he cried into my embrace.

We continued our walks for years until my family and grandparents moved to separate states. For fifteen years, that special walk with Grandpa remained our secret.

After my grandmother passed away, my grandfather began to suffer from memory lapses and bouts of depression. I tried to encourage my mother to let Grandpa come and live with us, but she and Grandpa had drifted apart.

One day, when I really harped on her to bring Grandpa back home, in a fit of rage she replied, "Why? He never cared about what happened to us!"

Little did she know, I knew precisely what she was talking about. "He has always cared and loved you," I said. "The hardest thing he ever did was put you and your brothers in the orphanage."

"You don't know what you're talking about!" my mother replied. "Who told you about that?" My mother had never discussed her days there with us.

"Mom, Grandpa told me that he came every week to see the three of you. He used to watch you play from behind the one-way glass. He used to bring you sweets every visit. He hated not being able to hold you for that year!"

"You're lying!" she snapped. "He was never there. No one ever came to see us."

"How could I know about the visits and the treats he brought if he didn't tell me?" I said. "He was there. He was always there. But the nuns wouldn't let him in the room with you because they said it would be too hard for you when he had to leave. Mom, Grandpa loves you and always has!"

I saw her eyes widen. She held her breath and then, suddenly, released it in a sigh that was almost a wail. Tears started to gather in the corners of her eyes. Suddenly, she realized that all along, years ago, Grandpa had stood behind that mirrored glass, hoping his children could somehow sense his presence, feel his love. The anger and sadness faded from her face. She could finally let the warmth and strength of his love get through the one-way glass.

Not long after, my grandfather came to live with us. At last my mom and Grandpa's love transcended the cold pane of glass that had remained between them for all those painful years.

Laura Reilly

Amazon Woman Becomes a Princess

*It is not the name that is important—it is what
it represents to you that is the key to its power.*

Laura Spiess

Family members traveled to New Brunswick from all over that summer: Winston-Salem, Colorado Springs, Kalamazoo and Daytona Beach. Our youngest daughter was about to marry a young man from Washington, D.C., and all of us—uncle, aunt, two sisters, nieces, nephew, brother-in-law and parents—were present to witness the event.

The groom had been married before. With the divorce settlement, he gained custody of the two children, a boy, five and a girl, three.

Not only were we gaining a new son-in-law, we would become instant grandparents to two adorable children, David and Stephanie.

On the afternoon before the wedding, family members from both sides gathered in the groom's apartment to pass the time and get acquainted. The two youngsters were a part of this homogeneous group.

From previous conversations with my daughter, I knew these children came fully endowed with six living grand-parents. They had two grandmothers, two grandfathers and two great-grandmothers.

How would we fit into this galaxy of grands and great-grands? I wondered. *How would the children designate which* grand per-son *they were talking about or talking to? And, by what names would they call me and my husband?*

During a lull in the chit-chat, I became bold and expressed my thoughts out loud.

Young David looked at me with a shy grin on his face and spoke as if he had already figured this out.

"I'm going to call you 'Princess,'" he said.

The room grew very quiet. I suspect this announcement shocked them as much as it did me.

For some unknown reason, David had looked at me and decided I should be called "Princess."

All through school, I towered inches above my short girlfriends. I weighed more than I should, even with the added height. Consequently, I grew up thinking of myself as the Amazon Woman, never as a princess.

"What a lovely name," I gasped. "I'm honored and delighted that you want to call me by that name."

Then and there, I became "Princess." Soon after, they christened my husband "Pop-Pop."

Ten years have passed since then. Young David is fif-teen, his sister Stephanie is thirteen, and they have a little sister named Rebecca. She is eight.

I often look back at that moment and consider it a turn-ing point in my life. Yes, I had evolved from the tall, awk-ward young girl, into a more graceful woman with streaks of gray in my hair, and a calm, self-assuredness that only years of living can produce.

From time to time, someone might pay me a compli-ment, but no one, not even my husband, had ever called me "Princess." No one, that is, except David.

I'll always be grateful to him. He helped me replace the clumsy, gargantuan image I'd carried in my mind's eye, too long, with the image of a princess.

On some days I know I look more like a bag lady than a princess. But on a day, ten years ago, a five-year-old thought I looked like a princess.

Perhaps it was the yellow summer dress I wore, or the jubilant smile on my face that said I approved of my daughter's choice of a life-mate. Whatever it was, the name thrilled me then as it does now.

Whenever I pick up the phone and a voice at the other end says, "Hi, Princess. Guess what happened at school today," a big smile spreads across my face and joy fills my heart.

And that's chicken soup for my soul!

Adeline C. Erwin

Through the Grandkids' Eyes

If you think the things that matter is the stuff that money
    buys,
Then spend a day with children, see the world through
    the grandkids' eyes.
They find the greatest joy in the smallest little things,
Like running through the sprinkler and the way that
    Grandpa sings.

You buy them toys at Christmas; they'd much prefer the
    box.
They like to wade through puddles and search for pretty
    rocks.
They'll climb a tree and skip a rope and never miss a beat.
They're filled with awe and wonder, and the world is at
    their feet.

To them there is no difference between dandelions and
    flowers.
They'll touch and smell and feel them and gaze at them for
    hours.
To have those kind of values we had when we were small,
Looking back in time it seems we really had it all.

We need to watch the children and look into their eyes,
To understand what matters most is not what money buys.
Reach back into the past this day; remember what you
  knew,
And you will find your inner peace in the child that lives
  in you.

Jill Grubb-Travoss

Hershey's Dark Chocolate

If my heart can become pure and loving, like that of a child, I think there probably can be no greater happiness than this.

Kitaro Nishida

I guess we all know of the one person in the neighborhood who stays by himself, or herself, and has very little to do with everyone else in the community. You know the type, right? Well, that is not exactly me, although I am not far from it.

I have been married too many times to talk about. In fact it would be embarrassing to say the exact number. All of the marriages were very good, as far as I was concerned, yet ended because I was unable to fully show love or affection. I found it very easy to be nice, kind and responsible. I mean, what else is there other than being good, kind, honest and responsible? That is all I ever knew or was even taught as an orphan in the orphanage in Jacksonville, Florida.

One day this little girl showed up at my door with dirty hands and chocolate all over her face. "Don't move, and I mean don't move a muscle," I yelled at her, as I ran to get a washrag. *Darn kids can't do anything without making trouble for me,* I thought, as I returned to wash her hands and face. For the remainder of the day I worked as a prison guard making sure this little troublemaker did not touch any of my personal stuff. All day long all I heard was, "Can I have this?" and "Can I have that?" I thought I would pull out what little bit of hair I had left before the day was over. Thank God, the phone finally rang and they were on their way to pick her up. But, oh no! They had not made it back to town and wanted to know if I would keep her for the night. Reaching for the aspirin, I shook my head and told them, "I guess I have no choice."

Later that evening I put Chelsey to bed, and as I was about to leave the room she looked at me and said, "Poppa, do you love me?"

"Of course, I love you!" I hollered. "I'm your Poppa!" and then I closed the door.

"I love you, too, Poppa," I heard through the door. I stood for several seconds with my head leaning against the wall. I immediately opened the door and just stood there looking at her at the end of her bed. She walked over and kissed my hand. I grabbed that three-year-old little baby girl and I hugged her as tightly as I could. I had never known, until that very moment, what the feeling of love felt like, and I never realized that—I hadn't known.

Now Poppa and his little sweetheart eat Hershey's dark chocolate in Granny's favorite recliner, until Granny gets the broom and chases Poppa and Chelsey to the bedroom where they watch cartoons together and get chocolate all over everything. That little baby will never have to ask her Poppa, ever again, if he loves her.

It is true that we must learn to love before we can truly begin to live, even at age fifty-three.

Roger Dean Kiser, Sr. (Poppa)

FOR BETTER OR FOR WORSE. ©UFS. Reprinted by Permission.

Dial H for Heaven

Children are the bridge to heaven.

Persian Proverb

After my fourth child was born, distance and deteriorating health prevented my mother and daughter from knowing one another very well.

In the beginning, Grandma could make the flight from New Jersey to Colorado for a visit, but as time passed, the high altitude became detrimental to her well-being and she was forced to stop her trips.

So began a mailbox/telephone relationship for the two of them. Amy sent her special pictures to her grandmother and learned to dial the long-distance phone number. With some assistance, she phoned her grandma two or three times a week to chat, however brief it may have been. When Amy learned her letters, she also wrote short notes.

For a year, the pair enjoyed their unusual friendship. When Amy's grandmother died, she asked a lot of questions. Several stood out.

"Where is Grandma? Why doesn't she call? Isn't there a phone where she is? Why can't I call her?"

Of course I tried to explain death and its permanency as gently as possible and ended with, "Grandma went to heaven."

It was hard to know if my little girl understood, but I felt I did my best.

One day while folding laundry Amy asked, "How do you spell heaven?"

Her tiny fingers struggled, and it did take her a while, but she wrote it down, letter by letter, as I told her.

She thanked me and scooted off.

Shortly after, while putting the clothes away, I found her in the bedroom crying.

Sitting next to her on the bed, I asked, "What's wrong? Why the tears?"

Picking up the phone she said, "Watch." I did.

Between her sobs she dialed: H E A V E N.

"There's no one there. Listen." She handed me the phone. "I even did her area code, like you taught me."

I hung up the phone, wrapped my arms around my daughter and explained the best I could, again.

"There's no phones in heaven?" Amy asked. "Then how do I talk to Grandma?"

The only answer I knew to give was, "In your prayers."

"You mean like I do when I talk to God?"

I nodded.

"You mean Grandma is with God?"

I nodded again.

Amy wiped her wet cheeks, replacing them with a smile.

"That'll work," she said.

Helen Colella

Grandma and the Chicken Pox

What children don't understand, they fill in the blanks.

Shirley Muck

My twin boys were only seven years old when their paternal grandmother announced she was getting remarried. We were all thrilled for her, since she had seemed so lonely since Grandpa passed away a few years before. We broke the news to our boys, who were sitting in the back of the car. "Grandma is getting married again," we said.

Jon had a look of thoughtfulness on his face for a while. He finally asked, "Is she going to have more children?"

Before we had a chance to respond, his twin brother Mike shot back this answer: "No! She can't. She already had them. It's like chicken pox. Once you get them, you can't get them again."

Susan Amerikaner

Somewhere, Babe Ruth Is Smiling

How old would you be if you didn't know how old you were?

Satchel Paige

They were two chairs from Yankee Stadium, number fifteen and number twenty-two, and they sat in the basement of his grandparents' home for years, unnoticed. Now and then, family members would come upon them and be told the story of how they were purchased. It seems when Yankee Stadium was rebuilt in the early seventies, thousands of these chairs were sold at a modest price. Fans sitting in number fifteen and number twenty-two watched the likes of Babe Ruth, Mickey Mantle and Lou Gehrig as they made baseball history. Perhaps one of them even caught a ball hit by one of the all-time baseball greats.

Someone approached my son-in-law about buying the chairs. A generous offer was made, and the family met in the basement to make a decision.

Grandson Ryan, a nine-year-old Little Leaguer just returning from a baseball game and wearing Lou Gehrig's number four on his uniform, protested.

"I don't believe you're selling those chairs," he said. "You can't give them to someone else." He approached his grandfather, the original owner of the chairs, with puzzled young eyes. "Why are you going to do that now?"

His parents, being much wiser about such things, explained that they could all make a healthy profit if they sold them. And now there was a buyer.

"You don't understand," Ryan was told as he persisted. Of course, the grown-ups understood better. They were older. They were wiser. And they were certainly more realistic about financial matters. Everyone would benefit from the money received.

The chairs were lifted from the dust and cobwebs that had gathered about them and placed in the center of the basement. They were chipped and worn. There were no fans sitting in them now, no cheers throughout the stadium surrounding them, no baseball greats to look down at with wonder. And yet they held a majesty that silenced even the adults for a few thoughtful moments.

The debate concentrated on whether to keep the chairs until they gathered more value or sell them now. But while the conversation continued, the Little Leaguer with the number four on his shirt sat down in seat number twenty-two. And while the family decided that it was the best thing that could have happened to them, and that the money sure would come in handy, and that a bird in the hand was worth two in the bush, while all of this was coming about in the basement, the Little Leaguer began to cry. He didn't usually cry in front of an audience. It made everyone uncomfortable.

"I think we'd better go upstairs," his father said. The discussion was over. The decision made. The chairs would be sold.

But his son didn't move. It was as if Ryan were glued to

the chair. "I can't get up," he said. It seemed he couldn't, even if he tried.

It was his grandfather who approached the boy. "Would you explain to me why you are so upset?" he asked.

Grown-up words came from Ryan's mouth when he spoke, as if they were delivered from somewhere else. "The people sitting in these seats got to see them all, the great ones, Gehrig and Mantle and Ruth. Right from this seat." His young hands caressed the chair. "Sitting here, I know just what they felt like," Ryan said. "What a great feeling."

Of course, everyone knew the wise thing to do, and the realistic thing to do. And the prudent thing to do. But no one wanted to remove this young baseball player from his chair, especially his grandfather who remembered what it was like to be that young and in love with baseball.

It was Ryan's chair now. Everybody in the basement realized it. And they finally understood what he was trying to tell them. There wasn't enough money in the world to buy seat number twenty-two now that Ryan had found it, and there wasn't enough money in the world to equal the look on Ryan's face when he threw his arms around his grandfather to thank him.

That night a nine-year-old boy wearing a number four on his baseball shirt took home Yankee Stadium seat twenty-two.

And somewhere, Babe Ruth was smiling.

Harriet May Savitz

Rainy Day Rainbows

*To us, family means putting your arms around
each other and being there.*

Barbara Bush

Unless we live amongst the sand dunes of the Sahara,
which we don't, the rains must fall. They have chosen
today, the day when K. C. is home from day care. I've only
to look out the window to know K. C. and I will travel no
trails outside our four walls this morning.

The rain has not deterred the ladies of the house;
they've decamped for an enclosed mall. K. C. and I have
been abandoned to map our own course.

We seek no guidance from such tomes as *101 Things to
Do with Your Toddler Grandchild on a Rainy Day*. Our genes
bubble with creativity; our imaginations delight in its tangible expression. In other words, a rainy day to us is just
another challenge on our chosen high road.

K. C. opts to begin in the kitchen. Sure, we'd already
eaten our Corn Pops and milk, our scrambled eggs and
maple syrup, but that was at seven o'clock right after
Blue's Clues. It's now nine-thirty, two to three hours before

lunch. K. C. and I make some peanut-butter cookies.

She works from a dining-room chair pushed flush with the kitchen counter. She cracks the egg; I pick the broken shell out of the bowl. I measure; she pours. We mash and stir together.

A small ball of dough is set aside for her, and quickly as I can, I form cookies on the baking sheet. Briefly, she idles, reminiscent of her play dough, forming curious shapes, perhaps voodoo dolls, perhaps cartoon creatures; it's hard to say, but her intensity is keen. I have to hurry because as soon as the modeling is over, K. C. starts eating the cookie dough. I can't blame her; I like it, too. My mother used to tell me it would give me worms. I didn't believe it then; I don't believe it now. Adults' ploys can be so naive!

The cookies are in the oven. We have demolished the kitchen. Onward we go to the dining room. K. C. has decreed, "Let's paint!"

I tape newspapers over the dining-room table while K. C. struggles into her plastic Pooh Bear smock. Now, I may be approaching geezer-hood, but I've still a dash or two of daring. From my secret place I bring out the materials that strike dread into the hearts of maternal neatness freaks everywhere. Big sheets of paper. Fingerpaints.

"Look what I found," I proclaim. K. C. looks. Her grin is so wide it wiggles her ears. She has instantly recognized the paint pots I have in hand. She's seen them at day care. We belly up to the table and get to work.

Things go well for a time. We out-Dali Dali. Van Gogh would wish his ear back to hear our merry banter as we do gaudy smears and flourishes, handprints, blurs and blots.

In her exuberance, K. C. accidentally brushes some paint on my forearm. Royal blue. When she sees the smear, she laughs. Never a challenge unmet, I retaliate with apple green on her arm. So it begins. No question, this is more fun than paper.

From fingertips to armpits, on the face and in the hair. In ten minutes we're pretty much a mess. Nor are the dining-room chairs unscathed. Nor the kitchen counter and cookie sheet, for I've been making cookies all the while.

To begin eating cookies we need to first wash up. No problem. K. C. pushes her dining-room chair up to the kitchen sinks. We slosh and swab, splash around a bit of water . . . some puddles on the floor; we'll clean it up later. Several towels look somewhat tie-dyed now. True artistry finds expression everywhere.

We aren't quite perfectly clean; clean enough for cookies and milk, but not clean enough to pass inspection when the ladies get home, as, inevitably, they do.

They spot our artwork still drying on various pieces of furniture and taped to the kitchen cupboard doors. Eating cookies distracts them, but not for long. They have seen the state of their kitchen; they have seen the dining-room chairs; they have seen our technicolor hair, for I'd not had time to wash that.

K. C. is summarily escorted to the bathtub. I detour quickly to the basement to change the kitty litter. I am never pursued when I undertake that task.

Much later, after lunch, chastened, K. C. and I are hiding out in her room watching *Teletubbies*. As luck would have it, the real life sequence of the show is about painting. The scene opens on a floor covered with paper, washbasins full of paint and a dozen kids, all barefoot. K. C. watches intently.

The kids wade in the basins, dance and slide across the floor, footprints, handprints, kneeprints, bumprints. Darn, but that looks like fun!

"I wanna do that someday," says K. C.

Cautiously, I reply, "Some day."

"Not by myself. With you."

"Okay, we'll do it together."

K. C. is pulling off her socks. "Now!" she shouts.

I wonder if maybe the kitty litter needs another change.
I start humming, "Rain, rain, go away . . ."

Arthur Montague

PICKLES. ©2001, The Washington Post Writers Group. Reprinted with permission.

What's a Grandma to Do?

What's so simple even a small child can manipulate it? Grandma.

Janet Lanese

One of the most pressing problems for grandparents these days is knowing how to be a grandparent. I certainly don't wear cotton flowered dresses and big full-sized aprons and bake molasses cookies every week like Grandma Kobbeman did. I don't sit on a porch swing and rock the evening away or watch soap operas like my Grandmother Knapp did. When I was fifty and a grandmother, I water-skied behind my brother's boat in Kentucky and snorkeled for hours in the ocean off the coast of two Hawaiian islands. The next year I rode every scary roller-coaster ride at Disneyland.

Grandparents are different nowadays. We have full-time careers. We run corporations and marathons. We belong to clubs, watch the stock market, eat out a lot, exercise regularly and still have the energy to do the Twist at wedding receptions.

My five grandchildren live out of town, and I don't see

them on a daily or weekly basis. In fact, since their parents have busy careers and whirligig lives like I do, I'm lucky if I get to see my grandchildren once or twice a month.

When Hailey was four years old she came for her very first "all alone" visit. She would be alone with me Saturday night, all day Sunday, all day Monday and half of Tuesday before her mother arrived to take her back home. Saturday night and Sunday were a breeze. Hailey, her favorite blankie, latest Beanie Baby and I, snuggled together in my big bed. We slept just fine until Hailey sat up in the middle of the night and whispered, "Gramma, you were snoring."

All day Sunday we kept busy with my daughter-in-law and other granddaughter who were visiting for the day. But on Monday morning when Miss Hailey and I woke up and she assured me that I didn't snore at all that night, I began to fret. *It's Monday, a workday. I have books to read and review and a book proposal to get out. I need to be in my home office! How am I ever going to get it all done if I have to entertain Hailey all day?*

I'll worry about it later, I thought. For at that moment there were little girl hugs to be had, waffles to toast, and birds to feed on the deck with my four-year-old helper.

And so we hugged and rocked and ate, and I held the bird feeder while Miss Hailey scooped up six big cups full of tiny seed into the feeder and only a half-cup or so landed on the deck.

As we sat in the glider swing on the deck watching the squirrels eat the bird feed I began to worry again. *I have a column to write and a talk to prepare.* And yet I wanted to be with Hailey. After all, we only had a day and a half left before her mother came. But my work. I needed to work. Or did I?

"Grammie, can we put up the hammock? We could take a nap in it!"

"Let's go to the shed and find the hammock," I said

gleefully. We hung the chains on the hooks in the big trees in the backyard and hopped aboard. As we watched a yellow finch and two cardinals flit around the branches high above us as we lay on our backs in that big double-wide hammock, I knew for certain that I was taking the next day and a half off work. Completely.

Hailey and I drew huge pictures on the driveway, using up a whole bucketful of sidewalk chalk. Then she wanted to climb up into her Uncle Andrew's old tree house. She swept all the leaves off the tree-house floor and only about half of them landed on my head. We took a long bike ride on the bike path near my house. I walked while Hailey rode her tiny two-wheeler with the training wheels.

"Grammie, can we go down by the creek?" Miss Hailey squealed when she saw the water.

"Sure! Maybe we'll catch a frog!"

Later that morning we jumped in the car, went shopping for shoes and found just the perfect pair for my wide-footed grandchild. Then we headed to the playland at McDonald's for lunch. Later that afternoon we ate Combos and candy at the $1.99 movie as we giggled at the funny songs in *Cats Don't Dance*.

"Grammie, are you sure there aren't any rules at your house?"

"I'm sure."

"No bedtime?"

"Nope."

"I can stay up until you go to bed?"

"Yup."

"Until late?"

"Sure. We can sleep late tomorrow. You just sit here in my lap so we can snuggle, and I'll read you a couple of books."

"I love you, Grammie."

And so, that's how I learned the true meaning of the

words I have laminated on top of my computer: WRITE THINGS WORTH READING OR DO THINGS WORTH WRITING.

I learned that doing things like spending an entire day and a half playing with a granddaughter is infinitely more important than sticking to a work routine and getting things done in the office. I learned that grandmothers today often need to abandon their schedules, meetings, clubs, activities, workload and appointments, and sometimes spend hours at a time drawing silly animals on the driveway or staring at the leaves from a hammock with a four-year-old's head snuggled in the crook of your arm.

Patricia Lorenz

Courtney's Love Lesson

Life is not dated merely by years. Events are sometimes the best calendars.

Benjamin Disraeli

The July day was bursting with sunshine and warmth. The kind of day that whispers, "Let's go to the beach."

Fridays were dear to my heart because Friday was my day to baby-sit our beloved grandchildren, Mikey, three years old, and Courtney, two years old. Taking them to the beach could only make the day more heavenly. Well . . .

What seemed like a wonderful idea at 10:00 A.M. didn't seem quite so wonderful at 11:00 A.M. as I began unloading the car with all the beach necessities: a blanket, cooler, sand toys, beach towels and two very rambunctious toddlers. What in the world had I been thinking? How could I manage all this by myself from the parking lot, which was a city block away from Lake Michigan's edge?

"Oh! Dear God, help me," I prayed as I stood there a wee bit overwhelmed, waiting for the morning's estrogen to kick in and calm me down. Just then a group of young, strong (note the keyword, strong) men walked by.

"Excuse me," I said. "You look so healthy and strong. Would you like to carry some of these things for us? The children are so excited, and I just can't do it all."

The taller of the three, blond and tanned like a California surfer, smiled and answered, "I'd be happy to help. I remember, as a kid, my Gram taking me to the beach."

A short time later, we wished our godsends a happy day as we staked out our homestead a foot from the water's edge and began building a secret tunnel that would take us to Disney World. Mikey was eager to play in the water, splash and "swim," but not so for Courtney, for the vastness of Lake Michigan and the rolling waves seemed to frighten her little heart. Mikey and I played in the water, as Courtney sat in the sand contentedly digging, filling and emptying her pail. No amount of coaxing, no offer to hold her in my arms could persuade her to come into the water. Fear shone through her big, brown eyes.

Suddenly, a strong wind came up, and within a second Gramma's straw beach hat took wings and sailed out across the waves.

"Gram, Gram, your hat!" Mikey screamed excitedly.

"I guess it wanted to go swimming, too." We laughed, watching as the waves carried it further out. And then out of the corner of my eye, I saw Courtney step into the water, her little body taking small, determined steps.

"Court, you're in the water?" Mikey shouted gleefully.

"Me get Gramma's hat," she answered as one little foot was placed in front of the other.

I stood there in the presence of our God, the Lord who had created this beautiful day, and these grandchildren who lived within my very soul, and tears fell from my eyes. Here was a child, so filled with pure love, that her fears were overlooked as she stepped into the water hoping to rescue her Gramma's hat.

Scooping Courtney into my arms I whispered, "I love you so much," as we waved good-bye to the beach hat. It had been a five-dollar special at Kmart, but it had taught me a million-dollar lesson.

Love conquers all things.

Alice Collins

Grandma's Report Card

*Every generation passes on a lasting memory
that sticks with pride and admiration. What will
your legacy be?*

Theodore N. Greenough

Grandma's Report Card		
Subject	**Comments**	**Grade**
Reading	Grandma's been reading to me for as long as I can remember. I have always loved sitting on her lap as she reads stories to me. And sometimes she stops and tells me one of her own stories. I like that a lot.	A
History	Grandma is excellent at recounting family history and can be counted on for fascinating and embarrassing stories about Mom and Dad.	A

Writing Skills	Grandma writes me letters and notes. She always says she loves me in them. I get cards from her on my birthday and on holidays. And she encourages me to write, too. She pressures me to write my thank-you notes and, even if I hate to write 'em, I've learned how important that can be.	A
Math Skills	Grandma knows when things "just don't add up" and is not afraid to tell me. She also knows how to save and is still able to contribute to my education.	A
Social Studies	Grandma understands that "what goes around, comes around." She does many acts of kindness, every day, for relatives and friends, for neighbors and even for strangers. She contributes to charity because she knows it's the right thing to do.She involves all us grand-kids in doing these acts of kindness because she knows we've got to learn this, too.	A
P.E.	Grandma plays well with others. She exercises, walks, rides her bike, goes on hikes, takes a kick-boxing class, pushes loaded shopping carts through miles of aisles. She owns a rocking chair, but is too darn busy to use it. Even though she complains sometimes about aches and pains, she's out there, moving and doing, every day.	A
Home Economics	Grandma really knows how to cook! She knows my favorite foods and has them ready when she knows I'm coming to visit.	A

Attendance	She shows up. She's there for every event that's important to me. I know that she'll be there on the sidelines cheering for me. She listens to me really well.	A
Personal Qualities	Grandma is just FUN! She seems to be always ready to play, just a little bit. When everyone else seems so serious, she'll give me a look with a twinkle in her eye and I know that we're on the same wavelength. She can be very serious, but she doesn't take herself seriously. She's my "bud."	A
General Comments	Grandma passes with flying colors. I'm looking forward to being with her for a very, very long time.	

Meladee McCarty

"Every time I get an A my grandma
puts it on her Web site."

My Grandchild's Hand

In your eyes I see the future
And a need to save the Earth . . .
So that you might walk the fields of God
And know that life has worth.

In your presence I can see now
That God continues on . . .
And he sent you as a glimpse of hope
When I thought all hope was gone.

When I plant a tree now I will know
Though the shade won't cover me . . .
I have offered you a shelter here
For all the world to see.

When I was young I questioned God
I had to know the truth . . .
And he closed his eyes and bowed his head
And he sent you down as proof.

It was deep inside your laughter
That I learned what life's about . . .
For the miracle of knowing you
Has left me without doubt.

As time passed by how could I know
The best was yet to be . . .
Through my grandchild's hand my God reached out
And he found the love in me.

Jill Grubb-Travoss

6

BECOMING A GRANDPARENT

A friend of mine was asked how she liked
having her first great-grandchild. "It was
wonderful," she replied, "until I suddenly
realized that I was the mother of a
grandfather."

Robert L. Rice, M.D.

CLOSE TO HOME   JOHN McPHERSON

"The maternity nurse let me borrow the other eight.
I just want to see the look on my mother's face when
she walks through the door."

Life, What a Beautiful Gift

Better to lose count while naming your bless-
ings than to lose your blessings to counting your
troubles.

Maltbie D. Babcock

It was the first week in December. My daughter Julie and
I had decided to go Christmas shopping. We have always
been extra close, and I always looked forward to this special time together. We would do some "serious" shopping,
go out for lunch, and catch up on what was happening in
each other's lives.

Over lunch, we discussed what gifts we would buy our
relatives and friends. I always felt this was a real chore, as
I was always worried about treating all five of my children
equally, finding something they didn't already have. Julie,
on the other hand, is a person who always seems to find
the perfect gift for everyone. Everything has to be the perfect color, the perfect size, the perfect scent! She goes back
and forth, from store to store, to get the best bargain.

That day, while eating, our conversation somehow
switched from Christmas gifts to life's blessings. This

made both of us think of my illness. Although I had been extremely sick several times, for the most part, I still considered myself truly blessed. In fact there had been several times when my M.S. or lupus were out of remission, and my doctor said it was indeed a miracle that I was still alive. Maybe it was a miracle, or maybe God just had other plans for me.

Realizing how lucky I was, when Julie asked me what I wanted for Christmas, I tried to tell her without ruining her Christmas spirit, that I didn't expect or even want a present. I explained just getting together with my beautiful family was all I could hope for.

Julie looked disappointed in my reply. "Oh, Mom," she said, "you are always so darn practical! There has to be something little you want."

I repeated what I had said, "I have a fantastic husband, beautiful children, and now two beautiful granddaughters. I have it all! What more could anyone want in one life?" I was speaking with my entire heart. I truly felt that way. I loved my family so much that little else was important. Each day I thanked God for giving me yet one more twenty-four hours to share with them.

Suddenly, without even thinking, I added, "I know this is selfish, but you know, I really would love to have a grandson before I die! Now that would be neat!"

Julie just shook her head, and said, "I give up!"

"Well, you asked what I would like, didn't you? I have always wanted a grandson! I love little boys! I'll never forget how happy I was to have your brother after all you girls! Oh, I love all of you equally, that is for certain, but there is something very special about little boys! Now if you can find a way to get me a grandson before Christmas, I will take him and love him without complaining!"

"You're impossible!" Julie added. "Let's finish our

shopping. You won't accept a little gift, yet you ask for the world! Mothers!"

Hours later, Julie dropped me off at my house. Exhausted from shopping, I hugged her and promised to let her know if I thought of anything "easier" for her to get for me.

When I went in the house, the first thing I did was check our new answering machine for messages. The blinking red light indicated there were several.

The first message was another daughter whose voice assured me that she was concerned because I had gone away for that long without first obtaining permission! I thought it was ironic remembering the times my children had forgotten to call me when they were going to be late. Funny how time changes roles. The second message was to remind me of an upcoming craft auction at church, and the third to confirm a dental appointment. Who needed to be reminded of such things? I started to walk out of the room, when I heard the last voice, that of my husband. He sounded more than a little confused.

"Barb! Are you home? If you are home, then pick this thing up! Can't you hear me? I need to talk to you . . . Q-U-I-C-K!" Frustrated, when at last he realized he was talking to an electronic piece of equipment, he lowered his voice and said, "Please, Honey, when you get home . . . CALL ME!"

Wow! This was so unlike the cool man I was used to! What could be wrong? I knew I had to call him back at once.

Call I did. It was not only a shocking call, but also an unplanned answer to a prayer, and that something little I had wanted for my Christmas gift. About the same time I was telling Julie that I would like a grandson before my life was finished, a young girl in a nearby town had called my husband at work to tell him that she was the mother of a little grandson we had never met! We were both in shock. This woman explained she had a brief relationship with our son, had gotten pregnant, and had a little boy who was now seven months old! She said she had pleaded with our son to tell us about the baby. However, he was afraid we would be disappointed in him if we knew, so he had made her promise not to tell.

For some unknown reason that day, she had decided that it was unfair to us to keep this grandchild a secret any longer. Since our home number was unlisted, she had called the place my husband worked and told him the story.

My husband gave me the woman's number, and said she had told him I was free to make arrangements to meet our little grandson if I liked. Grandson! Liked? I was a doubting Thomas. I had to see for myself. I called the woman, and within an hour, I was on the way to see this baby. If she was telling the truth I had a grandson! No matter how complicated the details of his conception were, I knew I would love him. I was happy, sad, excited and tearful all at the same time.

When I arrived at the given address, I was met at the door by the woman and her other children. I sensed all of them were trying to evaluate me, and this made me feel terribly uncomfortable. My first impulse was to turn and run. Something within me told me I had to stay. I offered her my hand; she took it. She invited me inside. Walking ahead of me to a nearby table, she picked up an envelope and handed it to me. "Here are the paternity papers," she said. "Here's proof that Toby is your grandson!"

I had just learned something else: Her baby's name was Toby. I questioned the baby's last name, and I was told he had received my son's last name the previous day in court.

Nearly collapsing, I lowered myself to the nearest chair. I didn't realize the girl had left the room until I saw her return, carrying a little boy. She walked up to me, placed the most beautiful little baby into my arms, and said, "Son, I think it is time you meet your grandma!" Toby looked right up at me and gave me the biggest smile . . . I cried.

At that moment, little Toby became a very important part of my life. My son and the baby's mother had made a big mistake. However, God himself had created little Toby, and God doesn't make mistakes. I had a grandson! A beautiful bundle of joy! What a precious Christmas gift!

Later that evening, my husband and I had a long talk with our son. We told him we knew about Toby, and I was hurt that he could even think for a moment that his father and I could have loved him less for having made a mistake. I told him if we only love our children when they live their lives the way we feel they should, then that isn't really love. He told me that when Toby's mother first discovered she was pregnant, she had considered an abortion, and we cried together, thanking God she hadn't. Later, we even laughed a little over the speedy way in which God seemed to answer my Christmas gift request!

Since then many Christmases have passed. Toby spends a lot of time with his father and with us, as well. Every day, but especially on Christmas, I am so thankful for this very special gift I received eight years ago.

Barbara Jeanne Fisher

Half-Listened

A good message will always find a messenger.

Amelia Barr

So many of our friends were becoming grandparents, and we kept hearing, "You're going to love being grandparents. There's nothing like it."

These are the same people who have "Let Me Tell You About My Grandchildren" bumper stickers plastered all over their car bumpers. The same people who refer to themselves as "Evan's grandmaw" or "Ashley's grandpaw."

I didn't doubt for a minute that they relished their roles. But that wasn't for John and me. We were entering the senior citizen's discount stage of our lives, looking forward to the day when we might be able to actually get that motor home and do some traveling. I enjoy my quiet time, and John would truly love nothing more than to be able to wander off to his favorite fishing hole and linger awhile under the shade of a big ol' magnolia tree with a cold adult beverage in hand.

Now we've raised two perfectly beautiful sons for whom the phrase "boys will be boys" was most certainly coined. There are no more messy diapers or cutting teeth or endless nights of worrying when one of them came down with a fever or the chicken pox. We wanted to trade our family car in for a spiffy little two-passenger candy apple red Corvette—no room for a car seat or diaper bags or any of the necessary gear one needs when taking a day trip to Disney.

Then, along comes Quinton—eight pounds, thirteen ounces of pure joy—double dimples and a smile that would melt your heart. A little bit of feistiness that comes from, well, several sources on his daddy's side and a sweetness that is most assuredly a combination of his precious mommy and daddy.

Okay, you pals of mine—you tried to tell us and we half-listened. We never dreamed that the depth of love we could feel for such a tiny human being could run so deeply. Or that we can hardly wait to hear the phone ring and to be asked, "Can you come over and watch Quinton while we eat?"

Holding that sweet little bundle brings a sense of calm over me, the likes of which I can hardly believe. Even if he's having a fussy spell, I still marvel at the softness of his features, the smell of that oh-so-soft baby skin. So, maybe I'll just get used to the fact that my graying hair and wrinkled skin qualifies me for the role of someone's grandmother.

Now, will someone please tell me where I can buy one of those silly "Let Me Tell You About My Grandchildren" bumper stickers?

Debby Stoner

CLOSE TO HOME   JOHN McPHERSON

Having spotted some acquaintances,
Vera activates the Instant Grandchildren-Photo
Display™ in her purse.

Gramma Jan

When one door of happiness closes, another door opens; but often we look so long at the closed door that we do not see the one which has opened for us.

Helen Keller

When I drove into the park, I noticed and recognized Grace right away. She sat on a bench watching the children romp and play. *Why did she have to come?* I thought. *Couldn't she let me be "Gramma" for the day?* I'd waited so long.

When I walked up, Grace looked at me tenderly. "I've thought about you so much these last few years."

She was constantly in my mind, too—the woman who is grandmother to my daughter's child.

My mind went back to when Amy, just seventeen, told me she was pregnant. I had struggled as a single mom after Amy and Jennifer's dad left us seven years before, and I thought the worst was behind us until that day.

Amy decided to place the baby for adoption. I agreed it was the right thing for this confused, young girl, and I was touched that she asked me to help her choose the parents through an open adoption process. I was fine until I saw the ultrasound, the life growing inside Amy. Then it hit me. In a few months I would have to let go, say good-bye to my granddaughter.

Leslie, the prospective adoptive mom, assured me, "We want you to be a part of her life." But what role could I possibly have? Leslie's mother, Grace, waited sixty-three years to spoil a grandchild. How much would she want me involved?

After little Nicole was born, Amy insisted on bringing her home for a week. "I need time to say good-bye." Those were special days, days to make memories with her first child, hold her, sing to her, write her a loving letter and then let her go. Yet, I couldn't even cuddle her as I wanted, fearful that bonding with this child would only increase my sorrow when she left us.

The first time I met Grace, she came to my house for the adoption ceremony. "I know you'll love her very much," I said, stiffly, biting my lip as they were about to leave with the baby. Grace said nothing but just hugged me. After everyone left, Amy and Jennifer couldn't stop crying, and I kept assuring them it was the right thing to do, that blessings would come from it.

Amy's tears started coming right away when she shared her story with other pregnant girls.

The first year I saw Nikki often, fussing over her like any grandparent does, buying frivolous department store dresses she'd only wear once. Then it happened—the family moved to Florida. What would I do now?

Leslie promised endless pictures and videos of special moments, but what did it matter? I was bonded with Nikki, and they were whisking her away. How would she ever get to know me at three thousand miles away?

The years went by, and as I tore open every letter I ached as I put the photos in an album. Why did Nikki have to look exactly like Amy? Suddenly, I was struck with baby radar, tuning in to every toddler with brown eyes and dark curls, struggling to squash the tears.

Then came the telephone call. The family was coming to California for a visit. Would I like to meet them at the park? Of course! All week I was as anxious as a grasshopper. It had been five years!

As my car sped down the freeway, I wondered, would Grace be there? Was it selfish to hope not? Couldn't I have Nikki to myself just for a few hours and make believe I was her only grandmother?

Nearing the off ramp, I thought, how will Nikki respond to me? I'm just a stranger to her. Should I hug her or play it cool?

"She knows she's adopted," Leslie had told me earlier on the phone. "We're not sure now much she understands, but to her, you are her Gramma Jan."

What a delightful, loving child I met that day. We played "hide n' seek" and fed the ducks. She sat on my lap and let me fuss with her ponytail. Grace didn't say much. She sat quietly in the background and let me relish those precious hours.

In the afternoon, she nudged my side. "You've done better than I thought you would, Jan. I know how hard this must be for you."

The tears stung. Oh, Grace, this is making me cry.

"She's a special child, Jan. She's such a blessing to me."

It was easy to see. Nikki was secure, adored by her father and thrilled with two little brothers. (Six months after the adoption, Leslie was miraculously pregnant.)

"Please come and see us in Florida when you can," Keith said as he gave me a big bear hug. It was as if God reached down with comforting arms to say, *This day was my gift to you, Jan. She will know you, and you will be an influence in her life. Just be patient.*

As Grace said her good-byes to me, she glanced over at Nikki feeding the squirrels. "Thank you," she said, squeezing my hand.

She was thanking me?

I pondered that for a moment, then I understood. Nikki was a gift to Grace from God, a gift that came directly through me. Sitting back to watch me connect with Nikki was Grace's way of honoring me.

To think I almost missed the blessing.

That day in the park I finally let go.

As I glanced back at Nikki chasing another squirrel, I put my arm around Grace. "Thank *you* for having room in your heart to let me be 'Gramma Jan.'"

Jan Coleman

Good News, Bad News

Happiness and love are just a choice away.

Leo Buscaglia

"Hi Mom, get Dad on the phone, too." John seldom called from his temporary New Zealand home.

"What's the matter?" I asked, then frantically motioned to Bob and mouthed, "It's John!" My breathing quickened.

John waited until his dad greeted him then asked, "Are you sitting down?" I slumped on the bed in our dark room. My mother's intuition kicked in. Something was wrong.

"I have some good news and some bad news," John said. I held my breath.

"I'll give you the good news first. You're going to be grandparents." A long moment of silence deafened our connection.

"Are you there?" he asked.

I voiced the bad news. "John, you're not married."

But John ignored my comment and continued, "Do we have any twins in our family? Cathy's family does. You're going to be grandparents of twins."

We'd learned about Cathy earlier in the year. From the

way John talked, we knew in our hearts that she was his true love.

I don't remember how Bob and I got through the conversation. After we hung up, I sensed John's worry of being forced into a situation he hadn't planned and couldn't control, much less afford on his teacher's salary. I didn't sleep much that night. Yet, my tears refused to flow.

In the morning, I attended a meeting in body, but not in mind. On the way home, the dam broke; tears blurred my vision. I struggled to see where I was going. As I passed our church my car seemed to turn into the parking lot on its own.

Once inside, I asked the secretary if I might speak to the parish priest.

"He takes Mondays off." She stared at my tear-stained face, then added, "You can call him at home."

"No, I won't bother him." Embarrassed, I rushed to my car. But at home, I recognized the need to talk to someone other than Bob, dialed the church and asked for Father's number.

"Don't push them into a marriage. Two wrongs don't make a right," my priest consoled calmly. "This doesn't have to be bad news. But let them make their own decision."

So Bob and I refrained from submitting advice. After Christmas, we received another call. "I gave Cathy a ring. We've decided since you're coming to New Zealand in March, we'll wait until you arrive to get married. The babies will be born in May."

Elated by the wedding news, we looked forward to meeting and getting to know Cathy, if only for a few days. When we arrived, we could see her Western Samoan heritage contributed to her outer as well as inner beauty. She proved to be all we'd hoped John might find in a partner.

Although disappointed we wouldn't be present for the birth of our first grandchildren, we returned to the United

States. The knowledge that John, Cathy and the babies would follow within the year and call Colorado home appeased us.

At last we waited at Denver International. I stared through the large windows at the gate. Another plane filled the space where John, Cathy and our eight-month-old granddaughters would eventually arrive.

Departing passengers occupied all the seats in the gate area. I leaned against a pillar afraid to talk to Bob for fear of crying, not from sadness but joy. I'd never been so nervous. How long before the babies would accept us? Could we hold back and give them the space and time they needed? Out of necessity, their family would share our home. Could we make it work?

I wrung my hands and wiped them on my skirt.

"I can't do this. I'm shaking inside and out," I blurted. "Why are planes always late?"

Bob draped his arm around my shoulders and squeezed. "You can do it," he assured me.

I laid my head against his arm and fought the tears that stung my eyes. Had it only been a little over a year since we'd lamented about our having four granddogs and two grandhorses rather than grandchildren? How quickly things change.

A voice screeched from the speaker over our head. "The flight from L.A. has landed and will wait for the gate to empty. It won't be long. Thank you for your patience."

I walked away from the gate and paced back and forth. My thoughts turned to the Christmas lights on the cul-de-sac still adorning our neighbors' homes. Usually, they take their decorations down the day after New Year's. But this time, they agreed to wait until January 5th so the lights might illuminate a warm welcome for our family.

At last one plane backed away and another took its place. Arriving passengers hurried through the doorway.

We waited. My heart thumped in my ears. More people exited. We waited. Several times I gulped air and released it with a heavy sigh. We waited until no other passengers stepped through the doorway.

When a flight attendant appeared, I grabbed Bob's arm. My knees weakened. My stomach churned. I stammered, "Maybe they missed the connection in L.A."

Hand in hand we rushed to the attendant. "Is anyone else on the plane?" Bob's voice quaked. "A family with twin babies?"

I looked around. Passengers waiting to depart watched us, curiosity evident on their faces.

"Yes." The attendant smiled. "We misplaced their stroller. They'll be out in a minute."

Then John sauntered through the doorway with one baby in a large pack on his back. He stepped aside. Cathy shyly walked toward me cuddling the second baby. Tears gathered in my eyes.

Several flight attendants surrounded our family. "We wanted to see your reaction to these precious babies," one offered. "If you don't want them, we do!"

My hands quivered, and my legs felt like cement. I slowly moved toward Cathy and hugged her. I touched the dark hair of her baby. Black eyes questioned as they looked at me. I turned to John. From around one side of John's head and then the other, black eyes, a carbon copy of her sister's, peered at me. The beginning of a shy smile sparkled from her beautiful olive-skinned face. Her plump little hand stretched toward me.

I threw my arms around both John and baby and sobbed. Sobs so loud they echoed through the terminal. I stretched to include Cathy. I couldn't hold all of them close enough.

"I'm so sorry," I stuttered. "I'm sorry to embarrass you this way." Hiding my face in John's chest, my body shook uncontrollably.

After the embrace, John placed his hands on my shoulders and pushed me away enough to look into my eyes. He smiled. "Mom, you should see all the people behind you. They're crying, too."

I returned John's gaze and remembered when he'd called to share his "good news and bad news." As I hugged my son, my daughter-in-law *and* my grandbabies, I realized it was all good news.

Linda Osmundson

She'll Call Me "Ma"

When doubts filled my mind, your comfort gave me renewed hope.

King David

"Guess what—I'm pregnant!" My stepdaughter phoned. Her joy was obvious. "That's wonderful," I said. "I'm going to be a grandmother!" We had always been close—bonded together by our mutual love for her father. I was sure that my love for this child was big enough to share with her child. What I wasn't sure of was my grandmothering ability.

I had often witnessed these women at church fellowships—huddled in a circle like football players planning their next play. They all had sweet names like "Mimi," "Nana," "Grammy" and "Grandma." Their purses bulged with photos that could be wielded out at a moment's notice. Their conversations revolved around sippy cups, Big Bird and onesies (which I had already mispronounced at a friend's baby shower as "o-nee-zees"). I, on the other hand, was young (only forty) and inexperienced and the stepgrandmother. I had lots of questions and all the fated answers. Would my stepdaughter pull away from me? It would only be natural that she grow closer to her real mother in the coming months. Would I suddenly feel like an outsider when my husband stepped into his role as grandfather? Blood is thicker than water. Would I ever get to be involved in this child's life? Never mind quality time . . . I would take any time. What would I be called by this child? "Stepgrandmother" would definitely not conjure up any warm, fuzzy feelings. And I knew that "Mimi," "Nana," "Grammy" and "Grandma" would quickly be claimed by the two grandmothers, two great-grandmothers and one great-great-grandmother who waited in the wings.

My relationship with my stepdaughter deepened as we talked our way through the months of waiting. "I just found out I'm having a girl," she cried. "You are coming to the baby shower, aren't you?"

"Of course I'll be there . . . if it's okay with your mom," I replied. Silence. Neither one of us needed to be reminded of our situation.

Two months later, it was finally time. "We're leaving for the hospital," her voice quivered. "We're on our way," I said. As my husband and I stepped off the elevator, we were greeted by our blended family. Time seemed to crawl as we all awaited the blessed arrival. Finally, she was here. "I'm a grandma!" I blurted out. All heads snapped to attention in my direction.

Had I said that out loud? I hadn't meant to. I suddenly imagined a sign over the hospital room door: "Only blood relatives admitted." I sheepishly smiled and stepped back as we all entered the room.

She was the most beautiful child (other than my own) that I had ever laid eyes on! I stood by as each one took his or her turn holding the tiny, red-faced stranger. Flashbulbs popped at every turn. She was so perfect. So tiny. And she possessed an unmistakable feature that drew me to her instantly . . . my husband's loving eyes. I knew I was falling in love with her and longed to cradle her in my arms like the others. Instead, I moved toward the door, trying to stay out of the way. All too soon it was time to go and let Mama and baby rest. My eyes filled with tears. I hadn't gotten to hold her. With all the passing of the baby, I had gotten passed over. Just an oversight during all the confusion, I rationalized. Shouldn't get too attached, anyway. That night, my prayers overflowed with pleas for a true relationship with this child. Opportunity for motherhood well behind me, all I had were memories buried under the difficulties of a bad first marriage. There had never been time for filling in baby books with first steps or first words. My daughter had basically raised herself, while my energy was spent just getting through it all. I desperately wanted a second chance.

The next day, I woke up anxious to get to the hospital and see my stepdaughter. I secretly hoped that no other relatives would be there so I could have her and the baby all to myself. When we arrived, all was well. Mama and baby rested as my husband and I exchanged labor and delivery stories with our son-in-law. When it came time to go, I felt a lump rise in my throat. I still hadn't held the baby, and I felt silly being that emotional over what seemed like such a small incident. No one could have known how I longed to hold that child. I certainly didn't feel like a stepgrandmother. As far as I was concerned, that was my child and my grandchild in that bed. As I turned to leave, my son-in-law caught my eyes. He saw my emotion and somehow he knew what I had missed the day before. He walked over to the bed, reached in and picked up the baby and handed her directly to me.

More than two years have passed since that day. I now fit in quite nicely with the other grandmothers at church.

You see, we have so much in common. I, too, have earned one of these sweet names. Shortly after her first birthday, my granddaughter reached out to me as "Ma." It stuck. Sippy cups now crowd my tea glasses and "o-nee-zees" abide in my lingerie drawer. Big Bird makes a daily appearance in my living room, and a larger-than-life version of Tinky Winky has taken up residence under my bed. And I am always armed and ready for any photo contest that might break out at one of those church fellowships.

I have cradled my granddaughter often and have stored up enough laughs for a lifetime as I have replied to questions like, "Ma, can you come over every day and just paint my fingernails?" I receive more love in a day than I could give back in a lifetime. You see, we have always been close—bonded together by our mutual love for her mother.

As I write this, I am happily awaiting the birth of my second granddaughter and am sure that my love for my first grandchild is big enough to share with her sister. Gone are the doubts. Gone are the questions—she'll call me "Ma."

Jackie Davis

The Bathroom Mirror

I look forward to being older, when what you look like becomes less and less an issue and what you are is the point.

Susan Sarandon

As I approach the bathroom mirror today, I cautiously scrutinize the reflection staring back at me. I have recently been given a new name. The name is "Grandma."

I brace myself against the counter while squinting my eyes at the face in the mirror. How could this woman possibly be a grandmother? She looks nothing at all like the grandmother who had been in my childhood. This woman doesn't have a speck of gray in her hair. And there is not a trace of wrinkles or age spots to be seen. Of course to be fair, my grandmother didn't have fifty different boxes of hair coloring conveniently awaiting her at the grocery store or the wonderful selection of anti-aging creams that stand lining my counter like good little soldiers. Still it is difficult to believe that I have earned this title of "Grandma."

Where have the years gone? My mind wanders back to my own childhood. I did have a very nice childhood. I would dare say, nothing out of the ordinary. However, I do remember certain phrases that my mother used that I swore would never pass through my lips. I still gasp in horror when I remember uttering for the first time to my kids, "It's always fun and games until somebody gets hurt!" I swear, my head did a ninety-degree turn to see if my mother was standing anywhere near me. Had those words really come from my mouth? Those were my mother's words. Oh no, I was possessed! And the first time I heard my mother's laugh coming out of my throat, well it was almost as if a full moon was turning me into a werewolf. I was downright quivering with fear.

Then there's the memory when I was eight years old and I was storming down the hall, headed towards my bedroom in a real snit over one of my mom's judgment calls. I slammed the door behind me with all my strength, purging my rage. Mom appeared within seconds, demanding to know why I slammed the door. Being blessed with very large eyes that could widen to angelic heights, I softly whimper, "It was the wind, Mama. See, the window is open." It worked like a charm, and I am happy to report that it still worked when my kids used it on me.

There's something about the word "mama" when spoken by a child, that has the power to unleash a force so strong that it can turn a mother's heart into a puddle of quivering Jell-O. As I stand before the mirror this morning, I ponder what the word "Grandma" will do to me. I en - vision a huge bowl of mush with the words, "Help me. I'm drowning," written on top in brown sugar with two large eyes blinking through it.

How has my childhood blurred into my children's childhood and now into their children's childhood? Where has the time gone? I realize the answer is gazing back at me in the mirror. It is within me. It is in my spirit and within my heart. I have become my mother and, in turn, a grandmother. I no longer quake in fear over the transition. I embrace it with a smile. This girl, this mother and now this grandmother is going to be just fine.

Wanda Mitchell

Reflections of Hope

The capacity to care is the thing which gives life its deepest meaning and significance.

Pablo Casals

They didn't grow inside of me
Next to my heart,
But they have my genes
So they are my own.

Most of them hug me, giggle,
Clamor for attention,
Beg for stories, expect treats
Want to sing and sleep over.

In their world I build tradition;
I am Thanksgiving and Christmas,
A memory-maker serving cookies with praise
Encouraging their ambition.

To them I'm slow, old-fashioned
A helper of homework who speaks strange words
They tell me I sound "cool."
In their unstable world
I offer things that rarely change.

In them I see myself;
Two have my turned-up nose,
Another my moodiness, my laugh,
One has my passion for music
Still another, my fascination with words,
Some gather friends like flowers,
A mirror of me.

Each one is a reflection of hope
making rainbows
where their own light shines.

In this complicated world
I look to them with pride,
They look to me with trust.

This cherished brood is my treasure
I call them precious
They call me Gram.

Yulene A. Rushton

All in Good Time

Learn to get in touch with the silence within yourself, and know that everything in life has purpose. There are no mistakes, no coincidences; all events are blessings given to us to learn from.

Elisabeth Kübler-Ross

The crunch of snow, as our son-in-law's truck pulled to a stop in front of our home, was quickly followed by pounding on the door.

"Hi, Grandma," our two grandchildren chorused, falling into the house, as I opened the door.

Bradie, seven, hugged and kissed me. "I love you so much, Grandma," he said. "I'm glad we're staying here tonight." My heart swelled with love for him.

Shondie pushed past us. "Where's Grandpa?" she shouted, darting up the stairs as fast as her four-year-old legs could carry her. She catapulted into her grandpa's outstretched arms, a stream of animated chatter ensuing as she showed him her new dolly.

Will she ever feel that way about me? I wondered. I longed for a special relationship with her, like I'd had with

Bradie. It was wonderful that she loved her grandpa so much, but part of me felt a little hurt, and yes, a little jealous.

"Don't be silly," my husband would say when I voiced my concerns. "She'll come around. All in good time."

After a busy time of reading stories, playing games and making a craft, Bradie asked if they could watch the movie they'd brought with them.

"Sit here, Grandma," he said, patting the floor. With a smile, I flopped on my stomach next to him, that wonderful feeling of love rushing through me like a beautiful melody.

"Do you want to sit with us, Shondie?" I asked, patting the floor beside me.

"I'll sit with Grandpa," she said, clambering into his lap as he put down the magazine he was reading.

I sighed. Was I being foolish to feel rejected?

Bradie chattered on and on, trying to explain which Pokémon was which and how each evolved. But before the movie was finished he'd lost interest.

"Tickle time," he shouted, jumping onto my back and tickling my sides. "You don't like being tickled, do you Grandma?"

"Neither do you." I bucked him off and began tickling him.

"No, no," he squealed. "Don't. I'll get you for that." Wiggling away from me, he made a dive for my bare feet.

Grabbing him, I held him down, kissing him. "You're my favorite boy," I cooed. "My favorite boy."

"Oh, no," he choked, "girl kisses. Yuck." He wiped his face with his sleeve and escaped to the couch.

I lay on the floor laughing as Shondie slipped from her grandpa's lap and dropped onto the carpet beside me. "Tickle time, Grandma," she said.

With a laugh, I began tickling her. She giggled and

squirmed. "Say it, Grandma," she said. "Say what you said to Bradie."

"You're my favorite boy," I said.

"No, Grandma," she chastised me. "I'm a girl. Silly." Her arms went around my neck and she kissed me.

"You're my favorite girl," I told her, my throat suddenly thick.

She wiggled away from me and climbed back onto her grandpa's knee. With a cherubic smile she laid her cheek against his chest. "And I'm your favorite girl, too, aren't I, Grandpa?" she asked.

"Yes, you are," he told her. "And you're Grandma's favorite girl, too."

Then he flashed a knowing smile at me as I wiped happy dampness from my eyes.

Chris Mikalson

Crossing the Threshold

From where I stood to where you are. These are years of mystery that we can never share . . . yet love and understanding can build a bridge for us to cross and so reach each other in ways that matter to us both.

Lois Wyse

As my daughter grew larger, the happy thoughts of grandparenting grew on me. I began to get used to the idea, relishing my fantasies about the baby and thoroughly enjoying my daughter's interest in talking to me about pregnancy and parenthood. Although my trepidation was not completely assuaged, I was excited. With the reality of a new baby on the way, I began knitting a sweater and lingering in baby shops. The clincher was meeting the baby, a healthy little girl who arrived three weeks early while I was out of town. I couldn't return to Los Angeles fast enough. Driving to Santa Barbara, I could hardly contain my excitement as we rushed to the hospital.

There she was, Caitlin Lilly. The Lilly is after me. Carrie, my little girl, was holding her little girl. At that moment I crossed the threshold of grandparenthood, a crossing I'll never forget.

I feel a bit uncertain holding this tiny baby. She looks so fragile. I look for familiar features . . . her mouth, ears, eyes, the shape of her face. Who does she resemble? Could that be my father's chin? Are those my mother's eyes or, maybe, even mine? It seems easier to think about her looks in terms of others than of myself. Are her long fingers like her father's? Yes.

Reluctantly I recognize that I must share her with the "other side." They, too, have a claim on her. I feel possessive. She's mine—my grandchild. I'm her grandma. Although she has no idea who I am, she will. I will see to that. In her, I see my history carried forward. The experiences of my ancestors are now stored in her, and she doesn't even know it . . . or me. She is the future. She will carry the genetic thread forward, beyond me, beyond my time. This is breath-stopping. It is life, past, present and future all rolled into one six-pound, twelve-ounce person. It is difficult to give words to my feelings. A wave of time and emotion is washing over me. It is heady. I ask myself, *What I can do here? What is my place in her life?* I want to do so much. I want her to have everything . . . everything good and beautiful, only kindness and warmth and a pony. Yes, she must have a pony as her mother did. May she be blessed with a strong body and mind in order to savor life, a fine education, a peaceful world. We will not have to escape the pogroms of Eastern Europe as her great-grandfather, my father, did.

While I think of all I want for her, how I will guard the history she holds, how I will nurture all of the possibilities for the future she possesses, how I will protect her and keep her safe, her father approaches. It is time for her to be fed. An abrupt reminder that she is not mine, that it is not my will or vision that prevails. I must entrust her to them, my daughter and son-in-law, lovely children with no experience. How will they know what to do? They are going to raise this baby? This precious bundle who holds the key to continuity in my life, the link to my past and future? How can that be? Is that safe? Smiling, he takes her from me. I smile, too, to cover up my sense of loss. She is my link. But she is not mine. I must learn to share. But I will find a way to make my mark. I will put my two cents in. She will know she has a Grandma Lilly. She will have a wonderful life. I am resolved. But how do I do it?

Lillian Carson, D.S.W.
Excerpted from The Essential Grandparent™: A Guide to Making a Difference *by Dr. Lillian Carson*

7

CHALLENGES

If nothing is going well, call your grandmother.

Italian Proverb

Gabriella and the Trophy

If enough people think of a thing and work hard enough at it, I guess it's pretty nearly bound to happen, wind and weather permitting.

Laura Ingalls Wilder

The lights dim as the music level rises. Thirty children of assorted shapes, sizes and ages are presenting a dance recital in the school gymnasium/auditorium. All the parents, grandparents, aunts and uncles are there. Hundreds of them fill the seats. This is the first public performance of my young granddaughter, Gabriella.

Gabriella is two years old. She is appearing in the recital as a pink bunny in a routine called "Animal Crackers in My Soup." She executes her part admirably, even though the bunny ears have slid down her face during a particularly athletic sequence and hang around her neck by a piece of white elastic. After a few attempts to reinstall the ears, she leaves them where they are like an ear necklace and catches up with the rest of the chorus line of members of the animal kingdom.

Two hours pass, and the show is drawing to a close. Thirty children and young persons are lined up on stage, the two- and three-year-olds in the front and the sixteen-year-olds in back, with the other ages filling the spaces in-between for the finale and the presentation of trophies.

The pink bunny with the ears clenched in her left hand steps out of line, crosses front stage and stands quietly at the kneecaps of the trophy presenter. Her right hand reaches up toward the trophy and runs out of length about two inches from the base. The presenter seems totally unaware of the silent pink bunny standing directly under her gaze. As she reads the name on the trophy, a young lady breaks from the group and claims the trophy over the head of the pink bunny still standing with hand outstretched, waiting now to claim the next one.

Herein begins the most amazing display of group dynamics I have ever witnessed. The silent determination of that two-year-old unifies hundreds of people in a space of about ten minutes. Mental messages converge into one growing breath of encouragement to the pink bunny as each trophy passes over her outstretched hand to another. With infinite patience and assurance, she waits. Ten names, ten trophies, and still she waits with hand held high. Somewhere around trophy number twenty, a brief struggle within a pink bunny is read from her body language by an intensely sympathetic audience. The bunny's eyes drop to the ears she is holding in her other hand and for one brief moment, her face falls. I feel the silent thoughts of those around me join my own . . . "No, no, it has nothing to do with your ears falling off. You are not a failure; your trophy is coming. Take heart!" The message is received, and the expression on the bunny's face changes to annoyance. Both hands go to her lips, her lower lip is stuck out in a pout, and the tiny face tilts upwards to its most extreme angle, but still no trophy.

A two-year-old monkey from the same dance sequence joins the bunny at front stage right for a whispered conversation. The eyes of the bunny and the monkey travel from the box of trophies to the presenter . . . more whispering. The audience is adding the words in their minds to the scene on stage. "You could tackle her around the legs, and I could grab two trophies, jump off the front of the stage and run out the back door." Now, the audience is howling with laughter, some stomping on the floor as if to force the laughter out faster, some holding stomachs to keep the laughter from bursting out the seams of the body and wiping tears streaming down cheeks. After considering the plan, the pink bunny shakes her head "No" and the plan is discarded. The monkey steps back in line and the audience settles back tentatively in their seats. The presenter, for whatever reason, continues to ignore the pink bunny.

Twenty-three trophies and still no trophy for Gabriella. The bunny shows signs of losing heart; her eyes are downcast, the lower lip trembles. Again there are waves of silent encouragement from beyond the stage, and even a few murmured . . . "Don't give up" . . . and "It's coming." The bunny makes a decision. She is still at the kneecaps of the presenter. Her face is once more raised in expectancy and slowly the right hand reaches up as the bunny resumes the stance of the first fifteen to twenty minutes. A collective sound arises from the audience, which can only be described as one giant moan.

The twenty-ninth trophy is Gabriella's. When it is transferred to the hands of the pink bunny, the entire audience stands up and cheers the loudest, longest, most emotional ovation of the night. The ovation is for the two-year-old in the bunny suit who taught a lesson in faith, determination and patience this night.

Barbara E. Hoffman

[AUTHOR'S NOTE: *Gabriella Maria Kramer is the middle child of my son Robert and his wife Maria. Sara, Gabriella and Michael are miracle children, born after eight years of unsuccessful attempts to conceive. We see them as gifts from God in gratitude for the loving care given by their parents to the adopted sister they never knew, teachers of loving lessons and a constant reminder that God's plan is greater than our own. I dedicate this story to the memory of Rachel Emily Kramer, an HIV-positive infant abandoned in a hospital at three months of age and taken into the hearts of this family.*]

The Moses Connection

If you listen carefully to children you will have plenty about which to laugh.

Steve Allen

When my children were in kindergarten and first grade, my husband and I owned and operated a family-type restaurant in a beach resort town.

Every weekend it was hectic as vacationers descended upon the town to enjoy their "fun in the sun," go out for an evening meal and enjoy the amusements and activities along the boardwalk.

During the busy times, my mother would come down from the city by train to baby-sit my children allowing me to work.

My mother's petite stature and pure white hair made her look quite a bit older than her chronological age.

But needless to say she was a wonder with the children.

Grandma Sissy, as my two sons called her, would arrive after work on Friday evening and leave Sunday evening.

Every Sunday morning, before our business opened, we'd all head to church.

More times then not, because of the summer crowds, we'd have to sit in two pews, usually one behind the other.

One morning in particular, when my husband, my five-year-old son and I sat in the row directly behind her and our other son, we noticed Andy seemed unusually fascinated with her hair.

He kept caressing it.

Finally, after a few minutes he turned to us and asked in a loud voice, "Is Grandma Sissy Moses?"

Before I could respond in any way, several nearby parishioners smiled; a few even giggled.

Totally unaware of the stir he caused, our son continued. "I bet she is," he declared. "She's got the same long, white hair." He gently patted it once again.

I smiled and whispered, "No, she's not Moses."

"Well," he continued. "Grandma looks just like the picture in Sunday School."

More smiles from those unsuspecting listeners. Andy grew silent.

I assumed my answer satisfied his curiosity.

Several minutes passed then we heard, "Grandma, are you Moses' mother?"

No one in close proximity, including Grandma Sissy, could hold in the laughter.

I quickly tried to explain the timeline, but Andy wouldn't have it.

He didn't give up.

He countered with, "Well, is she his grandmother?"

By now, laughter being highly contagious in the most unlikely of places, had spread to more folks than needed.

It could have been called a small commotion.

I noticed the priest stretching his head above the congregation trying to locate and identify the disruption and could see several people on the other side of the aisle looking in our direction.

Within a few seconds one of the ushers whisked past us and made his way to the pulpit.

Oh boy, I thought, *we're going to be asked to leave.* But to my surprise, the priest smiled and addressed his audience.

"I've just been informed that one of our very young parishioners believes his grandmother is related to Moses. Will our special guest please rise and satisfy our curiosity?"

Grandma Sissy stood.

The entire assemblage broke into laughter and applauded.

"See, I was right," said Andy. "Everyone else thinks so, too."

Helen Colella

Twenty-Nine and Holding

Nothing is better than the unintended humor of reality.

Steve Allen

Our family had always been big on birthday celebrations and other special occasions. On each and every birthday, my entire family gathered together to share a meal, gifts and a song. My mother wasn't fond of her own birthdays. Like many women her age, when her birthday rolled around she only admitted to being twenty-nine, just as she was the year before.

At the ripe old age of twelve, my twin sons had figured out that Grandma was much older than she admitted, but didn't question her when she once again announced that she was twenty-nine and holding. My younger daughter, Becky, took her seriously, however. She believed every word that her grandmother told her. If Grandma said she was twenty-nine, as far as Becky was concerned, she was twenty-nine. There was no question about it.

A few months went by, and we joined together as a family to celebrate my thirtieth birthday. After everyone sang

"Happy Birthday," we enjoyed heaping helpings of cake and ice cream. Finally, the time came for me to open my presents. Becky had been unusually quiet during the entire birthday celebration. She carried a worried look on her face.

After all of the guests left, she couldn't stand it any longer and sadly informed me, "Mamma, you're thirty, and Grandma is twenty-nine. I hate to have to tell you this, but you must've been adopted."

Nancy B. Gibbs

Mrs. Malaprop's Kin

"Grandma!" yelled four-year-old Cody from my bathroom. "There's a spider in the bathtub! Hurry! Can you fix it?"

Pans clattered as I rushed to get the Thanksgiving turkey ready for the oven. I hadn't wanted to baby-sit this busy morning. But I was drafted. Both parents were working. "Yes, I'll fix it as soon as I can. Don't worry." Grandmas are great fixers. "That faucet is hard to turn, but I can do it and the spider will go right down the drain."

"More Valium," came the worried voice from the bathroom. "I can't hear you."

In a few minutes, I rushed into the bathroom to confront the spider.

"Fixed it!" Cody proudly announced. "Grandma, close your eyes. I don't have my *wonder wear* up yet."

Shutting my eyes, I squinted toward the tub as the last of the yellow stream went down the drain. "You're right, Buddy, that spider is gone."

Firsts are memorable—first bike ride, first evening gown, first kiss, first grandchild. I couldn't wait to become a genuine grandma.

At long last, I got my wish. Cody was born. What an

angel. I loved his pink cheeks, bright blue eyes, tousled hair and chubby arms wrapped around a stuffed bear. It was a fact: This was the most adorable grandchild in the world. He was perfect.

When Cody began talking, however, the problem surfaced. He had Mrs. Malaprop's biological genes. You remember Mrs. Malaprop from Richard Sheridan's play, *The Rivals*. She made verbal blunders an art by replacing words similar in sound with those different in meaning.

His ailment became confirmed. Cody, a daredevil on his tricycle, let out a yell one afternoon. I rushed to open the back door when I heard him fall. He was doubled over.

"It really hurts a guy when he hits his tentacles," he cried.

I hugged him and said the reason for his accident was that his jeans were too large and had slipped down. He agreed. "Maybe I should wear expanders to hold them up."

Further proof of his malapropism came when we went to get my driver's license renewed. "Grandma," he warned me, "make sure your license doesn't perspire. I think you might get unrested."

As his condition advanced, he asked me an important question. "Will Santa's little dorks still make me toys when I'm older?" He paused. "Wait a minute . . . I forgot. The dorks live with Snow White. I mean the other little guys."

Yes, Cody definitely had the affliction, but I hope he has it for a long time. It's wonderful having a grandchild with this enigma. He gives me so many good chuckles.

Since the spider invasion had been resolved, Cody and I went back into the kitchen. I groaned. My giblets had boiled dry and were turning black.

"Don't worry, Grandma," Cody suggested. "We could always get some food at the delicate intestine."

Sharon Landeen

A Fair Trade

I've learned . . . it's not what you have in your life, but who you have in your life that counts. It gives you an opportunity to be counted on.

Ann Richards

"Keep away from children." That's what my matchbook cover says. Gladly. I'm seventy-four years old and heavily into the osteoporosis-and-angioplasty scene. But how can I keep away from children? We have a ten-year-old adopted granddaughter.

Nobody likes to be one of life's clichés. But we are. Startling statistics these days tell how many grandparents adopt grandchildren. My husband and I are two of them.

Our car has no bumper sticker that says, "I'm spending my children's inheritance." We are. But not on travel.

So this grandmother's life revolves around Girl Scouts and choir, dance and piano lessons. She's a much-ignored advocate for good manners. A much-resisted fashion consultant.

Well, you get the picture.

If ever there was a Don't Ask, Don't Tell situation, this is it. You get questions, or looks.

At the clinic, at the school office, wherever. "You're her . . . mother?" Well, yes, legally speaking. You keep explaining, like someone in a Zen riddle. "I'm her mother. I'm also her grandmother."

The kid gets questions, too, from other kids. "Why do you live with your grandparents?" "What's wrong with your parents?" My advice to her: "Tell them it's none of their business." But she came up with a better one: "My parents couldn't take care of me."

That's true.

Every adoptive grandparent and grandchild has some kind of soap-opera scenario. And it's nobody's business.

Culture shock bombards adoptive grandparents. There are two kinds. Math and sex.

Math first. Let's say you did bring up five children. Your oldest is now fifty-three. Your youngest is now thirty-four. That means you've been out of the loop for a while.

So you find that elementary-school math is a big culture shock.

You never mastered the so-called New Math thirty years ago. Now you find yourself clueless when confronted by a fifth-grade math book.

Go ask your granddad. Never mind. He's clueless, too.

Sex at the modern ten-year-old level is an even bigger culture shock. The words! The jokes! The casual, offhand reports of startling playground shenanigans.

Everything has speeded up. Now ten-year-olds act like teenagers. The giggling gender awareness. The raucous music. The constant sass. If this is fifth grade, what lies in wait in middle school?

And there are little ironies in the fire.

Take sewing. I can't sew. But now I have to sew Scout badges on vests, initials on dancewear, tails on costumes, buttons on many things. A real seamstress could do this in minutes. It takes me hours.

It doesn't help to have arthritic hands.

So here I am with a ten-year-old who's bigger than I am and wears bigger shoes that are getting even bigger. And more expensive.

Here's the part of the soap opera I'll tell: We were her foster grandparents for several years before we adopted her. Adoption took some doing. And yes, our advanced age was questioned by social workers, lawyers, the works.

But in the end, after some hassle, the kid was ours.

She's pretty. She dances and sings. She makes friends. She gets good grades. Well, if you don't count spelling. They have something now called "creative spelling," and you'd better believe it's creative.

So we're statistics—grandparents who have adopted a grandchild. And when you're in your mid-seventies, and your child is ten, you may rightly wonder about another kind of statistic: What are the chances you'll be around for her high-school graduation, her college diploma, her wedding day, her first child?

Luckily, the kid's beloved aunt and other relatives are standing by, ready to take over when the time comes.

Sometimes statistics end up cutting it pretty close. But the kid's with her own family. You wouldn't take that for anything.

Luise Putcamp, jr

CLOSE TO HOME   JOHN McPHERSON

"Now, now, sweetie. That was an *outdoor* voice.
We need to remember to use our *indoor* voices
when we're inside."

Love Times Three

Life's challenges are not supposed to paralyze you; they're supposed to help you discover who you are.

Bernice Johnson Reagan

The morning had passed slowly as I tried to busy myself to keep my mind off my youngest daughter Jenny. She thought she was pregnant, had been experiencing some problems, and was out to the hospital for an ultrasound. Jen, the youngest of my five children, was twenty-three, and yet to me she was still my baby! It was hard to believe that she might soon be a mother herself.

A short time later I was sitting at the table across from Jen and her husband. Both were unusually quiet. The suspense was killing me. "So, are you pregnant or not?"

Jen looked at Scott, then calmly answered, "Yes . . . with three . . . I am going to have three babies!"

At first I thought this was some crazy joke of their to get a reaction from me, but as we sat there a little longer, I knew it was the truth. Jennifer was carrying three babies! She was going to have triplets! I was ecstatic. I had never

seen triplets, and now I was going to have some for grandchildren. Wow! I had always believed that a new baby is
like the beginning of all things—wonder, hope, a dream of
possibilities. In a world that is cutting down its trees to
build highways, losing its earth to concrete . . . babies are
almost the only remaining link with nature, with the natural world of living things from which we spring. Three
babies . . . In the next hour I called everyone I had ever
known, and maybe a few that I had just met in passing! I
wanted to tell the world about these babies.

The weeks passed and because of the multiple embryos,
the doctor did an ultrasound every few weeks and had a
copy made of the video. At first there were only three little pockets, or sacs, then later we could see three little
heartbeats. They were called babies A, B, and C, which
seemed so common for something so phenomenal—these
were my grandchildren, not A, B, and C! Call them what
they may, but those little heartbeats belonged to three
very precious little human beings. As I watched them
growing inside my daughter, like so often in the past, in
still another way, my belief in God was reinforced.

Then somewhere near the end of the sixth month, my
daughter started having some serious problems. The doctor put her on complete bedrest, and we prayed and
waited. . . . I can't remember ever praying any harder. But
for some reason we might never know, God decided to
take my grandbabies home. Joey, Michael and Bradley
died shortly after birth.

No heartache can compare with the death of one small
child, and the pain was indeed tripled with the boys. They
were so tiny, so adorable, so perfect in every way. They
were so precious and soft, ten little fingers and toes. Sadly,
we would never know the color of their eyes. . . . To see my
beautiful daughter laying there with her three lifeless sons
was the closest to hell I have ever been. I couldn't imagine

her pain. With tear-filled eyes, my daughter took my hand and whispered to me, "Maybe God is tired of calling the aged, Mom, so he picked my three little rosebuds before they could grow old. Can you imagine how much more beautiful heaven will be with my babies there?" Then we cried together.

A short time later the doctor asked me if I wanted to hold the babies, and at first I said, "No." But he reminded me that once they took them away I would most likely never get another chance to hold triplets. I thought about it and decided I would try. He wrapped the three of them together in a little blue blanket and led me to a room where there was a wooden rocking chair. I sat down, and he handed me the babies. "Take as long as you need."

I rocked the babies and talked to them, and told them that I would come someday to heaven to find them. Although the human part of them was gone, I somehow felt I was bonding with their three little spirits . . . in fact, three little angels.

When a nurse finally returned to take my grandsons away, once again I began to cry, for surely the saddest word that mankind knows will always be "good-bye."

A friend of the family who runs a funeral home donated one little casket, and the boys were all buried together. Our pastor had a beautiful service at the cemetery. Like before, to see the pain in my daughter's heart was the hardest thing I had ever been through, and yet there was nothing to be said or done. She had done her best to carry her babies, and now all she had left was a sheet of paper filled with statistics, a certificate with smudged footprints and three tiny bracelets marked "Boy/Leighton." People who came to the service mopped their eyes and told us that they knew how we felt, but they couldn't know, because we didn't feel—not yet.

The story isn't ended yet. One year to the month after losing the triplets, Jennifer gave birth to Scott Edward.

Scottie is the joy of her life. Since then she also gave Scottie a little brother, Brandon Michael, and after five boys, she is going to have a little girl! Nothing can ever replace the triplets, but we believe they came into our lives for a reason and stayed just long enough to make us appreciate life and the little people more.

Occasionally, we might look for too big a reason for something we don't comprehend in our lives. Often the reason may seem small but have big consequences. Mostly, we don't see the results. Sometimes, we have to accept these heartbreaking things with faith.

I have four incurable diseases. Sometimes when things get really tough, I find peace in knowing that there are three special angels in heaven helping me get through the day. There is a real sense of contentment in knowing that someday, once again, I will hold my three little grandsons and complete our talk. . . . For certain, our first one was entirely too short.

Barbara Jeanne Fisher

Not Enough Hands!

The most rewarding thing about being a grand-parent is watching your children become loving parents. It is our assurance that we did something right, after all.

Jean Wasserman McCarty

Sarah was my first grandchild—the firstborn of my first-born—and her parents, Rogie and Steve, did all the things necessary to provide a safe, nurturing environment for their daughter. I was so proud of their efforts and abso-lutely devoted to being the best grandparent possible! But despite every precaution that grown-ups can take, some-times horrible things still happen. At the age of two years and two months, our precious Sarah was killed in a house fire caused by faulty wiring.

Our family has relived that tragic night over and over again, trying desperately to think of a way it could have been prevented. Each of us has, secretly, felt responsible. Not that anyone was, of course, but there's just something about being an adult, caring for a child, that makes you feel that you should have been able to prevent anything bad from happening. Children have ear infections and skinned knees—*they aren't supposed to die!*

God has blessed us with many beautiful grandchildren since then, and they are all miracles to us. But, of course, there is no Sarah. And until recently, I have had recurring nightmares in which I am desperately trying to protect or hide our other grandchildren from some unnamed danger. Finally, after still another terrifying dream, I turned my fears over to God and asked him to show me what I needed to do.

In answer to my prayers, he sent me one more dream:

I dreamed that my husband Ron and I had several of our grandchildren with us, and we were walking along a beach. There were other people passing by, some with their families, some in couples, some alone. A few spoke to us—most didn't—but that wasn't important. I sensed that everyone who walked there was, like me, silently reflecting on the mighty ocean and its overwhelming power.

Ron and I were holding hands, but of course the children were running all around, as inquisitive children do in a place full of things to discover. We were trying to keep an eye on all of them, and I remember thinking, *I don't have enough hands!* I wanted so much to hold the hand of each one and explain things about the beach as we went along, but they were eager to make their own discoveries.

Ryan was running ahead of all of us, but he was looking back to check in and call out comments about what he was finding on his way down the beach. Tiffani was following him, but staying much closer to us, sometimes running back to hold my hand a while for reassurance. Becky, Justin and Jessica were holding hands and talking together while they pulled each other this way and that. Big Benjamin was looking under logs and rocks for any interesting creatures to watch or play with, and Little Benjamin was toddling along, holding T. J.'s hand. T. J., the oldest of the grandchildren, was the guide, the caretaker. I knew she would see that the baby remained safe.

A crowd of people suddenly swarmed by—I hadn't seen them coming down the beach—and they were all traveling in the opposite direction from us. We momentarily lost track of the children, and when the crowd drifted on down the beach, Ron and I quickly inventoried each of our own. They were still playing, talking, traveling loosely in our family group, but at least in sight and still traveling our way—except for Little Benjamin, who came toddling up to us—alone! My heart froze! Ron and I looked at each other, and I could see his concern, too. T. J. would never let go of Benjamin's hand along a strange beach! Yet she was nowhere to be seen.

We called the other children together and started to search. I was frantic! I couldn't breathe! Pleading silently with God, I said, *Please don't take another child from us!* Familiar feelings of pain and guilt overwhelmed me. *Please let us find her!* We searched and called, but she didn't answer. Could she have been picked up and carried along by someone in the swarming crowd that had temporarily engulfed us? I climbed the hills overlooking the ocean to search in the tall grasses there. Looking out over the vast expanse of water, with its whitecaps bobbing, I was struck again at its power. She could be right there, bobbing with the whitecaps, and I might not even see her! I felt so frustrated! *I don't have enough hands!* I thought.

Suddenly, the urgency to pray came over me, and God's peaceful voice, out of the depths of the ocean—out of the air itself—spoke to me: *No human has enough hands—you're not supposed to. Don't expect yourself to be responsible for everyone and everything. That's where I come in. Let me have her—let me have all of them. Their spirits belong with me, just as Sarah's does—and yours. I love them even more than you do, and I know what each of them is capable of achieving. Give them to me each day—I have enough hands for everyone.*

I knelt and prayed in the tall grass, *Thy will be done.* I gave T. J. to God, just as I had turned Sarah over to him so many years ago. And for the first time, I forgave myself for not having enough hands—then and now. As I lifted my head, I heard shouts from down on the beach. Ron and all the children were hurrying toward a smiling T. J., who was running to catch up with the rest of her family! She had been temporarily swept along by the clamoring crowd and she, too, had not had enough hands to keep her hold on little Benjamin!

As I ran back down the hill to hold her in my arms, I thanked God for letting us keep her for a while longer. And I thought to myself, *I must tell her it's okay that she wasn't able to keep track of Benjamin. She needs to know that God is the one who has enough hands!* I need to remember that, too.

Cathie Collier Hulen

Birthday Girl

The very least you can do in your life is to figure out what you hope for. And the most you can do is live inside that hope.

Barbara Kingsolver, *Animal Dreams*

Several years ago, while I worked for Visiting Nurses, I made an initial home visit to a family in a poor part of the city. Misty Harper (not her real name), my new patient, was five years old. She had been born with defects of the heart, liver and kidneys. The doctors predicted she wouldn't survive long enough to leave the hospital.

Anna Harper, a large, smiling woman, introduced herself as Misty's grandmother. She sat me down on the well-worn, overstuffed sofa in a living room crowded with furniture. Mrs. Harper had something she wanted to show me before Misty's assessment. She pulled out a huge scrapbook full of photos, articles and newspaper clippings. The first was a newspaper article reporting Misty's birth, the damage to her internal organs and the sad predictions for the future. Her daughter, Misty's mother, had been so stricken with grief that she was afraid to bring her baby home from the hospital. She believed that if Misty came home, her older three children would grow too attached to the baby and would be devastated by the loss.

"What happened?" I asked, suddenly understanding the closeness of this family.

"I took her home myself," Mrs. Harper said. "My instincts and my faith just told me she was not going to die."

We sat together for a while longer looking at the album. It held photographs of a sweet infant, then of a beautiful toddler growing up to be a lovely little girl.

She pointed to little newspaper clippings that filled the album. "Every year I send an announcement to the newspaper to celebrate Misty's birthday. It's just my way of telling everyone who cares that Misty is still with us."

Then she opened the door to the kitchen, and I saw a happy little girl eating breakfast with her sister and two brothers. A younger version of Mrs. Harper, Misty's mother, Coral, was spooning out more cereal. She smiled and beckoned me into the kitchen.

"My mother watches my kids every morning before school starts. In a few minutes, I go off to work."

Not wanting to disturb them I told her I didn't think I'd do an assessment that day. Next week I would come back. I closed the door quietly. Mrs. Harper walked me to the front door. As I was leaving she said, "Whenever a new doctor or nurse comes to our home to check Misty, I show them my album. Children are more than statistics. They are love and faith and what you put into them."

I felt humbled. She was right. Misty was proof of that.

"She will be six next May. Be sure to check the paper," Mrs. Harper teased.

In May I searched the announcements. There I found it. MISTY HARPER WILL CELEBRATE HER SIXTH BIRTHDAY. THANK YOU LORD FOR ANOTHER MIRACLE YEAR.

Every May, I still look for the announcement and remember the family telling me in their own good-humored way, "Medicine doesn't know everything."

Barbara Bloom

8

SPECIAL CONNECTION

Perfect love sometimes does not come until grandchildren are born.

Welsh Proverb

"My mom wouldn't give me money for ice cream,
so I went over her head to Grandma!"

Reprinted by permission of Glenn Bernhardt.

Gramma, Please Don't Make Me Put Them Back!

My granddaughter and I are inseparable. She keeps me wrapped around her little finger.

Gene Perret

When my first granddaughter Lacy was about three or four years old, she was my favorite shopping buddy! I could take her for an afternoon of shopping, and unlike a lot of young children, she never asked for anything.

On one of these shopping outings in early spring, Lacy and I had been in several stores and now we were in a Wal-Mart. As always I had put her in the front of a cart so she could stand and reach all the pretty items. We went up and down several aisles looking at everything. When we got into the children's section, she would reach out, take a dress off the rack and say, "Oh Gramma, isn't this one pretty?" After we both admired it she would hang it back up. This is always how we shopped: We looked, commented, returned the item and moved on. She never asked for these items; she just enjoyed looking at all the pretty things!

We then moved on to the shoe department and as I pushed the cart through the little girls section, she picked up and admired several pairs of shoes. Then she saw a pair of hot pink (pink being her favorite color), high-top suede boots. Slowly reaching for them, she picked them up and cradled them in her arms. Looking up to me, still holding those boots, she said, "Gramma, please don't make me put them back!"

I was surprised with this sudden pleading and asked, "Miss Lacy, what do you need boots for?" After all it was April, winter was over, and it was almost time to start wearing sandals, not boots.

She replied so sadly, "Gramma, they're huntin' boots!" Trying to conceal my laughter, I asked her, "Exactly why do you need huntin' boots?" I knew this dainty, feminine little girl had never gone hunting with Daddy.

She looked at me with an expression that implied God had given her the dumbest of grammas to raise and she said, "For huntin' Easter eggs!"

I'm not sure how another gramma would have handled this situation. I do know Miss Lacy proudly left that store carrying the sack that held her new hot pink huntin' boots!

Karren E. Key

"What's the magic word to get what you want?" "Grandma!"

Thoughts from a Three-Year-Old

Children are unpredictable. You never know what inconsistency they're going to catch you in next.

Franklin P. Jones

Because of adult perspectives, our expectations from children, when they answer us, can be quite different than what actually takes place.

My three-year-old son had been told several times to go into the bathroom to get washed for bed. The last time I told him more assertively. His response was "Yes, Sir!" Being his mother, I didn't expect the "sir."

"You say, 'Yes, Sir,' to a man. To a lady you would say, 'Yes, Ma'am.'" So to quiz him on his lesson I queried, "What would you say to Daddy?"

"Yes, Sir!" came the reply.

"Then what would you say to Mama?"

"Yes, Ma'am!" he proudly remarked.

"Good boy! Now what would you say to Grandma?"

Being used to his usual question posed to Grandma, he lit up and said, "Can I have a cookie?"

Barbara Cornish

Princesses Need Jewels

All I can say about life is, oh God, enjoy it.

Bob Newhart

My grandmother's washstand, a small dresser used years ago to hold a china pitcher and basin for washing, is the first thing you see when you enter my front door. Whether because its austere lines seem in disharmony with the delicate curving legs of the wing chair across from it or because its golden hues clash with the deep tones of the intricately carved wardrobe looming beside it, the stand seems an oaken mismatch in the midst of overpowering mahogany. I planned it that way. I wanted it to stand out and whisper, "Notice me." For preserved within its layers of polish and simply cut lines are memories of my grandmother. And I like to think that the warmth of those memories emanates from her washstand to greet those who cross my threshold.

My grandmother wasn't an easy woman to know. Maybe it was because smiling didn't come easy to her. The lack of an upturn at the corners of her lips made the lines etched around her mouth more pronounced and consequently, she often wore a stern look.

My mother once told me that a hard life gave my grandmother her look of sternness. I learned the story of the high hopes my grandparents had when they immigrated from Iowa to Canada early in the 1920s to raise wheat on the windy plains of Manitoba. And how those hopes were smashed by an endless cycle of blight, locusts and bitter cold that forced them to return to Iowa, only to discover more hardship in the wake of the Depression. "She took in wash and scrubbed out the dirt from other people's laundry to help feed her five children, and then helplessly watched my brother Howard die before his twelfth birthday," my mother said. "She earned her lines."

Despite her stern demeanor, I knew my grandmother loved me. And it was never made clearer to me than one summer day in 1957 when I was eight. Having been left behind while my family went on an errand, my cousin Joyce and I helped our grandma make chocolate-chip cookies. Eating the batter was an indulged treat at Grandma's, and since there were two youngsters gorging on dough, the cookie sheet remained bare. Finally, Grandma shooed us out of the kitchen to make a batch for the oven, and Joyce and I went in search of something to do.

"Let's play dress-up," suggested my cousin, spying white sheets hanging to dry in the Iowa sun. "We can be Greek princesses." Pulling the sheets off the clothesline, we draped them around our bodies and, giggling happily, vainly tried to regally walk while the dragging bottoms of our "gowns" twisted around our ankles. Suddenly, Grandma shouted from the open window, "Girls, come here!"

I was sure we were in trouble. As we slowly tripped up the porch stairs, I imagined the worst possible punishment—being forced to go down into Grandma's dark cellar to rewash the sheets in her wringer washing machine. The thought of it made my knees turn to jelly. With its low ceiling, dark corners and earthen ledge extending above clammy stone walls, I was sure that cellar was a haven for huge, hairy spiders and long-legged bugs with spindly antennae. Being sent down to the cellar to get a jar of her homemade apple butter was hard enough, but I could do that in one quick dash. Washing sheets would take a long time—long enough for "things" to fall in my hair and wiggle up my socks.

When we opened the screen door, I shivered with fright. But Grandma wasn't standing by the cellar. Instead, she sat beside the open cabinet of her washstand, rummaging through boxes and pulling out a treasure of brightly colored scarves, bangly bracelets, huge amber brooches and ropes of necklaces.

"Princesses need jewels," my grandmother said, dispelling my fears and erasing the deeply etched lines of sternness around her mouth with a smile that filled the room.

I will never forget that day when my grandma put aside her work and laughingly played dress-up with her granddaughters. Covered in lipstick and rouge and bedecked in treasures from Grandma's boxes, I felt wickedly beautiful and ever so loved.

Now, more than forty years later and nineteen years after her death, I still see her face when I touch the satiny finish of her oak washstand. But I don't see the face of the stern woman whose mouth is etched with the hard lines of life that is preserved in our family album. Instead, I see a woman whose face is softened by a smile and laughter on a day of dress-up magic. And maybe one day, when I have granddaughters of my own who come to visit, they will walk in the front door and notice my grandmother's washstand. Together we will turn the brass key, and I will pass on the warmth of my memories. Then we will play with the treasures I have collected over the years and stored in the cabinet, and my granddaughters will make their own memories of magic at Grandma's.

Kris Hamm Ross

Other Grandpa

We cannot live only for ourselves; a thousand fibers connect us to those who are present and those throughout the generations.

Violet George

Like the dandelion seeds we used to blow into the wind when we were children, my family has scattered across the country and rooted in so many places that my children rarely see their many aunts and uncles, their cousins—even their grandparents. In fact, the remembrance of "Other Grandpa," whom we can no longer call or write, flourishes in my oldest son's heart through the cultivation of a single story.

Robbi met "Other Grandpa" only once, when he was four months old. I had flown to California to introduce my baby to some more of his family—to my parents, to two of my brothers and to a sister who came from Montana with her baby girl. But since his condition was so uncertain, I could make no advance plans to see my husband's father. He had been in a nursing home for a year, cut off by his silence and confusion like a flower pulled from its roots.

When I called the nursing home to schedule a visit, I was not surprised to hear that I would probably not be recognized by Morris, whom I had met only once when Bernie and I were married. And certainly, I was told, I should expect no response from him. Hardening of the arteries and the hardening of life had left him limp and listless. Still, there was no question in my mind that Robbie and I would make the hour-long drive to see "Other Grandpa." I did not even give much thought to why I was making this trip or for whom: for "Other Grandpa" who would not know us, for my infant son who wouldn't remember it, for my husband who couldn't leave his work, or for myself—to try to satisfy my need to bind this scattered family together.

We drove the busy and breezy California freeways to the place where my father-in-law had been transplanted for the last time. How he came to be in a nursing home three thousand miles away from his only child is one of those stories that I would like to undo, to rewrite with a different sort of ending. It is a complicated, horrific and lonely story which began in his native Poland and unfolded across a continent, an ocean and another continent, through a history of pogroms and racism and then struggle in a new country with a new language, a new life. He left most of his relatives behind in Hitler's Europe— never to hear from them again. To escape from Poland, he was married by proxy to the daughter of a friend of his family, a New Yorker he had never met. They lived in Brooklyn until she died of cancer, and his burlap bag business failed, and then his son went off to college, leaving him to begin yet again. It was his second wife who wanted to move to her girlhood home in California. After that move, Morris walled himself up inside his old age, where it seemed nobody could reach him.

I pulled into the parking lot, nearly empty of cars, and parked in the meager shade of a palm tree. The home was a brick building, smaller than I'd expected, pleasant enough on the outside. Yet, as I pushed Robbie's stroller through the front door, I could feel the unmistakable quality of the place that made it a home for the aged. It was sterile. Maybe there was easy-listening music being piped through speakers; maybe there were silk flowers on the reception desk and still-life prints on the walls. I do not remember these things. I remember only that there was no sound of children laughing.

Mumbling something about how the air conditioning would be repaired tomorrow, a nurse's aide led us down a hall into a lounge. "He's over there," she said, pointing to one of three people in the room, to the one in the wheelchair near the center of that vast space, his back to us and his head bowed. Apparently asleep. Then, thinking better of it, she walked with us the remaining few steps to tell him, "Morris, there's someone here to see you."

Morris turned his head in slow motion to look up at her and then at me. I had made no plans for that moment. Spontaneously, I scooped up my son as I said, "I'm Bernie's wife, and I've brought your grandson to meet you." I handed Robbie to his grandfather without even thinking that this wilted old man, nearly eighty, might not have the strength to hold him. There was a brief instant when we were all on "pause/still"—and then Morris lifted Robbie up, struggling to raise him to his face, to kiss him again and again. He knew!

My first son was undoubtedly the most smiley, giggly baby in all of babydom, and he squealed with delight as he was lifted heavenward, flapping his arms joyfully as though he were being given his first flying lesson. I watched without taking a breath, helplessly captivated by Robbie's gleeful shrieks and Morris's hands—hands trembling with emotion and with the weight of my little boy, fully fifteen pounds by then. Yet, I couldn't take

Robbie from him. My heart stuck in my throat as I watched my son balanced in the air, and I prayed I could catch him if he should fall. I was caught myself, stretched taut between the sparkle in Robbie's eyes and the glistening tears falling in great drops down my father-in-law's hollow, unshaven cheeks.

I don't know how long that moment lasted—one minute, five—but it will stay in my memory forever, and I pray I can graft it to Robbie's as well. I will always regret that as I gathered up all the baby paraphernalia for that trip, I did not remember to pack a camera. Without benefit of photographs, I must illustrate this story for my son through the words I choose.

I describe to him that room, barren and white and tiled, with side doors open to let in whatever breeze might mercifully come our way. We sat at a stark white fiberglass table, Morris in his wheelchair, Robbie in his stroller and I between them in a yellow plastic contoured chair, in a room that must have been designed for parties, yet I could imagine no parties there. I talked to Morris about our life in New York, about how well Bernie was doing, about the house we were going to buy, about my work as a teacher. I talked to Robbie about his "Other Grandpa," his daddy's daddy, about how he had come in a ship across a great ocean from far away. As I babbled on, not expecting any reply from either of them, I was struck by how similar they were, grandfather and grandson, diapered and bibbed, strapped into strollers, neither of them able to use words to express the feelings they held inside. How I longed to hear all the stories my father-in-law could never tell me, stories of the "old country," of this boyhood, of a mother-in-law I never knew, of my husband's childhood . . .

The other two occupants in the room came toward us and soon others were coming through the doors of the patio, residents and staff, and then from other rooms, all to see "Morris's grandson." Robbie, who on other days would have been fast asleep by then, must have sensed the importance of his role. He showed no sign of tiring as he was passed from one set of arms to another. They cooed to him, and he cooed back. They told him stories, and he crinkled up his baby eyes to match their crinkled, wrinkled ones. My little son breathed—and life went back into them.

After nap time or game time finally called our company away, the three of us sat alone in the reception hall, feeling the California heat and listening to Robbie's soft sucking noises as he nursed. I looked up at my father-in-law. He bore the same sculptured cheekbones and high, wide forehead of his son. He saw that I was studying him, and he leaned toward me as far as his harness would allow. I sensed that he wanted to say something even before his lips began to move. His mouth struggled with the formation of a word. Then—in a thick, cracking, parchment voice, one that had not been used for a very long time—he spoke. He looked at me and my nursing child and said, finally, simply, "Good."

Katharine St. Vincent

Paula Alone with Her Grandpa

The sixteen-year-old granddaughter arrived.
Alone.
Her dad, pink slip sweating in his hand,
Not unexpected, downsizing was air breathed,
He had hung on longer, but the timing was lousy.
The Florida trip was off right now.
Her mom wouldn't go without him.
It was decided. Paula would fly
Alone.
Grandpa was not happy about all of that.
He didn't know what to do with a teenager.
But they had always liked each other.
When Grandma was alive, she did the feelings.
Grandpa supplied the laughs and the money.
Girding himself for Paula, he missed his Sarah,
Alone.
"I want to go to the pool, Grandpa.
I brought four bathing suits."
"You're only going to be here four days,
So that should be enough."
Grandpa rounded up the sunscreen
And the towels and waited for Paula.

And thought about Sarah, his swimmer.
Alone.
He wasn't ready for Paula.
For how stunning this granddaughter was.
"That bathing suit fits you like
The designer knew you by your first name.
He certainly knew how beautiful you are.
Like Grandma was," he added.
"Oh, Gramps, you old flatterer.
I got this one at Goodwill. Cheap."
"You're my kind of girl, Paula.
I could never see spending money
On clothes. No moving parts.
They're nothing that needs fan belts."
The sun burning like the heater
In a pickup truck, the cement steaming.
Paula turned a few polite heads,
And Grandpa proudly introduced his granddaughter.
"She's not only beautiful,
but she's smart, too."
Paula dove into the water,
Her body knifed the water, splashless.
Alone.
Later, they cooked together,
He read her poetry while they ate,
And they watched "Jeopardy" side by side,
Decided with a little more practice
They'd try and get on the show,
Hell, they knew the answers.
The sun had made her sleepy,
She called home, laughed her private jokes,
Brushed her teeth, flossed, squeezed a blackhead,
And asked him to hold her hand and read her
A story, like he used to when she was little.
Alone.

Their second night together he asked
Her some brave questions, and she in turn
Asked him two big ones, her eyes hard on him.
"What is it like without Grandma, Gramps?
Are any widows nibbling at you? I sure would."
At that, they both cried for a while,
Soft as petals falling from roses.
Grandpa found the first words out of tears.
"I may reach out for company, Paula,
maybe even for touch, it does get lonely.
But I know I will never find love.
I've had that with your Grandma.
You don't get it twice."
Alone.
The four days went faster than palmetto bugs
At midnight, and all the bathing suits
Got worn and admired. Paula made everyone think
About their youth and about love.
She was a tonic to the whole condominium.
We saw her Grandpa grow younger.
And we knew that when he got really old,
Paula would be here. She'd hold his
Hand and read him a story before he closed
his eyes on the night he would die.
Not alone.

Sidney B. Simon

Real Magic

The courage of life is often a less dramatic spectacle than the courage of a final moment, but it is no less than a magnificent mixture of triumph and tragedy.

John F. Kennedy

Ten years ago my grandfather, who was then eighty-two, told me a story about a book he had studied in college. It was a children's book, the kind with a profound message only children and extraordinarily wise people seem to grasp. He confessed that over the years his memories of that book had intrigued him, and he wished to read it one more time before he passed away. As he was in ill health, I began searching for that book. For the next five years, on and off, I met with no one who had ever heard of, let alone possessed, a copy of *Behind the North Wind.* Book dealers in New York, Los Angeles and Chicago shrugged it off as an impossible search.

On October 6, 1995, I received word that my grand-father had taken a drastic turn for the worse. I felt ashamed that I had given up so easily on my search. In a last-ditch effort, I made a few phone calls. Many messages were left on many answering machines requesting a book called *Behind the North Wind,* a book that apparently did not exist.

The next days I received numerous calls. It seems the book I requested had never been written. However, each of these dealers told me about another book called *At the Back of the North Wind* by George MacDonald, a book all of them had, some in multiple copies. Where were these people five years ago?

Regardless, one was ordered and sent to my parents. The book, as my grandfather related to me, tells the story of a young boy who is terribly frightened of the North Wind. It is cold and dark and completely unexplainable. But somehow the North Wind befriends the child and takes him on a number of adventures. Eventually, the North Wind allows the boy to come visit the land in which it lives. The boy returns with a sort of sublime wisdom rarely encountered in our day and age. He has gained a new understanding of the wind; it is not something to be feared, but accepted.

The book arrived and was taken to my grandfather. All the machines had been turned off, the IVs removed. He had days, maybe hours left. No more could be done. My cousin sat beside him and began reading, reading this tale of a child's understanding of death.

The book was finished, the covers closed. My cousin said, "Well, you got to hear your book one last time." My grandfather, for the first time, looked up from his semi-conscious state, a faint smile forcing its way past his lips.

The relatives in the front yard, I am told, had just commented on how unusually calm this autumn's afternoon had been. At that moment, they were surprised to see the tops of the trees begin to sway as a soul-chilling blast of wind came up over the hill and blew through the yard.

The curtains in the bedroom pressed in and a silence coursed through the house as it was filled with this gale from the North.

And with that, my grandfather closed his eyes and went to sleep . . . forever.

I make my living as a magician. And I'm always asked if I believe in magic, if it is real. I'm always amazed why someone wouldn't. Sure, guys like me have to use tricks and deception, but ultimately our goal is to remind all of us, magician and audience alike, that there are mysteries in the world around us, and there is magic in our lives every moment should we only be willing to open our eyes and see.

Why could I not find that book until right then? Why were so many copies practically thrust upon me? Why did my family who never listens to me choose to do so now? And why was the name of the company from which I purchased the book, a company whose name I did not learn until the credit card statement arrived a month later, why were they the ABRACADABRA book company?

Why did it all happen the way it did?

My grandfather was the one member of my family who always supported my early efforts of performing. He'd tell tales of magicians he had seen in the past, and was always tolerant of a new trick. It is only fitting that he left me with an experience of magic I try so hard now to convey in each and every performance I give. I can only hope this story will help all of us realize the magic our grandparents are in our lives so we may choose to revel in those moments—or memories—while we can.

"That's how she would look when she thought I might be afraid of her," he said to himself. Then he spoke aloud. "I am not afraid of you, dear North Wind," he cried. "See! I am not a bit afraid of you!"

*Stretching out both hands to clasp her he pressed up
close against her and laid his head upon her breast and
then he fell asleep.*

*In the morning, they found little Diamond lying on
the floor of the big attic room—fast asleep, as they
thought, and with such a happy smile on his face. But
when they took him up, they found he was not asleep.
He had gone to that lovely country at the back of the
north wind—to stay.*

Brad Henderson

Sophie's Kids

Live so that your children and grandchildren model your understanding of joy, laughter and love as the elixirs of life.

Laura Spiess

On a warm summer day in late August, I stood with a group of mourners in a small cemetery in the central valley of California. I could hear the pulsing beat of sprinklers in the background overshadowed by the minister's words of condolence to those gathered. Most of us present were Sophie's kids. Although not biologically her children, nonetheless we were loved and cared for by her.

In my case, my brother suffered from a rare bone disease that forced him to be a regular resident of Shriners Children's Hospital in San Francisco. Although the doctors, nurses and other staff gave him wonderful treatment, it was not the same as healing in the comfort and love of your own family. My mother, having recently been diagnosed with M.S., was in another hospital across town ever since delivering me. The pregnancy, once thought to help an M.S. patient, sadly had the reverse effect, depleting her of what little stamina she possessed. My father was working three jobs to pay for the necessary hospital bills and numerous expenses encumbering our family.

Sophie and her husband Emil were friends of our family and lived across the street from us. Sophie loved children. Her children were grown and had children of their own whom she volunteered to care for while their parents worked. I think it was her childlike view of the world that drew her to the care of children. She always thought the world was out to do her good. She was quick to laugh and made time to play every day.

It was about this same time that Sophie began to take in foster children. She simply enjoyed the company of children, and her tender heart went out to the kids who needed a safe nurturing haven. It was her way of making a positive imprint on the world. Sophie was the mama and grandma that every child dreams of having.

My father was really struggling. He would begin his day at six in the morning by feeding one hundred and twenty head of cattle. From nine to five, he sold real estate and insurance and then went directly back out to the farm to feed the animals for the evening. Two or three times a week, he kept the books for several businesses in town in order to earn much-needed cash. I was only eight months old when the majority of care fell on his shoulders. As my mother's health deteriorated to the point of critical care, he felt his whole world was crashing in on him. My father's sister took care of me when she could, as well as a revolving door of baby-sitters trying to pick up the slack. One day his prayers were answered by the advent of Sophie.

He drove his pickup truck into our driveway late one evening only to be greeted by Sophie waving him down with her familiar apron. "Eric, I've got dinner cooking on the stove, and it will be ready for you and the baby as soon as you wash up." An immediate lump formed in the back of his throat as he thanked her for her unsolicited kindness and tried hard not to reveal his emotional state. As Sophie hurried back across the street to tend to dinner, he paid the baby-sitter, then showered and tried to spend a little precious time with me. As much as he wanted to be a good daddy and put up a good front, he was overcome with emotion and shuddered with tears.

He later told me that it was as if his grief and burden were so great that it passed somehow from his heart to mine. Although I didn't understand why he was so sad, I nonetheless began to cry also. He desperately tried to compose himself and me as Sophie knocked on the door and then let herself in with our dinner. Sophie allowed him his dignity by not mentioning the obvious, but instead casually began setting the table while filling him in on the day's wild and hilarious adventures of her brood of kids across the street. He caught himself laughing out loud in spite of the mood he was in and then thought momentarily, *When was the last time I had a good belly laugh?* Sophie, sensing the burden clouding his face again, interrupted his thoughts with an amazing offer. "Eric, why don't you bring little Meladee over to my house in the morning on your way out to the ranch and pick her up again at the end of your day? I start the coffee at five-thirty right on the button, and I've got so many kids playing around my house, one more won't make a bit of difference," she said.

And so I became one of Sophie's kids, a draftee. She fed us breakfast and dinner for almost five years, on and off, and because my father was an accountant, the only form of repayment she would allow was for him to do her yearly taxes.

Sophie loved to sing to Patsy Cline on the radio as she cooked for us in her small, clean kitchen. I felt cherished by her because she called me her "little dolly." I looked forward to her daily dose of laughter, which was her way of coping and poking fun at the mistakes humans make without taking them to heart.

Knowing my mother would be terribly sad being all alone in a hospital away from her family, Sophie started taking pictures of me and would put little footnotes at the bottom of each picture: "This is Meladee taking her first step." "This is Meladee all dressed up to go to church on Easter Sunday." "This is Meladee blowing you a kiss and telling you to get better because she misses you."

As my mother and brother recovered enough to return home and our lives took on at least some sense of normalcy, I took my daily trip across the street to play among that elite tribe of Sophie's—because I belonged. She bought a doll in honor of each child who stayed with her. The collection grew so large that her husband Emil eventually built her a big dollhouse in their backyard to house them all.

As I connect with all the many children turned adults who have come this day to pay their respects and tributes to Sophie, I'm overwhelmed with emotion like my father so many years ago, not because at age eighty-seven she passed on, but because here was a woman of great love, a lifeguard without a pool, who threw us a lifeline of unconditional kindness and hope. Sophie made the world a better place—one kid at a time. Sophie, my foster grandma.

Meladee McCarty

The New Family on Walton's Mountain

I had always dreamed of having a big family. I loved watching *The Waltons* on television during my childhood, and especially loved the part when the family bid each other a good night.

"Good night, John-Boy."

"Good night, Elizabeth."

"Good night, Grandma."

The notion of multigenerations living within the same household fascinated me. I longed to come home from school and have a "Grandma Walton" to make me homemade cookies and help me with my homework.

Close to thirty years after the Waltons set up housekeeping on Walton's Mountain, I am at long last living my dream. My friends think I'm crazy, but I am finding it to be a wonderful experience—for me, as well as for our five children.

It all happened quite by chance. My husband and I lived a busy life—as parents to five children, my husband owning his own business, and me running a business within our home. Weekdays were a barrage of shuttling children from dawn until well past dusk. Weekends found us in church and Sunday school, as well as completing a seemingly endless list of household tasks. Life was good. We were all very happy.

Shortly before Thanksgiving, my father-in-law suffered a mini-stroke and began a rapid decline. His health was poor. By December, he was in a nursing home. We bolstered my mother-in-law's spirits and got her through the holidays. Life was a bit more chaotic, but we managed quite well. However, shortly after Christmas my mother-in-law become ill, too.

By January she was confined to a nursing home, although we were told her complications would eventually subside. By March she came to live with us.

"How can you find the time to do that?" surprised friends would ask.

"Isn't it an awful lot of work?" others would insist.

"What do the kids think about this?"

I must admit, I was a bit astonished by their reactions. Everyone seemed to automatically assume that this sudden change in our lives was a negative one, and that our lives would be forever changed by it.

Things certainly have changed. However I have yet to discover the negatives in this situation. For starters, this is the life I dreamed of living. It doesn't sound glamorous, or even particularly exciting, but it's one that has appealed to me for decades. My mother-in-law is a wonderful addition to our household, and quite frankly, I hope she's with us for a long time.

I guess you could say we were in an optimal point in our family life to endure such a lifestyle modifications. Our oldest son had an apartment. Our oldest daughter was away at her freshman year in college. We had a spare bedroom.

We did a bit of shuffling around to accommodate Grammie. It was decided that our youngest daughter, Elizabeth, would move into Judy's (our college-age daughter) bedroom. Grammie would take Elizabeth's room. It was closer to the bathroom, and nearer to our own room, should she need help in the night.

This was a smooth transition, as a nine-year old moving into her eighteen-year-old sister's bedroom is deemed "pretty cool." Some of the other transitions weren't quite as smooth, such as scheduling showers and bath times. Grammie needed the bathroom frequently, and was automatically given first dibs on the option to use the bathroom. Grammie also has an oxygen tank for round-the-clock use, and our home is filled with oxygen lines. That was a slight problem at first, but we quickly convinced the dog that chewing on them wasn't an option.

Mealtime in our home has always been an ordeal. With five kids, a couple of friends, plus the adults in the family, there were very few evenings when I fed fewer than eight people. Most nights there were ten. Adding one more to our table was a breeze. And adding one who enjoyed and praised my meals was a treasure!

I still believe to this very day that the addition of Grammie to our household has far more benefits than complications. I am thrilled to pieces for our children. They are learning firsthand the fine art of compassion for the elderly. They are learning patience and tolerance, too. I am so proud when I observe them talking slowly and clearly so that Grammie can understand them, and I am proud of how my youngest boy always asks Grammie first, before he takes his turn in the bathroom.

"Grammie, do you need the bathroom?" Jonathan will ask. "I'm going to take a shower now if you're all set."

He's seven.

Grammie, on the other hand, is a joy. I have never met a more appreciative person in my life. She is grateful for her meals, her room and the company she now has twenty-four hours a day. And I am thrilled to get to know the woman who gave me my precious husband. It has been a bonding experience based on gratitude, respect and love. I look upon caring for her as a privilege, and I enjoy the time I spend with her.

We may not be living on the top of a mountain. And we don't grow our own food or sew our own clothes. I'm not nearly creative enough for that. However when we go to bed at night, I feel doubly blessed. No, we're not the Waltons. In fact we're a long, long way from reaching an ideal such as that.

But when our lights go out at night (probably much later than the Waltons' lights did!) I whisper a prayer of thanks for the many loved ones underneath our roof. And we typically say our good nights in the kitchen, or while tucking a child into bed. However late at night, when I'm ready to fall asleep, I smile. And I am able to convince myself that the sounds I hear are merely those of my loving family and their appreciation for one another.

"Good night, Jonathan."

"Good night, Elizabeth."

"Good night, Jim."

"Good night, Grammie."

And with that I close my eyes in peaceful respite.

Kimberly Ripley

9

TOO BUSY FOR THE ROCKING CHAIR

There is a fountain of youth and it is in your mind, in your talents, in the creativity you bring to your life and the people you love. When you learn to tap this resource, you will have truly defeated age.

Sophia Loren

The Rodeo Grandmas

The sky is my ceiling and the ground is my carpet.

Judy Golladay

Did you ever read an article in a magazine or newspaper about someone so very interesting that you really wished you could meet them personally? Me, too. That has happened many times, but I thought I'd never have the opportunity to follow through. Recently, however, I read a story about four ladies called, "The Rodeo Grandmas." Dressed in boots, ten-gallon hats, chaps, vests and carrying lariats, they seemed to be the embodiment of all that was and is good about the West. Tough enough to work outdoors on the range, skilled enough to win trick roping contests, tender enough to touch the hearts of so many people—these ladies had a twinkle in their eyes and an openness in their smiles, which came jumping off that magazine's pages and simply got to me. I decided that this was it, the moment to take thought and turn it into action. I ordered an airline ticket to Ellensburg, Washington, and called the Rodeo Grandmas to see if I'd be welcome.

"Come on ahead! The ladies will be delighted to meet you!" said their spokesperson, Mollie Morrow, a photographer in their town. Molly picked me up at the airport and treated me to a short history of the group on our ride from Yakima. Even with her thorough introduction, I was not quite prepared to meet these unusual ladies.

Molly took me to her studio where I met Lorraine, Janis, Chloe and Peggy. Sitting around the small studio were the smilingest, most welcoming group I've met in a very long time. The Rodeo Grandmas, from sixty-five to eighty-nine, had been selected by an advertising agency that was designing a new series of ads for the Washington Mutual Bank in 1993. The agency had wanted a series of unusual people to highlight—trying to make the connection that their bank was "something different" from the ordinary. They'd put out a call for grandmas—grandmas who could ride and rope and even compete in rodeos. Nearly thirty women from this area had shown up and, within a few hours, the producers had unerringly selected four women who seemed to embody a special spirit—independence, high energy, high skills and toughness mixed with tenderness.

They shot their commercial and left. It was a one-shot deal. Washington Mutual's series would show many other kinds of special, unusual people. But when it aired, the reaction was dramatic: Everyone wanted to see more of those "rodeo grandmas"!

The agency came back and shot more commercials. And, bit by bit, the Rodeo Grandmas became a tight-knit group. The producers had chosen well. Somehow they clicked as a group. One of their number, Judy Golladay, had revealed to the group, and to the producers, that she'd just been diagnosed with breast cancer. Despite that, they all agreed she'd continue as a part of the group. She was having radiation and chemotherapy even as the commercials were being shot. For five months out of every year, she had lived out on the range, with just her horse and dog as company. She was simply a cowgirl, in touch with the earth as few modern Americans are anymore. She spoke of the sky as her ceiling and the ground as her carpeting. Perhaps that sounds corny to someone citified, but Judy meant it and lived it. When the going got tough, she'd climb up on her horse and head out for the hills with her dog and soak in the peacefulness she found in that environment.

There was good news: The treatments had worked! Judy's cancer went into remission. And the Rodeo Grandmas began a series of appearances all over the northwest. Wherever Washington Mutual needed them to appear, they'd show up in full regalia, riding in on horseback, roping and hollering, "Yippie-ty-yi!" and "Howdy, Buckaroos!" They enjoyed playing with the stereotypes and making them real. Pretty soon they began receiving invitations to lead the opening parade at rodeos or to appear at shopping malls and hospitals and retirement homes.

What a deep chord they struck in western hearts! As they'd ride into the arena leading the parade, you could hear the crowd noise change: A dull roar became louder, more focused, more joyous. You could track their location by the change in the sound from the audience: "They're here, the Rodeo Grandmas!" Cheers rose spontaneously, children waved, everyone was excited. Little kids came up to them demanding (and getting) hugs.

Once, on the way to the airport for yet another appearance in another city, there was a major traffic jam. All cars were stopped. The grandmas were sitting quietly in their van waiting for the jam to clear. Suddenly, the occupants in a nearby car spotted them. There was a tap at the window of their van. "Are you the Rodeo Grandmas?" the driver of another car, standing in the road, asked. "IT'S

THE RODEO GRANDMAS!!!" he shouted to all the other cars. "IT'S REALLY THEM!" And there, in the roadway, cars stopped bumper-to-bumper, and a crowd formed, cheering for them and requesting autographs.

At their appearances, children line up to learn roping—throwing their lariats at a practice steer and lighting up with joy when they make it. And there, over at the end of the line of Rodeo Grandmas, is Lorraine, sitting comfortably, with a line of kids waiting to be taught how to yodel.

"Something about being a grandma and being up on a horse seems to be the attraction," said Peggy, seventy-four, an accomplished trick roper. "They just think that some-one on a horse has to be honest." At twenty she was a Rodeo Princess and met a famous trick rider, Monte Montana, who took a liking to her and sent her a gift of a trick-riding saddle. Her rodeo career took off. But life has a way of interrupting one's plans, and she got married, became a secretary and raised four children. "I used to do the Cossack Drag," she told me. "Some people call it the Suicide Drag, but I'm not doing trick riding now. I also used to spin four ropes at once. One I held in my mouth, one on my foot and one in each hand. Today I just do three. You've got to know what you're capable of," she confided.

Janis, at sixty-five, does team roping with a partner, catching steers in competition. In fact, she competes in events with her grandson! "When I was born, my dad sold a horse off for eighty dollars to pay the hospital bill. That was a lot of money then. So horses have always been in my blood. My dad didn't have any sons, so my sister and I became the boys of the family." Then she added an afterthought, as though I might think her too much the tomboy, "We can be real ladylike, too, you know." I nodded my agreement. "My dad called me, 'Toughie,' and he taught me how to ride. I've learned to draw strength from my horses. You have a relationship with your horse, you see, and if you've got tears to shed, your horse will listen and be there for you. It's hard to explain to anyone who hasn't had this experience, but it's really true." All the ladies agreed.

Chloe said, "I've heard it said that 'the best thing for the insides of a man is the outside of a horse.' The relationship with your horses is almost therapeutic. In fact, when Judy's cancer returned and she knew how bad it was, she saddled up and took her horse and dog up into the hills for one more time. She spent some weeks up there and it gave her a lot of peace."

Chloe replaced Judy in the group. "I was kind of the wrangler—Lorraine's my mom, and I was going to all the Rodeo Grandmas' events anyway, so they kind of corralled me into it. And I love being in the Rodeo Grandmas with my mom." She patted Lorraine's knee. "Kinda amazing, huh? Sometimes when we're at a show, and we get set up to teach roping and stuff, the kids come running at us in waves and surround us. It's an incredible feeling to see that, and they all seem to want to touch my mom." Lorraine grins at me.

Lorraine met her husband at a stock show in 1928 and is now not only a grandmother of eleven, she's a great-grandmother of nineteen. Her horse is a little too spirited for her now, but she does ride occasionally. Still, she is ready to teach you how to yodel and will give you a hug at the drop of a ten-gallon hat.

The Rodeo Grandmas are not media people, although they've been affected by their media appearances. They've retained their hometown values and style, despite being on *Entertainment Tonight, The Rosie O'Donnell Show,* and on countless radio and TV interviews.

You get a clear message from being with these ladies that they don't sit around fretting about "the meaning of life." Instead, they take action, and they know that life is meaningful. As Lorraine says, "We only did what had to be done. There's nothing special in that. You do the tasks the Lord puts in front of you."

Peggy added, "You have to have something to get up for in the morning." It was clearly the secret of these gals' healthiness and continued strength, that their lives had given them purpose and continue to do so. Chloe smiled and said, "I've learned to put my heart into what I'm doing." Her mom looked at her proudly, smiling, too. Janis continued, "When you sit in the rocking chair, you just don't get anywhere."

"I think I was born to be a Rodeo Grandma," Peggy declared, looking serious. "Everything in my life seemed to be aimed in this direction. I knew there was something special going to be in my life, and look, here it is!" And she tells me that none of the Rodeo Grandmas has ever broken more than a finger or a toe and that Lorraine has never spent the night in a hospital. "Builds your muscles, expands your chest, makes you breathe more deeply—and that's just when you get on the horse. Go riding a bit and you'll really get some exercise. It's a good, clean life."

It was the end of a glorious day, spent in the company of these tough and tender ladies, and I really didn't want to leave. Each one hugged me, and I readily hugged back. "Lorraine," I said, choking up a bit, "I've just about run out of grandmas in my life. I wonder if you'd be my grandma?"

She beamed at me and gave me an extra squeeze, "Why shore, honey, you can be my little buckaroo!"

On the trip back home I was still filled with the experience of being with them and pondered what I'd learned, or maybe relearned. It was clear that they'd lived a lifestyle that was healthy and unambiguous. What had to be done had to be done, no two ways about it. They had built fun and humor into every day whenever possible. They had been the kind of people you can count on—and there's something powerfully reassuring in being around people like that. They'd not retired from life but were still actively engaged in it, every day. Connecting with people and making a difference in their lives have kept them going, too. Although their lives had most of the same elements in them before, each had been profoundly changed by becoming a Rodeo Grandma. It enabled them to see themselves on a wider stage, and gave them an opportunity to be a model for others, whether they were kids or grandparents. How to live a life with integrity, how to organize yourself so that the important things got done— these were not inconsequential things. But they don't preach these concepts; they simply live them day by day.

I wasn't kidding when I asked Lorraine to be my grandma, for my own are long gone, and there's something missing in my life, too: someone older and wiser, someone who also knows when it's time to give a hug or share a grin. I'm making plans to go visit Grandma Lorraine, and, who knows, she just might teach me to yodel!

Hanoch McCarty

More Whipped Cream, Please

I have a new delightful friend,
I'm almost in awe of her;
When we first met I was impressed,
By her bizarre behavior.

That day I had a date with friends,
We met to have some lunch;
Mae had come along with them,
All in all . . . a pleasant bunch.

When the menus were presented,
We ordered salads, sandwiches and soups;
Except for Mae who circumvented,
And said, "Ice cream, please. Two scoops."

I was not sure my ears heard right,
And the others were aghast;
Along with heated apple pie,
Mae smiled, completely unabashed.

We tried to act quite nonchalant,
As if people did this all the time;

But when our orders were brought out
I did not enjoy mine.

I could not take my eyes off Mae,
As her pie à la mode went down;
The other ladies showed dismay,
They ate their lunches and they frowned.

Well, the next time I went out to eat,
I called and invited Mae;
My lunch contained white tuna meat,
She ordered a parfait.

I smiled when her dish I viewed,
She asked if she amused me;
I answered, "Yes, you do,
And you also do confuse me.

"How come you order rich desserts
When I feel I must be sensible?"
She laughed and said, with wanton mirth,
"I am tasting all that's possible.

"I try to eat the food I need,
And do the things I should;
But life's too short, my friend, indeed,
I hate missing out on something good.

"This year I realized I was old,"
She grinned, "I've not been this old before;
So, before I die, I've got to try,
Those things for years I have ignored.

"I've not smelled all the flowers yet,
And too many books I have not read;
There's more fudge sundaes to wolf down,
And kites to be flown overhead.

"There's many malls I have not shopped,
I've not laughed at all the jokes;
I've missed a lot of Broadway hits,
And potato chips and Cokes.

"I want to wade again in water,
And feel ocean spray upon my face;
Sit in a country church once more,
And thank God for his grace.

"I want peanut butter every day,
Spread on my morning toast;
I want untimed long-distance calls,
To the folks I love the most.

"I've not cried at all the movies yet,
Nor walked in the morning rain;
I need to feel wind in my hair,
I want to fall in love again.

"So, if I choose to have dessert,
Instead of having dinner;
If I should die before nightfall,
You'd have to say I died a winner.

"That I missed out on nothing,
That I had my heart's desire;
That I had that final chocolate mousse,
Before my life expired."

With that, I called the waitress over,
"I've changed my mind, it seems;"
I said, "I want what she is having,
Only add some more whipped cream!"

Virginia (Ginny) Ellis

Why Not?

A CD player headset drowned out the background noise as I worked in the living room at my computer. My fingers rushed over the keys as fast as my mediocre typing skills would allow, and my unblinking eyes stared at the monitor. Working in the living room of a small house that is home to three adults and two young children has forced me to develop a new level in my ability to concentrate. I was busy, very busy with my work. I had achieved that state of concentration that allowed me to block out just about anything, a tornado vacuuming up the room around me, if need be.

Then it happened. A tiny rift opened in my concentration as my eye caught a glimpse of an object flying upward through the air. I pulled my mind back to my work. I didn't even look to see what the object was, or what became of it as I sealed the rift. No sooner had I resumed my work, than laughter opened another rift in my concentration. Now I was getting annoyed. My seven-year-old grandson, Zach, was sitting across the room on the couch. His smile faded as I gave him my most stern, "Hush, I'm working" look.

Although I couldn't hear him, I could see that he said,

"Sorry, Nana."

Success—another rift sealed and concentration restored. Sometimes children don't understand that there is a time for play and a time for work. This time is work time and I must get back to it. Clickedy, clickedy over the keys my fingers raced.

Another object whizzed past my peripheral vision, and the music wafting through my headset was no match for Zach's hearty laughter. Now I was really annoyed. Zach was too busy to see my sternest "Hush, I'm working" look. I followed his gaze to the ceiling as he launched another object, a hair scrunchy. With a quick slingshot motion, the hair scrunchy was airborne—whiz, bump, stuck to the popcorn ceiling. Some people like popcorn ceilings. To me, they look as if someone forgot to smooth out the Spackle. I never had any use for a bump-filled ceiling. Zach, on the other hand, had found a use for the ceiling, which now was adorned with a half a dozen hair scrunchies.

Red, purple and green circles clung to the ceiling, some flat up against it and some hanging down.

I lightened up my stern look a bit. "That's very funny but you have to stop now. Scrunchies don't belong on the ceiling."

"But why not? It's fun! I won't break anything."

I was about to tell him to go get the broom so that I could remove the scrunchies, when his words sunk into my head and reminded me of a time when I would have said, "why not?"also. When had I gotten so serious and so busy that I couldn't revel in the joy of a moment? What happened to the woman who would send her young children's friends into fits of giggles upon meeting them for the first time by asking them what they did for work and if they were married and had any children? What happened to the woman who laughed herself silly when her children and husband got into a snowball fight in the kitchen with cookie dough? When did I become so rigid? When did I forget, "Why not?"

Why not indeed! I looked at Zach and couldn't help but smile.

"Can you show me how to do that?"

His face lit up as he showed me how to launch a scrunchy. His laughter filled the air and his eyes sparkled. The ceiling never looked so colorful and happy with all those red, green, purple and yellow circles, some laying flat and some hanging down. I have to admit, Zach was better at it than I. Most of his attempts hit their mark. Most of mine ended up on the floor.

The following morning, I sat at the computer, ready to begin my work. I looked at the scrunchies still clinging to the ceiling and smiled. I certainly had enjoyed our time putting them up there. I decided I would take them down later. That is, until the ceiling lost its grip on one, and it fell, bounced off my shoulder, and onto the floor. Zach's smiling face flashed in my mind's eye. I smiled again. I felt like that woman of years ago who laughed at the cookie dough fight. I picked up the scrunchy and plopped it into my pocket.

When Zach came home from school that day, I was ready. He had given me a precious gift, now it was time to show him that I appreciated it.

"Zach, I've been waiting all day for you. Look what I found on the floor. It's no wonder I can't find these scrunchies when I need them. Please put this away." I handed him the scrunchy and he headed toward the door.

"Zach," I called out to him, "where are you going?"

He turned to me, "I'm going to put the scrunchy away, Nana."

"Please put it where I can find it." I shifted my gaze from his sweet little face to the ceiling. A broad smile spread across his face as he realized what I was asking him to do. Whizzzzzz, bump—up it went. It was perfect!

If you come to my house, beware of falling scrunchies. You may wonder why I keep my scrunchies on the ceiling. Zach knows the answer to that question, and now, so do I—"Why not?"

Christina Coruth

A Grandma Takes Power

I am not afraid of storms, for I am learning how to sail my ship.

Louisa May Alcott

When my grandmother was eighty-nine years old she was having problems with her heart. My family went with her to the cardiologist who told her that she had a serious heart condition that required surgery. However, the eminent physician warned that because of my grandmother's age, complications could arise. He went on to say that because of her age, my grandmother would have a 40 percent chance of having a heart attack during the operation, a 35 percent chance of having a stroke, a 30 percent chance of dying on the operating room table . . .

My grandmother, shocked, quickly interrupted the doctor and said, "Doctor, as long as you're talking about statistics, I have one for you: THERE'S A 100 PERCENT CHANCE OF YOU NOT OPERATING ON ME!" With these words, my grandmother got up and left the doctor's office.

My grandmother might be stubborn, but she's no fool. So the next day she went to another doctor where he, too, told her she needed surgery. He also stated that her age might cause a problem, BUT he was telling her in a way that was positive as opposed to the negative way of the previous day.

My grandmother then asked the doctor, "If I were your mother, what would you recommend?"

The doctor walked up to her, smiled, put his arm around her, and said, "Mom, let's have the operation!"

She had the operation and came out fine! Her positive attitude (which is vital to her and everyone) added many wonderful, happy years to enjoy life and her family.

Michael Jordan Segal

The Granny Hook

The events of our lives happen in a sequence in time, but in their significance to ourselves they find their own order . . . the continuous thread of revelation.

Eudora Welty

In looking back upon it now, I believe it was sheer attitude when I confronted our grandchildren at various times and in various settings after an accident in which I lost my arm in 1993. It was essential that everyone, especially the twelve grands, feel perfectly comfortable around me. A good deal of this rested with their very loving and savvy parents. After all, their granny wasn't all that different. I hadn't suddenly sprouted two granny heads. The surgeons had done an admirable job remodeling my granny face and most of my granny ear, and as it turned out, children handled the granny makeover so much better than friends. I thought it remarkable.

Our youngest daughter, Katie, was a marvel. She had organized a soapbox regatta and neighborhood picnic at her lake home some six hundred miles from our Montana ranch. Because of my artsy ways and her dad's building skills, she informed me that the children had elected us to design and build a vessel from any scraps we could uncover in her garage and basement. It was a mere one month after a final prosthesis fitting, but I was so happy to be amongst the living, we quickly accepted the invitation.

Our darling grandkids greeted us that Friday night as we've never been greeted before. They giggled and laughed over my prosthetic clumsiness and wasted no time christening me "Granny Hook." I loved it. At bedtime there appeared four inquisitive onlookers who seemed fascinated watching me wrestle with shoes and zippers, buttons and earrings. They insisted upon helping and were dying to see how the new bunglesome and awkward contraption worked. After donning pj's I invited everyone in, and we had "Prosthesis 101" in the fine art of wearing and managing a hook with various attachments.

The next morning I showed up at breakfast wearing what I like to call my "go to meetin'" myoelectric arm complete with a soft rubber hand and painted fingernails. By flexing my muscles against electrodes inside the fitted arm, I could make the wrist turn back and forth and even around and around. This was a first major effort for me; I needed more practice but I made a huge hit. The girls were eager to begin showing Granny Hook off to the neighborhood and begged us to stay longer for their class show-and-tells. Maybe another time.

By mid-morning my "farm-and-ranch" hook was ready to go to work looking for building scraps. After gathering odds and ends of planks, inner tubes and a sheet for a sail, our pirate ship began to take shape. Somehow Papa anchored an eight-foot piece of PVC pipe for a mast at the bow, the kids painted a skull and crossbones on the flag, cut out black-paper eye-patches and appropriately painted all our faces. With the swing of a well-targeted plastic water bottle, the creation was christened "The Granny Hook." There was nary a breath of air for sailing so the boys found light pieces of wood for paddles, desplintering the ends with duct tape.

As the afternoon wore on, any number of crazy looking homemade vessels appeared at water's edge. Lavishly decorated one-man inner tubes seemed to populate the beach in great quantity. We wondered if our big cumbersome raft would be sluggish in the water. Nonetheless, the voyagers donned life jackets, and Captain Granny Hook hitched up her arm a notch and climbed aboard just behind the mainsail while the eye-patched maties were hoisted aboard from behind.

As we sat amongst the flotilla bobbing up and down in the water, it occurred to me that my husband, my daughter, my son-in-law and his dear folks still had confidence in my life-saving skills (arm or no arm) to entrust me with our four precious kids in the middle of a lake. It was a handicap moment in my life I'll not forget.

At last the whistle sounded and all were off like a herd of turtles, some happily capsizing and sinking ten feet from shore. We lagged behind until Captain Hook coached the crew to commence rapid rhythmic paddling. The Granny Hook picked up knots just before the halfway buoy but lost big water in the turn. Three ships now led, and our rhythmic paddlers were tiring. It would not be enough to win. What to do? What to do? In timely fashion the captain shouted an "abandon ship" order, and the crew reluctantly slipped over the side to hang onto the back and kick their hearts out.

The Granny Hook barely overtook the fleet and she won!

That glorious weekend was the beginning of many regattas on Katie's lake.

Kathe Campbell

Grandma Lois

We're only young once, but with humor, we can be immature forever.

Art Gliver

A few years ago my husband and I were riding in the car with our friends Denny and Laurie Montgomery and Grandma Lois, Denny's mother. Having known the family for years, we were always braced for whatever Lois would say. She was about seventy-five at that time . . . somewhat hard of hearing, but alert and spunky as anything. Driving through an older part of North Seattle, we passed some weathered brick buildings that had advertisements and pictures painted on the sides of them. Coming up on our right was an old-fashioned eye clinic or something . . . an optometrist's office, probably. On the side of the building was a graphic painting of a gigantic *eye* with very special details—the pupil, iris, eyelashes. . . .

Lois barked out from the back seat: "DENNY, WHAT IS THAT!?"

"On that building, you mean? It's a picture of an eye, I think, Mom."

"WHAT is it? A picture of what?"

"It's an EYE, Mom . . . a picture of an eye."

This irritated Lois for some reason . . . a giant picture of an eye evidently didn't sit right with her. She seemed to find it ridiculous and annoying.

"Well! (tsk!) An EYE?! Why on Earth would anybody paint an EYE like that on a building!?" She rolled her eyes and abruptly crossed her arms.

Denny loved Lois dearly, and he never seemed to tire of her cynical nature. He was patient no matter what was bothering her, and something usually was.

"Well, the guy's probably an eye doctor, Mom, and that's his advertisement. It's probably an optometrist's office, or something. Maybe he's an optician."

"Well for heaven's sake!" Lois sniffed, thoroughly disgusted. "Humph!" She was shaking her head. "Aren't ya' just glad he wasn't a gynecologist!!!?"

Patricia S. Mays

"I'm all dressed for our drive
to Grandma's house."

Ageless

You know you're getting old when you stoop to tie your shoes and wonder what else you can do while you're down there.

George Burns

It was Sunday morning. My grandmother and I were getting ready for church. Lately, I've been noticing her paying a little more attention to what she was wearing, examining herself for longer periods of time in front of the mirror.

"Is everything okay, Grams?"

She checked if her earrings were on straight and if her blush perfectly matched the color of her dainty pink dress.

"You have no idea what it's like," she said.

"What what's like?"

"To be old and wrinkled."

I chuckled. "Gram, it doesn't matter what you look . . . I mean, you're . . . seventy-five!"

She turned away from me and I immediately realized my insensitivity had hurt her feelings. "I'm sorry. I didn't mean seventy-five in a bad way."

"Oh, it's not you I'm trying to impress."

Without speaking further, we drove the short distance to church. I felt horribly guilty, wondering if I should have told her how I really felt about her attractive appearance.

I trailed into the church behind her while a handsome gentleman usher took her arm. Jim, a seventy-four-year-old widower, often walked my grandmother down to her seat. He was so sweet to her and always made sure he had saved a pew for us near the front so we could clearly see the pastor.

Then like a lightning bolt, I understood what was really upsetting my grandmother! She wasn't depressed or really mad at me! She was feeling insecure because she had fallen in love in her golden years.

"How are you, Loretta?" Jim inquired.

"Well."

"My brother came for a surprise visit," Jim explained. "I'm sorry I missed you at bingo. I heard you won, though. Congratulations."

I scooted down into our pew, determining that Jim must have been asking about my grandmother's whereabouts on Wednesday as well.

Tenderly gazing down into her dark brown eyes, he escorted her to my side. After a moment of embracing her hand, he shakily pulled a crumpled piece of paper out of his pocket and placed it in her fingertips.

I waited until he walked away. "What does it say, Grams?"

She blushed. "It has his phone number and says to call him if I'd like to go to the singles dance on Saturday."

I fought back tears of joy witnessing her brilliant smile wipe away all signs of wrinkles. "See, someone else knows how beautiful you are, too, Grams; you're still as perfect as you ever were."

"He just needs a dancing partner, that's all."

I countered, "Gram, he wants to waltz with someone who cares about him."

Her face lit up. "Maybe you're right."

"I know I am."

Watching my grandmother and Jim dance that night was something that took my breath away. My boyfriend Louis and I were worried about her and decided to drop by. With one glance, all our fears disappeared. They were swinging like teenagers, laughing and holding each other underneath the twinkle of the stars.

Nine months later, at the age of seventy-four, Jim dropped down on one knee and asked for my seventy-five-year-old grandmother's hand in marriage.

"Yes," she immediately replied. "But . . . there's just one thing."

"What's that?" Jim wiped the tears from her rosy cheeks.

"I don't do windows anymore."

He clapped with excitement. And before a man of God, my family and I came together, filling his house to watch them wed by candlelight.

It's been eight years now, and Jim and Loretta are still just as happy as the night they danced until dawn. Every time I see them together, I'm reminded that love is ageless. It's as priceless at eighty as it is at twenty, perhaps even more.

Michele Wallace Campanelli

The Marriage License

I think sometimes a person's spirit is so strong that it never completely leaves the Earth but remains scattered forever among all those who love them.

Chris Crandall

Grandpa was a practical joker. He was a successful businessman, farmer and entrepreneur, but his most memorable trait was his sense of playfulness. He made you want to be around him, and if nothing else, you wanted to see what was going to happen next.

Grandpa Eric, at eighty-seven, needed to renew his notary license and called upon his friend and partner Terry Parker to drive him to the Sacramento County recorder's office to complete the task. Terry and her father had worked with Eric in the real-estate business for years and were well acquainted with his shenanigans. They knew to look for the twinkle in his eye, which was their cue to go along with anything Eric said or did. The payoff for going along with the practical joke was a guarantee of a good belly laugh and a terrific story to tell anyone who came into the office.

Terry and Eric must have been a comical sight together. Eric's mobility was questionable, his sight was undependable, he was sporting a big Stetson hat, two hearing aids and an unlit cigar. Terry supported his arm walking up the steps of the county recorder's office, but it was challenging for the two of them to maneuver through the door. Terry was nine months pregnant with a sixty-inch waist, swollen feet and a bladder reduced by pressure to the size of a small cocktail olive. They just barely made it through the office door only to notice the long, long line up to the records and licenses window. Eric didn't mind waiting because he was already working on how to turn the wait into a little fun.

It was a busy day in the recorder's office and the staff were working as quickly as they could, fielding many questions, some ridiculous, handing out numerous forms and directing people who were completely lost to other offices.

After about a thirty-minute wait, Terry and Eric made it to the front of the line only to be coolly greeted by an exasperated state employee. Sighing impatiently, she asked, "How can I help you?" From her attitude, it was clear that she was thinking that this old man had probably come in with his daughter to get a power-of-attorney form and could have saved everybody a lot of time if they'd just called ahead and picked one up at their local stationery store. In spite of his age, Eric was a very sharp guy and figured out the woman's impression of him at first glance and couldn't resist the chance to have a little fun. He was thinking, *Let the games begin!*

"We're here for a marriage license!" he demanded loudly as he pounded his fist on the counter. "And speed it up! We've been waiting in line for a half an hour and as you can see my bride-to-be here can't stand much longer." The look of total shock (and negative judgment) on the clerk's face as she processed this bit of surprising information could have stopped a speeding locomotive in its tracks. She was so befuddled that she couldn't even muster up enough composure to cover her shock and said, "Why I thought I'd seen everything in my thirty years of working here, but this takes the prize!"

Eric pulled himself up to his full height, puffed his chest out, looked her in the eye and said, "I'm not getting any younger here, so let's not take all day about it." Terry had a decision to make: let this gal off the hook or go along with the joke. She was also doing everything in her power not to burst into laughter at the ridiculous request, not to mention the hilarious look on the clerk's face. She went for it. She put on her best game face, one that resembled a desperate gold-digging bride who'd found her sugar daddy at the eleventh hour of the game. She also looked very uncomfortable—which was not part of the joke, since she was afraid she was going to laugh so hard that her "tears" would run down her legs.

Eric let that poor clerk run all over that office looking for a marriage license. She was so disconcerted that a simple daily task turned into the search for the Lost Ark. The clerk stopped at each secretary's desk, soundlessly whispering to them, shaking her head and pointing to Terry and Eric. Shocked stares and rolled eyes refocused on the odd couple.

At long last the clerk came back with the necessary paperwork and with an incredulous expression asked Eric if he knew that in the state of California he needed blood tests to get married in case of infectious diseases. "I don't know where she's been before I got hooked up with her, but at my age I guess I'm ready to take the leap of faith. What do you think?" An unrecognizable sound came out of the clerk's mouth as she shoved the paperwork in his direction. Eager to go to the ladies' room, Terry was wondering just how long Eric was going to keep the clerk in suspense when suddenly he smiled and said, "*Gotcha! We're really here to renew my notary license!*"

At this point Terry was sure the practical joke had run its course and dashed to the ladies' room, not a moment too soon. When she returned to collect Eric and his renewed license, the entire office was laughing with him, including the clerk who was a good sport considering the joke was at her expense. After that day, whenever he had any business in the recorder's office he asked for her by name.

Meladee McCarty

The Gold Locket

There is no duty so much underrated as the duty of being happy.

Robert Louis Stevenson

It was a time of the Great Depression in the early 1930s. I was a boy of eleven years living on a small farm in northwest Missouri. That summer, it was decided that I would be sent to live with my grandfather, who had a farm some distance away. There were six of us children at home. My leaving would make one less mouth to feed, and besides, Grandfather could use the help on his farm. I tearfully packed my meager belongings and said good-bye to my mother and Beggar, my collie dog.

Things weren't so bad at Grandfather's. I had my own room, and there was lots of good food, which I relished. I did my best to help Grandfather that summer. I harnessed the horses, mowed and raked, and worked in the garden. Stacking hay was a big job for an eleven-year-old boy, and I worked from sunup until sundown. In those days, hard work was a virtue, and very quickly I earned my grandfather's respect and admiration.

Grandmother had passed away quietly in her sleep three years earlier. I could tell that Grandfather missed her terribly. At times he would get moody and quiet. At other times, he would sit for hours, oblivious to all things in the living room, except for the picture of Grandmother that sat on the buffet. Grandfather was getting careless about wearing the same overalls too long between washings, and not shaving or getting his hair cut.

One morning while we were in the garden hoeing weeds, a car drove in the driveway. It was my Aunt Lucille, my grandmother's favorite sister. She had another lady in the car with her. They both got out, and Lucille greeted Grandfather with a warm hug, and said, "Joseph, you know that your dear, departed wife would not have wanted you and this house to be so untidy so I brought my friend Mary Ann to help you once a week." Grandfather reluctantly nodded his head, but I could see that the idea of someone else coming into the house to clean up did not set well with him.

I liked Mary Ann. She was light-hearted and gave a new spirit to what had been a drab setting. Grandfather seemed not to notice her and would arrange to be away from the house while she was there. Despite Mary Ann's best efforts, Grandfather never complimented her good cooking or the fact that she kept the house sparkling. He kept any conversation with Mary Ann to a bare minimum, but I could still see the longing way that she looked at my grandfather. I knew that she wished for more attention from him.

One afternoon Mary Ann seemed unusually quiet. After lunch, she called me back into the kitchen. "I don't know why your grandfather doesn't like me, but he just doesn't seem to. I will be going to another job after next week." I watched as a tear spilled down her cheek. "What did I do wrong?" she whispered as she regained her composure.

"It's not what you did; it's what you didn't do," I replied. I told Mary Ann that I had known Grandfather all of my life. Number one: Never wash his pipe in the dishpan, no matter how bad it smells. Number two: A good mincemeat pie will turn him into putty in her hands. Number three: Grandfather liked Grandmother's hair best when she wore it down. And number four: Grandfather would make friends with a cactus if it would sit on a log with him on a moonlit night and listen to the hounds run. Grandfather always said that the sound of those dogs running at night was the sweetest music this side of heaven. I would listen and listen, but in all honesty, it just sounded like dogs yapping to me.

You might have guessed that the very next time Mary Ann came to the house, she brought the most scrumptious mincemeat pie that I had ever tasted. Her chestnut hair was flowing down her back. But the most amazing thing was the conversation that evolved across the kitchen table when Mary Ann talked to us about "Old Bugler," a silver-throated hound that she had raised as a pup.

I knew changes were in the making when Grandfather would dress up a little and always be clean-shaven on the day Mary Ann would be there. If I had any doubt, it all faded away when I looked out my open window at two in the morning, to see the two of them, hand in hand, walking back from a hunt with the dogs.

After that night, Grandfather found more and more excuses for Mary Ann to come to the farm. What had started as one day a week became nearly every day that they spent together. It also became apparent to me that my grandfather did not know the finer points of courting a girl. A date with Mary Ann consisted of taking her to the livestock auction in Maryville, but she never complained. I think she even liked it.

The days of summer were fast fading into fall when Grandfather took me with him to Maryville. I had no idea what the trip was for, until we went to the jewelry counter at Holtz. I watched intently as Grandfather selected a beautiful, gold locket with a gold chain. This would seal a relationship between Grandfather and Mary Ann for the rest of their years. They were married at Thanksgiving time, and happily lived out their years on the farm where they had met.

Today I treasure that gold locket and chain. When I look at it, it reminds me of a time long ago, when I played a small part in bringing two lonely people together to share life and love, and to rediscover the gold in their golden years.

Bruce Carmichael, D.C.

Who Is Jack Canfield?

Jack Canfield is one of America's leading experts in the development of human potential and personal effectiveness. He is both a dynamic, entertaining speaker and a highly sought-after trainer. Jack has a wonderful ability to inform and inspire audiences toward increased levels of self-esteem and peak performance.

He is the author and narrator of several bestselling audio- and videocassette programs, including *Self-Esteem and Peak Performance, How to Build High Self-Esteem, Self-Esteem in the Classroom* and *Chicken Soup for the Soul—Live.* He is regularly seen on television shows such as *Good Morning America, 20/20* and *NBC Nightly News.* Jack has co-authored numerous books, including the *Chicken Soup for the Soul* series, *Dare to Win* and *The Aladdin Factor* (all with Mark Victor Hansen), *100 Ways to Build Self-Concept in the Classroom* (with Harold C. Wells), *Heart at Work* (with Jacqueline Miller) and *The Power of Focus* (with Les Hewitt and Mark Victor Hansen).

Jack is a regularly featured speaker for professional associations, school districts, government agencies, churches, hospitals, sales organizations and corporations. His clients have included the American Dental Association, the American Management Association, AT&T, Campbell's Soup, Clairol, Domino's Pizza, GE, ITT, Hartford Insurance, Johnson & Johnson, the Million Dollar Roundtable, NCR, New England Telephone, Re/Max, Scott Paper, TRW and Virgin Records. Jack is also on the faculty of Income Builders International, a school for entrepreneurs.

Jack conducts an annual eight-day Training of Trainers program in the areas of self-esteem and peak performance. It attracts educators, counselors, parenting trainers, corporate trainers, professional speakers, ministers and others interested in developing their speaking and seminar-leading skills.

For further information about Jack's books, tapes and training programs, or to schedule him for a presentation, please contact:

Self-Esteem Seminars
P.O. Box 30880
Santa Barbara, CA 93130
phone: 805-563-2935 • fax: 805-563-2945
Web site: *www.chickensoup.com*

Who Is Mark Victor Hansen?

Mark Victor Hansen is a professional speaker who, in the last twenty years, has made over four thousand presentations to more than two million people in thirty-three countries. His presentations cover sales excellence and strategies; personal empowerment and development; and how to triple your income and double your time off.

Mark has spent a lifetime dedicated to his mission of making a profound and positive difference in people's lives. Throughout his career, he has inspired hundreds of thousands of people to create a more powerful and purposeful future for themselves while stimulating the sale of billions of dollars worth of goods and services.

Mark is a prolific writer and has authored *Future Diary*, *How to Achieve Total Prosperity* and *The Miracle of Tithing*. He is the coauthor of the *Chicken Soup for the Soul* series, *Dare to Win* and *The Aladdin Factor* (all with Jack Canfield) and *The Master Motivator* (with Joe Batten).

Mark has also produced a complete library of personal empowerment audio- and videocassette programs that have enabled his listeners to recognize and better use their innate abilities in their business and personal lives. His message has made him a popular television and radio personality with appearances on ABC, NBC, CBS, HBO, PBS, QVC and CNN.

He has also appeared on the cover of numerous magazines, including *Success, Entrepreneur* and *Changes*.

Mark is a big man with a heart and a spirit to match—an inspiration to all who seek to better themselves.

For further information about Mark, please contact:

Mark Victor Hansen & Associates
P.O. Box 7665
Newport Beach, CA 92658
phone: 949-759-9304 or 800-433-2314
fax: 949-722-6912
Web site: *www.chickensoup.com*

Who Is Meladee McCarty?

Meladee is a professional educator and dynamic speaker in the field of special education. She is a Program Specialist for the Sacramento County Office of Education. She works to provide inclusional education settings for children with disabilities and presents a variety of training to educators on Kindness in the Workplace; Communication and Team Building; Self-Esteem in the Classroom; Humor in the Learning Process, The Seven Habits of Highly Effective People and Focusing on the Disruptive Child. She has extensive experience helping schools and other institutions meet the needs of disabled students and workers.

Meladee is the coauthor, with her husband Hanoch McCarty, of *A 4th Course of Chicken Soup for the Soul, Acts of Kindness: How to Make a Gentle Difference, A Year of Kindness: 365 Ways to Spread Sunshine* and *The Daily Journal of Kindness.* They have traveled all over the United States and Norway together working with educators and business professionals on the goal of bringing more kindness and altruism into the world, workplace, home, community and classroom. Meladee and Hanoch have a wonderful time working and playing together. Meladee is a master at using appropriate humor to defuse tension and conflict.

Meladee and her husband Hanoch are the proud parents to McAllister Dodds, Stephanie Dodds, Ethan McCarty, Shayna Hinds, and their granddaughter, Rand Hinds. Of all the many opportunities she has had in her life, being the mother and wife of such a loving family is her most cherished role.

It is Meladee's goal to bring more humor and kindness into the world, creating a positive impact on those with whom she comes in contact. She is deeply touched and encouraged by the contributors to this book and the many wonderful kind and loving acts of altruism they have shared that keeps recreating a world that is a better place for all of us. To contact Meladee for more information about her programs:

The Kindness Revolution
P.O. Box 5
Galt, CA 95632-0005
phone: (209) 745-2212
fax: (209) 745-2252
To order autographed copies of Meladee's books,
call 800-KINDNESS

Who Is Hanoch McCarty?

Hanoch McCarty is an educator and motivator. He is well-known for his high energy and the appropriateness of his examples and stories; the drama and humor of his presentations, and the fact that he always interacts with his audiences in the most exciting way.

He researches and custom designs each presentation to exactly fit the themes and concerns of the group. He simply doesn't give a "cookie-cutter" presentation. He uses high tech to achieve "high touch"—because he believes that you don't reach the audience's minds and memories unless you touch their hearts and tickle their funny bones.

Hanoch gives many presentations each year all over the world. He has spoken in sixteen countries including Canada, mainland China, Japan, Israel and Norway. He has spoken in forty-eight of the fifty states—and he's looking forward to being invited to speak in Alaska and Idaho someday soon.

He speaks to school systems, governmental agencies, conventions, college faculties, professional associations, medical practices, health maintenance organizations, dental groups, hospital staffs, law practices and industry groups. He has spoken to over twenty college faculties in the past two years and to many more public and private school faculties, classified staffs and parent groups. He has spoken to church conventions, teacher training and school opening meetings.

His corporate clients have brought him in to sales meetings, employee and management seminars where his stories and research-based insights have empowered and enlightened audiences from coast-to-coast.

He is the author and coauthor of twenty books and training programs, including: *Self-Esteem in the Classroom; The Experts Speak: A Guide to Teachers of Adolescents;* and *Ten Keys to Successful Parent Involvement.*

Some people say that Hanoch "wrote the book" on motivational speaking—and it's true—he did. It's called, *Motivating Your Audience: Speaking from the Heart* and it's a great summation of all that he's learned in over twenty years as a motivational speaker.

His latest book, *Motivating Your Students: Before You Can Teach Them, You Have to Reach Them,* is an example of his lifelong commitment to the improvement of instruction on all levels.

With his wife Meladee, he is coauthor of four books, including the bestseller, *Acts of Kindness: How to Make A Gentle Difference; A Year of Kindness: 365 Ways to Spread Sunshine; The Daily Journal of Kindness* and the *New York Times* #1 bestseller, *A 4th Course of Chicken Soup for the Soul.*
To contact him, write or call:

Bestspeaker.com
P.O. Box 66
Galt, CA 95632-0066
phone: 209-745-2212
fax: 209-745-2252
e-mail: *hanoch@bestspeaker.com*
Web site: *www.bestspeaker.com*

Contributors

Susan Amerikaner is an author and television writer. Raised in Baltimore, Maryland, Amerikaner moved to California in 1979 to work for Walt Disney Studios. The freelance author and her husband now reside in San Luis Obispo. Their twin sons are both in college.

Faith Andrews Bedford's short stories and essays have been published in numerous magazines; her column "Kids in the Country" appears in *Country Living*. Her most recent book is *The Sporting Art of Frank W. Benson* (Godine, 2000). She divides her year between the Blue Ridge Mountains and Florida.

Sheryl Berk is the senior editor of *A&E Biography Magazine* and the former entertainment editor for *McCall's*. She is the author of numerous books including the *New York Times* bestseller, *Britney Spears' Heart to Heart* (with Ms. Spears). She resides in New York City with her husband, Peter.

Barbara Bloom has worked as a psychiatric social worker for the last twenty years in both the United States and Canada. About two years ago, she became hooked on writing. Now, when she chauffeurs her two sons to their various activities, she keeps a pen and paper handy. She lives in Kingston, Ontario.

Gail C. Bracy was born and raised in Central New York and attended college in Watertown and Geneseo. She returned to college when her children started school and earned a B.S. in Education. She works for the Department of Transportation in Watertown. Her hobbies include writing, singing and spending time with family and friends.

Karen Brandt resides in Ohio with her husband, Kenn. Her son, Anthony, lives in California with his wife, Gladys. Her daughter, Angela, lives in Maryland with husband, Darion, and their four children, Tanisha, Darian, Phyllis and Joshua. Family is an important part of her life, and she loves to write.

Michele Wallace Campanelli, a national bestselling author, was born on the Space Coast of Florida where she still resides with her husband, Louis. She is a graduate of Melbourne High School, Writers Digest School and Keiser College. She is author of *Hero of Her Heart,* published by Blue Note Books, *Margarita* by Hollis Books and numerous short stories. Michele welcomes fans to e-mail her with comments at *mcampanelli@juno.com.*

Kathe Campbell lives with her husband, Ken, on a seven-thousand-foot mountain near Butte, Montana, where they have raised national champion spotted asses. Kathe has contributed to the local newspaper as well as national magazines on the subject of Alzheimer's disease. She is a prolific writer of the month at *www.2theheart.com,* and her Montana artwork is featured as stationery at *www.outlookstationery.com.* Kathe and Ken have three grown children and twelve grandchildren.

Irene (Seida) Carlson is a middle-aged grandmother from Fort Worth, Texas.

She enjoys writing all types of stories from personal stories about her family and herself, to westerns, romance, horror, children's and poems. She is the mother of two daughters and the grandmother of five. This story is very special to her because it is about her oldest grandchild, Justin, who has always been Grandma's angel, and she would like to share this story with you all.

Bruce Carmichael, D.C., was a decorated fighter pilot. He has had a rich and colorful career as a writer, educator, builder, motion-picture producer and physician. He strongly embraces his Christian beliefs. He can be reached at 750 W. Madison, Lebanon, MO 65536. Call 417-532-5094.

Karen Carr lives in rural New Hampshire. She enjoys traveling, walking, reading and spending time with family and friends.

Dr. Lillian Carson is an authority on child development, parenting and grandparenting, and a national spokesperson on grandparenting. She is the author of The Parent's Choice Award Book *The Essential Grandparent: A Guide to Making a Difference* and the first in a forthcoming series, *The Essential Grandparent's Guide to Divorce: Making a Difference in the Family*. Visit her Web site at *www.essentialgrandparent.com*.

Helen Colella is a wife, mother, former teacher and freelance writer living in Colorado with her family. She's also a first-time "card-bearing" grandmother. Helen enjoys her family, traveling and reading. After twenty years in Colorado, she still marvels at the beautiful and majestic scenery of the Rocky Mountains.

Jan Coleman is a busy author whose work has appeared nationally. Her first book is *After the Locusts: Restoring Ruined Dreams, Reclaiming Wasted Years.* Jan is a dynamic speaker who tickles the funny bones and tugs at the heartstrings of her audience. In her speaking and writing, Jan merges her own life's lessons to inspire others. She and her husband live in Northern California. Contact her at *jwriter@hoothill.net.*

Alice Collins and her husband, John, have been blessed and perplexed by four fine sons and one lovely daughter. The aggravation was worth it all, because now they have ten wonderful grandchildren to spoil! Alice, a professional speaker, writes two weekly columns filled with the sentiment and humor of family life.

Barbara Cornish, in her thirty-second year of teaching and marriage, has three boys and one girl, aged twenty-four down to fifteen. She has a love of music, language, nature, photography and dogs. She and her husband have chaperoned their children's Chamber Singers' performances in the major Italian, French and English cathedrals.

Christina Coruth is a writer. She is a contributing editor and a managing editor at *Suite101.com*. Her passions include amateur astronomy and genealogy. She and her husband are lifelong residents of New Hampshire where they raised two children and now share in the joy of two grandchildren.

Brian Crane's daily comic strip "Pickles" was syndicated in April 1990 and the

Sunday version was launched the following year. In 1995 "Pickles" was nominated for "best comic strip of the year" by the National Cartoonists Society. It appears in over 300 newspapers around the world. Crane lives near Reno, Nevada, with his wife, Diana. He's the proud father of seven and grandfather of one.

Cookie Curci was born in San Jose, California, and has lived there for fifty-nine years. Her grandparents came to San Jose from Italy at the turn of the century. Their family stories inspired her to write a "Remember When" column for her local newspaper, *The Willow Glen Resident,* which she has been writing for twelve years. Her family is close-knit, not only emotionally, but also geographically. She considers herself blessed to be living in a community so rich in family heritage.

Michael W. Curry married his high-school sweetheart, Nancy, and with their two daughters, they live on five acres among the foothills of the beautiful Cascades. He teaches Spanish, art, photography and driver's education at a public high school in Washington State. He believes in the power of telling stories to reach and inspire his students. He was an extra in the Spielberg movie *Always* for about eight seconds. See more of his work at *www.writtenbyme.com.*

Angela D'Valentine is a native Californian. She loves children, dogs and houseplants—and as she frequently tells her loving husband, Matthew, she might write more if she had a larger computer monitor, though he thinks all she needs is a trip to the optometrist.

Jackie Davis resides in Weatherford, Texas, with her husband. She is the mother of one, stepmother of two and stepgrandmother of two. She is a member of North Side Baptist Church where she serves as Coordinator of the Ladies Ministry, and writes and publishes the Ministry's quarterly newsletter.

Kati Dougherty-Carthum is a writer and stay-at-home mom. She lives with her husband and children in Washington State. She has been published in *Jeopardy* magazine, as well as two *Sword and Sorceress* anthologies edited by Marion Zimmer Bradley. Previously, she taught junior-high English and drama.

Joe Edwards is a retired jazz musician now living in Springfield, Missouri. His stories regularly appear on *Heartwarmers,* an online e-zine. He is currently producing a collection of short stories, *Reflections,* to be self-published in the spring.

Virginia (Ginny) Ellis is enjoying her retirement years by indulging in a new-found hobby, that of writing poetry, and she loves it. Being published on the Internet is a special treat, enabling her to make many new friends worldwide, and adding a genuine luster to the gold of her golden years. She invites you to visit her Web site, Poetry by Ginny, at *www.poetrybyginny.com.*

Adeline C. Erwin is a native of Topeka, Kansas. She received her early, formal education in its public schools and graduated from Washburn Municipal

University with a Bachelor of Music degree. She is a retired schoolteacher, wife of a United Methodist minister, mother of three daughters, grandmother to seven children, and great-grandmother to two boys. Her hobbies include reading and writing poetry.

Barbara Jeanne Fisher resides in Fremont, Ohio. A prolific writer, she has published articles in numerous national magazines. Although fictional, her first novel, *Stolen Moments,* is based on her dealing with lupus in her own life. Her goal in writing is to use the feelings of her heart to touch the hearts of others. Contact her at *mentorsfriend@cros.net.*

Sally Franz is a corporate trainer, motivational speaker, author and radio talk-show host. She holds a degree in gerontology. In her early career she produced 150 TV shows focusing on how the elderly can stay active and young. Her grandmother was the inspiration for the TV series.

Susan Garcia-Nikolova, M.S., is an assistant principal at Eisenhower Elementary School in Clearwater, Florida. She is married to her husband, Emil, and is dedicated to both family and to inspiring children to be leaders with a tough heart and tender soul.

Nancy B. Gibbs is a pastor's wife, mother and grandmother. She is also an author, weekly religion columnist and freelance writer. Her stories have appeared in *Chicken Soup for the Nurse's Soul, Stories for the Heart, Honor Books, Guideposts Books, Chocolate for Women* and *Heartwarmer's, Angels on Earth, Family Circle, Woman's World, Decision, Happiness* and *Georgia Magazine.* Nancy may be contacted at *Daiseydood@aol.com.*

Jill Grubb-Travoss is the author of *Almost a Lifetime,* a complete work of poetry about "life passages." She is looking for a publisher for this book and is now working on a book entitled *Stolen Moments with My Mother.* Jill resides outside Atlanta with her husband, James. Together they have three grown children and four grandchildren. Jill works as the Center Administrator of the Griffin Radiation Therapy Center in Griffin, Georgia, and is a cancer survivor herself.

Brad Henderson, considered to be one of the finest magicians performing in the United States, develops entertainment marketing concepts for corporate events, and presents motivational and informational seminars that feature his critically acclaimed sleight of hand magic and mind reading. Brad resides in Austin, Texas, and may be reached through *www.bradhenderson.com.*

Barbara E. Hoffman is a public librarian, adjunct professor, editor, reviewer and contributing writer, public-relations professional, storyteller, author of children's picture books, folk singer, musician, foster parent and, most importantly, Nana to Sara Rose, Gabriella Maria and Michael David. She currently resides in Brookhaven Hamlet, Long Island, New York.

Darcie Hossack works as a freelance writer in Canada's beautiful British Columbia. Her grandparents, Jacob and Anna Friesen, were the most special influence of her childhood. Their lives, love and prairie farm of many cats will always live in memory. Darcie can be reached by e-mail at *allegro@cnx.net.*

Cathie Collier Hulen is a freelance writer/editor with experience in the fields of education, journalism, advertising and design. She believes that we must use every situation as a learning experience and share that knowledge to help others along the way. Her greatest lessons come from nurturing her large family.

Tinker E. Jacobs has scribbled stories since she first could print the alphabet, but she has only recently begun to submit her writings for publication. She is an adventure addict: Her passions include living, learning, loving, motion, traveling, spirituality, and family and friends. Tinker is her real name, a family name, and the last name of her grandparents about whom this story is written.

Pamela Jenkins lives in Henryetta, Oklahoma, where she works as an office manager for Stanley, her veterinarian husband. Her stories have appeared in numerous inspirational publications and on the Internet. She is a member of the Church of Christ, and can be reached by e-mail at *ramblinrabbit@juno.com.*

Brian G. Jett resides in Lexington, Kentucky, with his wife Tanya and daughter, Olivia. Brian is the author of many short stories and poems, and has fomented over three hundred quotations. He enjoys inspirational speaking. Brian can be contacted at 859-264-1808 or by e-mail at *hangtough@earthlink.net.*

Bil Keane created "The Family Circus" in 1960 and gathered most of his ideas from his own family of wife Thel and their five children. Now read by an estimated 188 million people daily, nine granchildren provide much of the inspiration for the award-winning feature. Check out The Family Circus Web site at *www.familycircus.com.*

Karren E. Key is fifty-two years of age and has a blended family of five children and thirteen beautiful grandchildren. Her husband Lacy's job moves them all over the United States, so they rarely are able to live near any of their family. She is making her special memories of each of them even more special.

Roger Dean Kiser, Sr. is the author of the book *Orphan: A True Story of Abandonment, Abuse and Redemption.* He was raised in a Jacksonville, Florida, orphanage for most of his youth. He vowed to return one day and tell the horrors of what it is like for innocent little children to be incarcerated their entire childhood just because nobody wanted them. He now owns and operates The Sad Orphan Child Abuse Web site located at *www.geocities.com/trampolineone.*

June Cerza Kolf, after raising her family, spent twelve years doing hospice work and began her writing career. She has six published books relating to grief and terminal illness and is a frequent contributor to inspirational magazines. Her most recent book, *Standing in the Shadow,* is for suicide survivors.

Sharon Landeen, a retired elementary-school teacher, is the author and illustrator of two bilingual picture books, *When You Get Really Mad* and *Really, Riley!* She enjoys working with youth, was involved for twenty years with 4-H, and is back in the 4-H program with her grandsons. She's a volunteer teacher in reading and art, but still finds time to be "grandmother superior." She can be reached at 6990 E. Calle Arandas, Tucson, AZ 85750 or at *SLLandeen@aol.com.*

Patricia Lorenz is the proud grandmother of Hailey, Hannah, Zachary, Casey and Riley. She's also a full-time writer and speaker who has been published in numerous *Chicken Soup for the Soul* books *(2nd Helping, 3rd Serving, 4th Course, 6th Bowl, Woman's Soul, Single's Soul, Unsinkable Soul, Christian Family Soul,* and *Writer's Soul).* For speaking engagements you may contact Patricia through Associated Speakers, Inc. at 800-437-7577 or e-mail her at *patricialorenz@juno.com.*

Lea MacDonald, forty-five, is a retired Manager of Applications Development. He left corporate life to pursue his passion for writing. His warm and nostalgic stories visit the early halcyon days of twentieth-century life. Currently, Lea is completing a book of heartwarming true stories called *A Simpler Place in Time.*

Marnie O. Mamminga is a freelance writer and teacher in Batavia, Illinois. Her essays have been published in the *Chicago Tribune, Reader's Digest, The Christian Science Monitor, Lake Superior Magazine* and *Chicken Soup for the Mother's Soul 2.* She has also been a speaker on essay writing at the University of Wisconsin's Writers Institute and the Northern Illinois School Press Association. She received her bachelors and masters degrees from the University of Illinois at Urbana-Champaign. She can be reached at *Mamminga@aol.com.*

Patricia S. Mays is a tremendous fan of the ordinary person and has a special ability to see humor in "life as usual" events. Born in a small town in Idaho, Patti is a member of a large family that loves to laugh. She has had previous stories published, including one in the "Life in These United States" section of *Reader's Digest.* Patti, husband John and daughter Natalie live in Atlanta, Georgia.

Terri McPherson lives in Windsor, Ontario, Canada, with her husband, Ray. She is the mother of two adult children, and a grandmother to the one and only Caitlynd. As the editor and contributing writer of an online newsletter, she writes about the small human threads that connect us to one another. She can be reached at *tmcphers@mnsi.net.*

Walker Meade began to write stories at the age of fourteen. When he was twenty-two, one of his pieces was published in *Colliers* magazine. He then wrote short fiction for the *Saturday Evening Post, Good Housekeeping* and *Gentleman's Quarterly,* among others. He then turned to writing nonfiction for magazines such as *Cosmopolitan, Reader's Digest* and *Redbook.* Later he became the managing editor of *Cosmopolitan* and then the managing editor of Reader's Digest Condensed Book Club. His last position in publishing was as president and editor-in-chief of Avon Books. Today he is retired and concentrating on writing longer fiction. Upstart Press published his first novel in August 2001. It has had exciting critical reception and is selling unusually well. The book, *Unspeakable Acts,* can be ordered from *www.amazon.com.*

Chris Mikalson is a fifty-two-year-old grandmother of three. By day she works as a bookkeeper for a car dealership. On nights and weekends she is a freelance writer and novice novelist. She and her soulmate/husband, Ivan, have been married thirty-four years and have two lovely daughters.

Wanda Mitchell is a wife, mother and grandmother residing in Alta Loma, California. She works as a librarian aide for Etiwanda Intermediate School. She is also a travel agent, specializing in cruises. Her passions include her family, reading, writing and seeing the world from a cruise ship. You may contact her at *Travel980@aol.com.*

Arthur Montague became a part-time caregiver to his granddaughter, K. C., in 1998, due to unexpected family circumstances. Nothing on Earth could have prepared him for the richness of this relationship despite having, earlier, raised four children to adulthood. In a very real sense, the stories he writes are K. C.'s heritage.

Doris Hays Northstrom is a nationally published author, inspirational speaker and creative-writing teacher, and acquires material from family, friends, forest, pets, solitude, books, biking and gardening. She has four children and five grandchildren, adding five more grandchildren to love since marrying Ron in December 1998. Write her at 1308 N. Cascade Ave., Tacoma, WA 98406 or call 253-759-9829.

Jay O'Callahan is a writer and a performance artist of international renown. He has performed his dramatic works at Lincoln Center, The Abbey Theatre in Dublin, at The Fine Arts Complex in London, and throughout the United States. For more information on his work and audio recordings call 800-626-5356, e-mail *jay@ocallahan.com* or visit his Web site at *www.ocallahan.com.*

Linda Osmundson is a freelance writer, former teacher and art docent in four art museums—Phoenix, Utah, Denver and Seattle. She lives in Ft. Collins, Colorado, with her husband of thirty-six years. She enjoys crafts, golf, writing, reading and grandparenting. You may reach her at *LLO1413@aol.com.*

Alison Peters, after passing the half-century-on-this-planet mark, is happy to report that honesty and standing up to face one's responsibilities are no less important now than then. She prays that her parents' Christian example is passed down through each generation.

Kenneth L. Pierpont is the senior pastor of First Baptist Church in Fremont, Michigan. He is a writer, storyteller, poet, songwriter, singer, humorist, husband and father of eight children. He speaks at camps, conferences and retreats. He can be contacted at 231-924-3110 or at *baptist@ncats.net,* Web address: *www.members.xoom.com/pinestreet/.*

Patricia Pinney is a forty-one-year-old grandmother who continues to learn life lessons "from the mouths of babes." She is working on a series of short stories and essays and hopes to someday enter the field of freelance writing. She can be contacted by e-mail at *pp40409@alltel.net.*

Kay Conner Pliszka, a retired high-school teacher, motivational speaker and author of humorous and inspirational stories. Her grandchildren bring love and laughter to her life, and compassion and joy to her writing. Kay may be reached at *K.PLISZKA@prodigy.net.*

Michael T. Powers resides in Wisconsin and is the author of the new book *Straight from the Heart: A Celebration of Life.* For a sneak peek at his book or to join the thousands of readers on his daily inspirational e-mail list called "Straight from the Heart," visit *www.MichaelTPowers.com* or e-mail *MichaelTPowers@aol.com.*

Luise Putcamp, jr, writes under her maiden name, though she's been married to Robert H. Johnson for fifty-four years. She got her first newspaper job at sixteen and has written for pay ever since. Her three books are: *Sonnets for the Survivors, The Christmas Carol Miracle* and *The Night of the Child.*

Carol McAdoo Rehme, a frequent contributor to *Chicken Soup for the Soul* and other inspirational books, is a full-time storyteller, speaker and author. Her latest passion is a pilot program, "Silver Linings for Golden Agers." It is the recipient of several grants and provides highly interactive, multisensory presentations at eldercare facilities. Contact her at *carol@rehme.com* or *www.rehme.com.*

Laura Reilly grew up in the Bronx just down the block from her grandparents. Her grandparents had emigrated from Ireland and gave her a great sense of family pride, as well as pride in their new country. Even after Laura's family moved to Long Island, the family remained close. Laura now lives in New Jersey and works in medical advertising.

Kimberly Ripley is a freelance writer and published author from Portsmouth, New Hampshire. A wife and mother of five, she shares many of her family's antics in her writing. Her dream is retirement with her husband in Fort Myers Beach, Florida.

The Rodeo Grandmas are a group of four women, Chloe Weidenbach, Peggy Minor Hunt, Janis Capezzoli Anderson and Lorraine Plass, who ride and rope and yodel and generally remind people that women can be tough and tender and that grandmas have no limits. The Rodeo Grandmas have written a cookbook, *Good Lookin' Cookin',* which is available on their Web site: *www.rodeograndmas.com.* A portion of the proceeds is dedicated to help support the hospice Friends of Kittitas Co.

Kris Hamm Ross is a wife, mother, writer and fifth-grade teacher living in Houston, Texas. Although she has had numerous articles published in educational magazines, her first love is memoir writing. The joy of collecting and preserving family memories on paper is a gift she hopes she has been able to pass on to her students and to her son.

Yulene A. Rushton lives in Utah. She is the mother of four, grandmother of eighteen and great-grandmother of five. She collects angels, believes in miracles, and loves gardening and music. Her greatest passion is writing short stories, articles, poetry and essays about life's experiences. She's been published in several magazines and newspapers, and loves journal writing. She can be reached at 4120 West 3100 South, Salt Lake City, UT 84120.

Ann Russell teaches composition at Lansing Community College in snowy central Michigan. She has two sons and two stepsons, ranging in age from ten to twenty-seven. Her grandchildren—Hilary, Corey and Wesley Allen—help keep her life full of happiness and constant activity.

Harriet May Savitz is the author of twenty books. They include: *Run, Don't Walk*, an *ABC Afterschool Special* produced by Henry Winkler, *The Lionhearted*, and *On the Move*, reissued by iuniverse.com. Also available is *Growing Up at 62: A Celebration*, a book of essays. She can be reached at 732-775-5628.

Hope Saxton is an author from Ontario, Canada. Her work has appeared in *A 6th Bowl of Chicken Soup for the Soul* and *Chicken Soup for the Preteen Soul*. Hope and her family were featured in a "Remembering Your Spirit" segment of *The Oprah Winfrey Show*. Her motivational speaking has taken her to schools and churches, where she speaks out on Child Abuse Prevention and School Violence. Contact Hope at *Hopewrites@yahoo.com*.

Michael Jordan Segal is a social worker at Memorial Hermann Hospital in Houston, Texas, an author, and an inspirational/motivational speaker. His "miraculous comeback" story has been featured on national television and magazines. Mike's story, "My Miraculous Family," was published in *Chicken Soup for the Christian Family Soul*. He is available for public-speaking engagements and can be reached via e-mail at *MsegalHope@aol.com*.

Sidney B. Simon is internationally known for his pioneering work in Values Clarification. Now retired as Professor Emeritus in Psychological Education from the University of Massachusetts, Sid still does dozens of workshops and keynote speeches around the world. He is working on a book that tells the stories of people aging gracefully, and sometimes not so gracefully, in a typical Florida condominium. You can reach him at 9471 Peaceful Drive, Sanibel, FL 33957.

Connie Spittler conducts workshops across the country, teaches at the University of Arizona Writing Works Center, and is working on her book *Writing the Wise Woman Within*. Also a writer/producer, you'll find her *Wise Woman Video Series* in the Schlesinger Library on the History of Women in America, Harvard University.

Debby Stoner lives happily in the Sunshine State with her husband and pets. Her two wonderful grown sons live close by. She spends her days taking care of Quinton, who at the age of eight months, has given new meaning to the words 'perfect love.'

Katharine St. Vincent has led a serendipitous life as the daughter of a naval officer, the wife of a psychologist, the mother of two sons, a teacher (of kindergarten, high school and college), a linguist and a life-long learner, having recently earned her third master's degree. Writing is one of her passions.

Scot Thurman is currently an assistant director with the Baptist Collegiate Ministry on the campus of the University of Arkansas in Fayetteville. He graduated from the University of Arkansas in 1992 and from Ouachita Baptist University in 1997. His love lies in helping people grow closer to Jesus Christ.

Sue Vitou is an award-winning writer living in Medina, Ohio, with her four children. She has over three hundred published articles, and her work has appeared in *The Plain Dealer, The Universe Bulletin, Cleveland Woman Working* and *The Medina County Gazette.* She is currently working on her first novel, *Fresh Eyes.*

Joseph Walker began his career as a staff writer for the *Deseret News* in Salt Lake City, eventually becoming that newspaper's television and live theater critic. Since 1990 he has written a weekly newspaper column, *ValueSpeak,* published in more than two hundred newspapers. His published books include *How Can You Mend a Broken Spleen? Home Remedies for an Ailing World* for Deseret Books, and *The Mission: Inside the Church of Jesus Christ of Latter-Day Saints* for Warner Books. Joseph and his wife, Anita, are the parents of five children. They reside in American Fork, Utah.

Dr. Selma Wassermann is Professor Emerita at Simon Fraser University. A widely published writer, she is author of the popular *The Long Distance Grandmother* (Hartley & Marks). Married for fifty years to her best friend, Jack, her two grandsons, now young men, continue to hold their hands around her heart.

Colleen Madonna Flood Williams lives in Homer, Alaska, with husband Paul, son Dillon, and Bouvier des Flandres Kosmos Kramer. She has written six children's nonfiction books, including *The People of Mexico* and *Native American Clothing.* Contact her at *coleenmwilliams@hotmail.com* or P.O. Box 3492, Homer, AK 99603.

Lynne Zielinski is "Nana" to thirteen grandkids in Huntsville, Alabama, and believes all children are a gift from God. Thrilled when a teenager seeks her advice, Lynne is astounded when they heed it. She writes inspirational stories, short fiction and enjoys freelance work. E-mail her at *Excell1047@aol.com.*

Permissions

We would like to acknowledge the many publishers and individuals who granted us permission to reprint the cited material. (Note: The stories that were penned anonymously, that are in the public domain, or that were written by Jack Canfield, Mark Victor Hansen, Meladee McCarty or Hanoch McCarty are not included in this listing.)

Orange Cheeks. Reprinted by permission of Jay O'Callahan. ©1982 Jay O'Callahan. A version of this story is available as a picture book illustrated by Patricia Raines and published by Peachtree Publishers.

I Love You, Grandma and *More Whipped Cream, Please.* Reprinted by permission of Virginia A. Ellis. ©2000 Virginia A. Ellis.

Everybody Knows Everybody. Reprinted by permission of Lea MacDonald. ©1999 Lea MacDonald.

The Antique and *Somewhere, Babe Ruth Is Smiling.* Reprinted by permission of Harriet May Savitz. ©2000, 1999 Harriet May Savitz.

Magic Snowball Time. Reprinted by permission of Colleen Madonna Flood Williams. ©2000 Colleen Madonna Flood Williams.

One Finger and *Good News, Bad News.* Reprinted by permission of Linda L. Osmundson. ©2001 Linda L. Osmundson.

Little Marie. Reprinted by permission of Angela D'Valentine. ©2001 Angela D'Valentine.

Raising My Sights. Reprinted by permission of Terri McPherson. ©2000 Terri McPherson.

Moe Birnbaum, the Fiddler and *Paula Alone with Her Grandpa.* Reprinted by permission of Sidney B. Simon. ©1999 Sidney B. Simon.

The Last Man on the Moon. ©1999 by Eugene Cernan and Don Davis. From: *Last Man on the Moon* by Eugene Cernan and Don Davis. Reprinted by permission of St. Martin's Press, LLC.

The Priceless Gift. Reprinted by permission of Irene (Seida) Carlson. ©2000 Irene (Seida) Carlson.

Same Agenda. Reprinted by permission of Patricia Pinney. ©2000 Patricia Pinney.

Buying Something for Herself. Reprinted by permission of Karen Brandt. ©2001 Karen Brandt.

The Gift of Giving. Reprinted by permission of Hope Saxton. ©1999 Hope Saxton.

Computer Granny. Reprinted by permission of Kay Conner Pliszka. ©1996 Kay Conner Pliszka.

Here with Me. Reprinted by permission of Gail C. Bracy. ©2001 Gail C. Bracy.

Marnie O. Mamminga.

He Was a Hero, Like All Grandfathers. Reprinted by permission of Sue Vitou. ©2000 Sue Vitou.

The Boys of Iwo Jima. Reprinted by permission of Michael T. Powers. ©2000 Michael T. Powers.

The Stories Grandma Told. Reprinted by permission of Susan Garcia-Nikolova, M.S. ©1997 Susan Garcia-Nikolova, M.S.

Worms and All. Reprinted by permission of Pamela Jenkins. ©2000 Pamela Jenkins.

Perennial. Reprinted by permission of Tinker E. Jacobs. ©2001 Tinker E. Jacobs.

The Silver Sugar Bowl. Reprinted by permission of Karen E. Carr. ©1999 Karen E. Carr.

My Grandmother's Shell. Reprinted by permission of Faith Andrews Bedford. ©1996 Faith Andrews Bedford.

Grammy's Gifts. Reprinted by permission of Sheryl Berk. ©1998 Sheryl Berk.

Grandma Hattie. From *As Far As You Can Go Without a Passport* by Tom Bodett. ©1985 Tom Bodett. Reprinted by permission of the author.

Finger Play. Reprinted by permission of Carol McAdoo Rehme. ©2001 Carol McAdoo Rehme.

Behind the Mirror. Reprinted by permission of Laura Reilly. ©1999 Laura Reilly.

Amazon Woman Becomes a Princess. Reprinted by permission of Adeline C. Erwin. ©1999 Adeline C. Erwin.

Through the Grandkids' Eyes and *My Grandchild's Hand.* Reprinted by permission of Jill Grubb-Travoss. ©1995, 1998 Jill Grubb-Travoss.

Hershey's Dark Chocolate. Reprinted by permission of Roger Dean Kiser, Sr. ©1999 Roger Dean Kiser, Sr.

Dial H for Heaven and *The Moses Connection.* Reprinted by permission of Helen Colella. ©2001 Helen Colella.

Grandma and the Chicken Pox. Reprinted by permission of Susan Amerikaner. ©1999 Susan Amerikaner.

Rainy Day Rainbows. Reprinted by permission of Arthur Montague. ©2000 Arthur Montague.

What's a Grandma to Do? Reprinted by permission of Patricia Lorenz. ©1999 Patricia Lorenz.

Courtney's Love Lesson. Reprinted by permission of Alice Collins. ©1997 Alice Collins.

Katharine St. Vincent.

Real Magic. Reprinted by permission of Brad Henderson. ©2001 Brad Henderson.

The New Family on Walton's Mountain. Reprinted by permission of Kimberly Ripley. ©2001 Kimberly Ripley.

The Rodeo Grandmas. Reprinted by permission of Chloe Weidenbach, Peggy Minor Hunt, Janis Capezzoli Anderson and Lorraine Plass. ©2001 Hanoch McCarty.

Why Not? Reprinted by permission of Christina Coruth. ©2001 Christina Coruth.

A Grandma Takes Power. Reprinted by permission of Michael Jordan Segal. ©2001 Michael Jordan Segal.

The Granny Hook. Reprinted by permission of Kathe Campbell. ©2000 Kathe Campbell.

Grandma Lois. Reprinted by permission of Patricia S. Mays. ©2000 Patricia S. Mays.

Ageless. Reprinted by permission of Michele Wallace Campanelli. ©1999 Michele Wallace Campanelli.

The Gold Locket. Reprinted by permission of Bruce Carmichael, D.C. ©2001 Bruce Carmichael, D.C.